The Lost Soul of the American Presidency

The Lost Soul of the American Presidency

THE DECLINE INTO DEMAGOGUERY AND THE PROSPECTS FOR RENEWAL

Stephen F. Knott

University Press of Kansas

Published by the University Press of Kansas (Lawrence, Kansas 66045), which was organized by the Kansas Board of Regents and is operated and funded by Emporia State University, Fort Hays State University, Kansas State University, Pittsburg State University, the University of Kansas, and Wichita State University.

Library of Congress Cataloging-in-Publication Data
Names: Knott, Stephen F., author.
Title: The lost soul of the American presidency : the decline into demagoguery and the prospects for renewal / Stephen F. Knott.
Description: Lawrence, Kansas : University Press of Kansas, [2019] | Includes bibliographical references and index.
Identifiers: LCCN 2019006955
ISBN 9780700628506 (cloth : alk. paper)
ISBN 9780700628513 (ebook)
Subjects: LCSH: Presidents—United States—History. | Executive power—United States—History. | Political leadership—United States—History. | Demagoguery | United States—Politics and government.
Classification: LCC JK511 .K66 2019 | DDC 973.09/9—dc23
LC record available at https://lccn.loc.gov/2019006955.

British Library Cataloguing-in-Publication Data is available.

Printed in the United States of America

10 9 8 7 6 5 4 3 2

The paper used in this publication is recycled and contains 30 percent postconsumer waste. It is acid free and meets the minimum requirements of the American National Standard for Permanence of Paper for Printed Library Materials Z39.48-1992.

For Amy and Donna Knott
and Kathleen Colpoys,
MaryKate Doherty,
Meg Harrington,
Mary and Kathryn Lysko,
Julie Moloy,
and Alexis, Laura, and Maura Walsh

A dangerous ambition more often lurks behind the specious mask of zeal for the rights of the people than under the forbidden appearance of zeal for the firmness and efficiency of government. History will teach us that the former has been found a much more certain road to the introduction of despotism than the latter, and that of those men who have overturned the liberties of republics, the greatest number have begun their career by paying an obsequious court to the people; commencing demagogues, and ending tyrants.

—*Alexander Hamilton,* Federalist *no. 1*

CONTENTS

ACKNOWLEDGMENTS

This book would not have been written without the encouragement of Laura Walsh and Patti Wade. Patti, a member of the highly professional staff at the Westwood (Massachusetts) Public Library, encouraged me every step of the way, while Laura's repeated friendly inquiries regarding the status of my book spurred me to complete it.

I also owe a debt of gratitude to Ellen Walsh, Pauli Lysko, Peg Colpoys, and Kathy Moloy. Madeline Doherty was also indispensable in providing valuable assistance in a remarkably timely manner. Justin Vaughn, Tony Williams, Jeremy Bailey, Edward O'Donnell, Thomas Karako, and Maura Porter all provided insightful advice. Special thanks are owed to David Congdon, Kelly Chrisman Jacques, Michael Kehoe, and the remarkable staff at the University Press of Kansas.

My wife, Maryanne, and my daughter Maura, as always, are the loves of my life, and I cannot imagine completing this project, or anything else, without them.

INTRODUCTION: THE LONG, DECLINING ROAD

I have always admired the American presidency and many of the occupants of the office. One of my favorite gifts as a child was a book about the American presidents given to me by my parents on my tenth birthday.[1] The official portraits of all the presidents were included, except for the recently slain John F. Kennedy and the new president, Lyndon B. Johnson, neither of whom had an official portrait just yet. My favorite president was Zachary Taylor because he was wearing an impressive military uniform and grasping a fearsome-looking sword. That was all that was necessary for Taylor to win my affection.

I was fortunate enough to pursue my interest in the presidency into adulthood, landing my first job after college at the John F. Kennedy Library in Boston. From there I pursued a doctorate in political science with a focus on the presidency. I taught for several years, and then accepted a position at the Miller Center of Public Affairs at the University of Virginia, where I eventually became the codirector of the center's presidential oral history program. I conducted oral histories of the Reagan, George H. W. Bush, Clinton, and George W. Bush presidencies. In general, I came away impressed by the intelligence of the people we interviewed and frequently discovered that an interviewee's reputation in the media, be they Democrat or Republican, was incomplete at best. I mention this because this book is a lament for what has happened to the American presidency, and more importantly, the American political order writ large. Things in that order, we might say, are out of sort. And this is not simply due to the election of Donald Trump. The American presidency has lost the respect it once held, and the roots of that loss predate Trump.

The American president was intended, at least in part, to serve as the nation's chief of state, as its symbolic head, not a partisan leader. An office envisioned by George Washington and others as a source of national pride and unity has devolved into a force for division and discord. Additionally, presidential candidates have exaggerated the powers and potential of the office for the last one hundred years, assisted by a cadre of scholars and biographers who embrace the notion of what became known as "presidential government." And, truth be told, the American people fall for this pitch almost every four years.

At its core, this book focuses on the contrast between the constitutional or framers' presidency versus the Jacksonian or populist, later progressive, presidency. The latter conception of the presidency has been in place since Teddy Roosevelt and was given its intellectual imprimatur by Woodrow Wilson. The legacy of Wilson's presidency persists to this day, but important elements of that presidency were seen as early as Thomas Jefferson's time, when the nation's third president refounded the office with his "Revolution of 1800." This refounding shifted the presidency from its intended role as a check on majority rule to a spokesman for and implementer of the majority's wishes. As an utterly predictable consequence, this meant the literal disenfranchisement, and worse, for African Americans and Native Americans.

The presidency of Jefferson and Jackson, and the elevation of "majority rule" into an unofficial constitutional principle, further entrenched slavery in the American political order and institutionalized an odious form of racial supremacy which existed well into the twentieth century, if not beyond. And it placed the presidency on an unsustainable path, a path of heightened expectations at odds with any limits on its power and contemptuous of checks and balances. It also diminished the important unifying role the president was expected to play as head of state, forcing him to become a party leader and policy formulator—in short, a perpetual partisan lightning rod. All of this contributed to an erosion of respect for the office.

What was lost under the process begun by Jefferson and Jackson was a conception of the presidency that would serve the nation well today. George Washington, Alexander Hamilton, and other members of the founding generation designed a presidency of "sober expectations," one that did not pander to or manipulate the public, one that was averse to the notion that it was the president's job to provide "visionary leadership," and one that was loath to implement the majority will at the expense of political, racial, and economic minorities. They also understood the importance of presidential character above all else, especially a sense of humility about one's own potential and the potential of the office they held.

The populist presidency transformed the office into the "tribune of the people," elevating the chief executive into the defender of "the common man" against the privileged few. The president was also expected to serve in the vanguard of change. Determined to liberate the American government from the constraints of the Constitution's antiquated checks and balances, the president (assisted by talented administrators) was to act as a visionary and lead the nation into the promised land.

It is my contention that a century of progressive disregard for the Constitution damaged our nation's polity. The progressive revolution promised too much of the federal government, especially of the presidency. The promise of the progressive presidency was most eloquently proclaimed by John F. Kennedy, who noted that "man can be as big as he wants" and that "no problem of human destiny is beyond human beings." While Kennedy's rhetoric inspired many Americans, this unbounded hubris contributed to the collapse of confidence in the presidency and in the entire federal government.

This book traces the evolution of the decline of the presidency, and offers an alternative conception based primarily on the principles and practices of George Washington and Alexander Hamilton. This book also argues that the academic community needs to reconsider its notions of what constitutes "presidential greatness." This community needs to reevaluate its reverence for "change agents" and acknowledge that there is a place for a John Quincy Adams, a William Howard Taft, and a Gerald Ford. Perhaps we need a new Mount Rushmore, and we might want to consider sandblasting the old one, or at least sandblasting two of the four visages.

Three final introductory notes: this book is not a call for a restoration of the "cult of the presidency" or the sort of mythical, semimystical worship of the office that took root during the twentieth century and was promoted by those who embraced the unconstitutional notion of "presidential government." The myth of the "glorious burden" carried by the "leader of the free world" was ably stoked by admirers of Franklin D. Roosevelt and John F. Kennedy. This was part of the progressive campaign to imbue the presidency with qualities it was never intended to possess and contributed to the inevitable disappointment that most Americans feel toward their government in the early twenty-first century.

I also do not share the view of many libertarians and those on the American left that the presidency needs additional restrictions placed on it by Congress or the courts. The changes that need to occur must come from within—from those granted the privilege of holding the office, and "within" the character of the American citizenry. Congress needs to reassert its constitutionally mandated role, but not at the expense of impairing the president's Article Two powers. I have always believed, and continue to believe, that in the realm of foreign affairs and national security, the president was granted considerable discretionary authority. That should remain unchanged in my view.

The Hamiltonian presidency, which was embraced by George Washington and Abraham Lincoln, among others, contributed to the emergence of the United States as a superpower in the early twentieth century. A restoration of the Hamiltonian presidency would continue this tradition of executive leadership while removing some of the odious features grafted on to the system first by Jefferson and Jackson, and later by Wilson and his successors. These features have damaged the office, and the entire constitutional system, perhaps beyond repair. But this book was written in the hope that restoration and renewal are still possible.

I also do not contend that the transformation of the American presidency was solely the result of pressures emanating from the occupants of the office. Yet I acknowledge up front that this book is "president-centric." The rise of political parties, the demands of special interests, and the entreaties of the public all generated momentum equal to or perhaps greater than the desire for change on the part of various presidents. The role of parties, of economic and demographic changes, and of interest groups and public opinion are beyond the scope of this book. I do contend, however, that this transformation was aided and abetted, and at times driven by, ambitious presidents who could have resisted external pressures, who could have defended the constitutional presidency, and chose not to do so. Some of these presidents acted on principle, others less so.

The nation's first "change agent," Thomas Jefferson, was under little pressure to alter the American presidency. It made electoral sense for Jefferson and his party to adopt such changes, but there was no overriding public demand that the system needed to be changed. John Adams and the Alien and Sedition Acts may have needed to go, but not the constitutional presidency. While I readily acknowledge many other forces at work in the abandonment of the constitutional presidency, the fact is that much of the damage to the office was self-inflicted by presidents motivated by a variety of motives, some rooted in self-interest.

This book is about those presidents who decided they knew better than the framers, who thought that they could control public opinion, shape it and direct it, and transform that opinion into policy, and thereby allow the majority to govern. These presidents annulled the intentions of the framers of the Constitution. Jefferson, Jackson, and Wilson championed the populist presidency because it suited their vision for the nation—sadly, throughout the history of the United States, these presidential "visions" have seriously damaged the American political order, as we shall see.[2]

The Lost Soul of the American Presidency

1

The Founders' Presidency

Washington, Hamilton, and an Office of Sober Expectations

The American founders, especially those who considered themselves Federalists, understood that moderation and stability have their place and that constant upheaval is not healthy for a political order. In light of this belief, they were averse to any form of government that simply translated the wishes of the public into law. The founders believed in consent, on a government based on representation, but it was the role of elected officials to refine and enlarge public sentiments. Public opinion was fickle and prone to the ill effects of passion, they believed, and subject to the siren call of demagogues. On occasion, perhaps most occasions, true leadership, statesmanship in fact, required defying public opinion.

The American founders also understood something many twentieth-century presidents did not: that the more you expand the roles and responsibilities of the presidency, the more you diminish it. The founders' presidency provided both a floor and a ceiling that protected but also energized the office; without this, the office would be trapped in a cycle of raised expectations followed by public disappointment and increased cynicism. Even strong nationalists like Alexander Hamilton acknowledged limits to what the presidency should do: administer the federal government, conduct foreign negotiations including those involving international finance, oversee military preparations, and if need be, direct a war. And perhaps most importantly for Hamilton, the president should not employ "the little arts of popularity," the pandering and demagoguery, that would undermine the dignity of the office and the Constitution itself.

"Commencing Demagogues, and Ending Tyrants"

While Alexander Hamilton was, of course, never elected president, he was George Washington's closest advisor and confidant throughout the latter's eight years in office. Hamilton's writings in what became known as the *Federalist Papers* provided a kind of rulebook to guide the nation's first presidency. George Washington had read the *Federalist* essays and expressed his "great satisfaction" with the collection, noting that "the work will merit the notice of prosperity" due to its candid discussion of "the principles of freedom and the topics of government."[1]

Hamilton was an advocate of, as he put it in the *Federalist,* an "energetic executive." He was not, as his critics often allege, an advocate for authoritarian or monarchical government. He is also often blamed for building the foundation for what would become known as the "imperial presidency." This idea was first broached by Thomas Jefferson and his followers, who believed that the cunning immigrant from the Caribbean was manipulating a somewhat feeble-minded President Washington. All of Hamilton's actions, whether at Washington's side or later as the de facto leader of the Federalist Party, were viewed by Jeffersonians as efforts to establish an American plutocracy or perhaps a hereditary monarchy. None of this was true, although this did not deter Jefferson or generations of progressive and libertarian scholars from endorsing this durable, pernicious myth.[2]

The evidence for Hamilton's alleged aristocratic authoritarianism was rooted in his speech at the Constitutional Convention in June 1787, in which he proposed a president elected for life, pending good behavior. Although the convention proceedings were supposed to remain secret, James Madison apparently allowed Jefferson to peruse his notes. Other myths circulated by Jefferson suggested that Hamilton was something of a closet Caesar, who, to add insult to injury, considered the people to be a "great beast."[3] While Jefferson and his lieutenants, including James Madison and James Monroe, considered Hamilton a threat to the American political order, George Washington believed Hamilton possessed the noblest kind of ambition, and sought to breathe life into the fabric of the new Constitution. As was frequently the case, Washington's assessment of Hamilton's integrity, and of his principles and practices, was correct.

Hamilton was determined to infuse into the new government, and into the presidency, enough elements of permanence and stability as republican principles would admit. While a president elected for life offends the sensibilities of modern Americans (as well as the sensibilities of Americans in 1787), it is important to note that Hamilton's lifetime executive would be elected and subjected to removal by impeachment. It is also possible, as historians such as Forrest McDonald have suggested, that Hamilton's somewhat radical proposal for lifetime presidential tenure made other proposals put forward by "nationalists" or "centralizers" appear more moderate. These proposals allowed for presidential re-eligibility albeit with a shorter term of office.

Nonetheless, while Hamilton's president was to be an "energetic" chief executive, he was not the president of twentieth-century progressives, all libertarian protestations to the contrary. Hamilton's chief executive was to serve as a check on popular opinion by acting in concert with the judiciary and with the Senate as a curb on the boisterous, passionately inclined House of Representatives. Nothing could be further from Hamilton's mind than the idea that it was the president's responsibility to shape public opinion or serve as a spokesman for the public at large. This concept came to be partially accepted by Thomas Jefferson, and reached its full flower under Andrew Jackson, who sought to convert the presidency into the "tribune of the people."

All of Hamilton's life was devoted to resisting delusional and at times dangerous trends in public opinion. As he would note later in his life during the Whiskey Rebellion of 1794, "I have learn[ed] to hold popular opinion of no value. I hope to derive from the esteem of the discerning, and an internal consciousness of zealous endeavors for the public good, the reward of those endeavors."[4] Hamilton was committed to the American Revolution, having risked his life for its success, but he was a revolutionary who understood the virtues of prudence and moderation, and the rule of law, which set him apart from contemporaries such as Thomas Paine and Thomas Jefferson. Paine and Jefferson's theoretical musings veered dangerously close to the revolutionaries of modern times who profess an abstract love for humanity and who envision mankind freed from the strictures of the past and reaching new levels of perfectibility. Hamilton never suffered from any illusions about the flawed nature of man and stood firmly for reason over passion and for stability over speculative change.

Hamilton first demonstrated his commitment to these principles when he was a twenty-year-old student at King's College, when an angry revolutionary mob stormed the house of the college's president, Myles Cooper, a Tory sympathizer. Hamilton apparently appealed for calm long enough to allow the frightened president to escape through a back door. This would be the first of many Hamiltonian appeals for reason over passion, a position to which he would adhere throughout his entire public life. In many ways, what happened on the steps of Myles Cooper's house epitomized Hamilton's conception of statesmanship—preserving order and holding the forces of passion at bay for as long as possible.[5]

Hamilton's aversion to mob rule can also be seen in his defense of the rights of Tories in the aftermath of the American Revolution. As with John Adams's defense of "redcoats" after the Boston Massacre, Hamilton risked his reputation to defend the rights of Americans who had remained loyal to the Crown. The most prominent case was *Rutgers v. Waddington* (1784) in which the youthful Hamilton argued that laws passed in New York targeting Tories violated both common law and the laws of nations and the laws of war. This case concerned a suit brought by Elizabeth Rutgers under these laws seeking back rent from Joshua Waddington for the use of her property that she had abandoned during the American Revolution. Hamilton, always vigilant when it came to the use of law as a weapon against unpopular groups, considered New York's actions to be politically motivated attempts to shame Tories and force them to undergo a form of "re-education." For Hamilton, the principles in the *Rutgers* case and the over seventy other cases he was involved in defending Tories, were the same principles at stake on the steps of Myles Cooper's home: "Nothing is more common than for a free people, in times of heat and violence, to gratify momentary passions by letting into the government principles and precedents which afterwards prove fatal to themselves." In these circumstances "no man can be safe, nor know when he may be the innocent victim of a prevailing faction."[6]

Hamilton won a partial victory for his Tory client Waddington in the end, but not at some expense to his public reputation.[7] In fact, his principled stance in defense of the rights of Tories and his rejection of law rooted in "momentary passions" would later fuel allegations that he was an Anglophile, if not an outright British agent. Character assassination is frequently the dues paid by those who defy public opinion and defend the rule of law. But it is a sacred obligation of those entrusted with great power, particularly American presidents.

Alexander Hamilton categorically rejected the belief held by some Americans that the people always reasoned correctly and that the cure-all for the problems of a republic was more democracy. Hamilton's candor regarding the fickleness and faultiness of public opinion stands in contrast to that of Thomas Jefferson, who wrote more often about the wisdom of the American people (although it should be noted that there are exceptions to Jefferson's rosy rhetoric that tend to be selectively ignored by populist historians).

As offensive as Hamilton's position may seem to modern Americans, he believed, rightly so, that the public "sometimes err[s]" and that while the people intend to do right by the common good, they do not always "reason right about the means of promoting it."[8] This was partly due to the ability of demagogues to flatter the people, which presented a constant threat in a republic; by appealing to public prejudices, demagogues were able to lead the people to betray their true interests. George Washington believed that this phenomenon had occurred during Shays's Rebellion in Massachusetts in 1786–1787. The future president blamed the uprising on the machinations of "men of consequence and abilities behind the curtain who move the puppets; the designs of whom may be deep and dangerous."[9]

Washington and Hamilton believed that the forces of populism at work in their day were prone to respond to "every sudden breeze of passion" and "temporary delusions," which were completely at odds with the permanent, long-term interests of the nation. They believed, as Hamilton put it, that the "deliberate sense of the community should govern," and that this was possible only through a government that allowed for "cool and sedate reflection." There would be times when statesmanship would require the president to resist the wishes of the people. This was the essence of Hamilton's political philosophy, and it is this that was slowly but surely undone by the Jeffersonian and Jacksonian movements of the first half of the nineteenth century and whose task was completed by the progressive movement of the early twentieth century.[10]

George Washington shared Alexander Hamilton's views of the flawed nature of man, and for the propensity of public passions to degenerate into mob action. In terms of a Judeo-Christian worldview, both men were adherents of the Old Testament perspective. Mankind was flawed, deeply so, and visionary talk of creating a new man through political action was futile, not to mention dangerous. Men are, in words guaranteed to shock any unreconstructed idealist, "ambitious, vindictive, and rapacious."[11] Moderation and prudence lay at the foundation of each of these men's political philosophy, and they were averse to visionary schemes offered by philosophic voluptuaries, or the latter's counterparts in the political world, demagogues.

As Hamilton observed in 1784 while defending the rights of an unpopular minority, "moderation rather than violence" should guide the actions of the body politic. That "justice and moderation are the surest supports of every government, are maxims, which however they may be called trite, at all times true, though too seldom regarded, but rarely neglected with impunity."[12]

During Washington's first year as the nation's president, he observed that his "greatest fear" was that "the nation would not be sufficiently cool and moderate in making arrangements for the security" of liberty.[13] Washington's commitment to reason and moderation began when he was a teenager, when he had copied by hand over one hundred "rules of civility" including the following passage, "let your conversation be without malice or envy . . . and in all causes of passion admit reason to govern."[14] In 1787, while contemplating whether to attend the Constitutional Convention in Philadelphia, Washington noted in a letter to Henry Knox that one of the failings of democracy was "that the people must *feel*, before they will see."[15] Feelings, passions, and emotions motivate political action, Washington believed, not appeals to reason.

As such, Washington, both as a general and as a president, was a firm proponent of the rule of law. For instance, in the early days of the American Revolution, less than a week after the issuance of the Declaration of Independence, Washington condemned the mob who pulled down the statue of King George III in New York City on July 9, 1776, and beheaded "His Highness": "Tho the General doubts not the persons, who pulled down and mutilated the Statue, in the Broadway, last night, were actuated by Zeal in the public cause; yet it has so much the appearance of riot and want of order, in the Army, that he disapproves the manner, and directs that in future these things shall be avoided by the Soldiery, and left to be executed by proper authority."[16] Washington's public service for the nation was bookended by pleas for moderation. He began just days after the Declaration urging restraint and obedience to law, and he ended on the same note. In his Farewell Address published on September 17, 1796, the ninth anniversary of the completion of the drafting of the Constitution, Washington warned of the propensity of demagogues to exploit factions or interests for their own self-interest. "Cunning, ambitious, and unprincipled men" will "subvert the power of the people" and "usurp for themselves the reins of government, destroying afterwards the very engines which have lifted them to unjust domination."[17] "Passionate attachments" as an element of statecraft were inappropriate, as much as they might be a fact of life in the interactions of individuals. This was Washington's way of accusing Jefferson and his followers of having, as Alexander Hamilton once put it, a "womanish attachment" to France.[18] Passionate policies were at odds with the national interest, and it was the duty of statesmen to resist these sentiments, Washington believed.

The sentiments Washington expressed in his Farewell Address regarding the dangers presented by demagogues were shared by the person who likely wrote those lines for Washington, Alexander Hamilton. In his very first *Federalist* essay, Hamilton noted that: "A dangerous ambition . . . often lurks behind the specious mask of zeal for the rights of the people. . . . Of those men who have overturned the liberties of republics, the greatest number have begun their career by paying an obsequious court to the people; commencing demagogues and ending tyrants."[19] Hamilton was dismissive of the "talents for low intrigue and the little arts of popularity" that sometimes prevailed in state elections, but he was hopeful that this phenomenon would not occur at the national level, primarily due to the Electoral College, which unfortunately no longer serves its original purpose. Hamilton also stood for moderation, a virtue that a currently divided nation seems to have forgotten. "All the sincere lovers of the union," he urged in his final *Federalist* essay, must judiciously reflect on the lessons of "moderation," particularly so as to avoid "the military despotism of a victorious demagogue."[20] And while a republican government must pay heed to the governed, or at least to the "deliberate sense of the community," republicanism does "not require an unqualified compliance to every sudden breeze of passion, or to every transient impulse which the people may receive from the arts of men, who flatter their prejudices."[21]

The condemnation of demagoguery found in Washington's Farewell Address was presaged in Hamilton's defense of the Washington administration's treaty with Great Britain, known as the Jay Treaty. Hamilton, with Thomas Jefferson likely in mind, noted in July 1795, that:

> It is only to consult the history of nations to perceive, that every country, at all times, is cursed by the existence of men, who, actuated by an irregular ambition, scruple nothing which they imagine will contribute to their own advancement and importance. In monarchies, supple courtiers; in republics, fawning or turbulent demagogues, worshipping still the idol power wherever placed, whether in the hands of a prince, or of the people, and trafficking in the weaknesses, vices, frailties, or prejudices of the one or the other.[22]

The Jay Treaty offered opponents of President Washington, as well as opponents of the Constitution itself, an opportunity to enhance their political prospects on the eve of a presidential election. The demagogue preys on divisive issues, such as the Jay Treaty, issues fraught with emotion, and seeks to inflame these emotions to banish reason and reflection from the public square. Hamilton believed that exploiting popular prejudices had been the modus operandi of demagogues throughout history, and that this phenomenon was quite apparent during the Jay Treaty "debate," if one can call it that. According to Hamilton: "It was to have been expected, that such men, counting more on the passions than on the reason of their fellow citizens, and anticipating that the treaty would have to struggle with prejudices, would be disposed to make an alliance with popular discontent, to nourish it, and to press it into the service of their particular views."[23]

Despite harboring some doubts about the Jay Treaty, President Washington was appalled at the displacement of reason and deliberation with zealotry and an appeal to prejudices. Washington told Hamilton "the cry against the Treaty is like that against a mad-dog." The final months of Washington's presidency were, as the president characterized it, a time of "folly and madness," an assessment shared by Hamilton, who wrote Washington that "in these wild times every thing is possible."[24]

One of the opponents of the Jay Treaty was James Madison, Hamilton's former *Federalist Papers* coauthor. And while the two men disagreed vehemently regarding the merits of the Jay Treaty, they were both in agreement that demagogues were toxic to republics. In his famous *Federalist* no. 10 essay, Madison warned of the existence of "men of factious tempers" whether out of an attachment to "local prejudices" or out of "sinister designs" may "by intrigue, by corruption . . . first obtain the suffrages, and then betray the interests of the people."[25] Later, in a less notable essay, *Federalist* no. 63, Madison argued that the proposed United States Senate would serve as a check on popular excess and a potential firewall against the machinations of a demagogue. The Senate was, according to Madison:

> necessary as a defense to the people against their own temporary errors and delusions. As the cool and deliberate sense of the community ought, in all governments, and actually will, in all free governments, ultimately prevail over the views of its rulers; so there are particular moments in public affairs when the people, stimulated by some irregular passion, or some illicit advantage, or misled by the artful misrepresentations of interested men, may call for measures which they themselves will afterwards be the most ready to lament and condemn. In these critical moments, how salutary will be the interference of some temperate and

respectable body of citizens, in order to check the misguided career, and to suspend the blow meditated by the people against themselves, until reason, justice, and truth can regain their authority over the public mind?[26]

The United States Senate, before its undoing by the Seventeenth Amendment in 1913 mandating direct election of senators, was one of many filters created by the framers to refine popular sentiment and ensure that cool and deliberate reflection prevailed in the affairs of the American body politic. It is worth noting that the *Federalist Papers* contain sixty-six separate mentions of the word "passion" or "passions"—the word is repeatedly mentioned by both Hamilton and Madison as scourge to avoid.[27] Madison and Hamilton differed on many of the great issues of their day, but they were united in believing in the primacy of reason and the debilitating effect of passion. Madison expressed his concern over the threat presented by demagogues at the Constitutional Convention, when he noted that checks were necessary to guard against the abuses of an overbearing majority, including "the followers of different demagogues."[28] As he would note later in his life, "in Republics, the great danger is that the majority may not sufficiently respect the rights of the minority."[29]

Madison's belief in the merits of deliberation and his fear of the politics of passion led him to support a system of representation, which he viewed as *the* distinguishing feature separating a republic from a democracy. He noted in *Federalist* no. 63 that representation would also set the United States apart from the ancient republics due to its "total exclusion of the people, in their collective capacity, from any share" in administering the government.[30] Public opinion would be filtered "through the medium of a chosen body of citizens, whose wisdom may best discern the true interest of their country."[31] Madison believed that the permanent interests of the community were enhanced through this republican form of government rooted in representation and resistant to the whims of public opinion. Madison rejected the notion of parroting the will of the public and would oppose the claims of present-day members of Congress who boast about using the internet as a tool to pressure their colleagues before casting a vote.

This is as far removed from James Madison's claim in *Federalist* no. 10 that representation will "refine and enlarge the public views" as one can get. Madison was opposed to pandering to the public, and rejected the type of populist, demagogic appeals that emerge from the cyber-pulpit. Madison, the architect of the Constitution, hoped that legislative deliberation would act as a filter, or at the very least, as political scientist Greg Weiner has suggested, slow the process down and allow for the passage of time to "season" public opinion. According to Weiner, Madison "portrayed passion through metaphors that suggested rapid and uncontrolled spread, including those of fires, fevers, pestilence and contagions."[32]

None of the founders, including Madison, would think that reducing complicated issues of public policy to 280 characters or less was a healthy approach to lawmaking, never mind using that same vehicle to rally the public to pressure their fellow lawmakers. The purpose of representation, and one could add, the task of a chief executive, was to serve as a "medium" by which the public's views were refined to ensure that the "true interests" of the country were protected, and not sacrificed to "temporary or partial considerations."[33]

Near the end of his life, in 1834, Madison warned a fellow citizen not to forget the lessons of history: "The ancient Republics, and those of a more modern date, demonstrated the evils incident to popular assemblages, so quickly formed, so susceptible of contagious passions, so exposed to the misguidance of eloquent and ambitious leaders."[34] Madison's letter was likely prompted by Andrew Jackson's pronouncement that the "majority is to govern" and that the president served as the "tribune" of the people. Madison believed, rightly so, that Jacksonian principles were undermining the framers' republic. The American republic stood for something beyond simple majority rule. "There is no maxim" he wrote in 1786, "which is more liable to be misapplied, and which, therefore, more needs elucidation, than the current one, that the interest of the majority is the political standard of right and wrong."[35]

Thomas Jefferson, always the more ardent revolutionary than his ally James Madison, seemed unconcerned about the prospect of the people being misled by a demagogue. In fact, during the heated battle over the Jay Treaty, Jefferson seemed to welcome the fact that a mob had thrown rocks at Hamilton at a pro-treaty rally in New York City. Jefferson informed Madison that the treaty opponents "appealed to stones and clubs and beat him [Hamilton] and his party off the ground."[36] Of all the key founding fathers, Jefferson veered the closest toward embracing the beliefs of Thomas Paine and other populists who believed the people could do no wrong and were capable of rationally discerning what was in their best interest.

All regimes, Washington and Hamilton believed, were subject to the designs of conniving individuals, although the targets of these designs differ depending on the nature of the regime. The Jay Treaty was just one episode where Hamilton and Washington were accused of threatening to replace republican government with either an aristocracy or a monarchy, or both. In fact, both men were attempting to create a permanent and stable republican government that would serve as a bulwark in defense of liberty. An energetic government would repulse foreign attacks, promote law and order, and provide for the security of property, which was the cornerstone of liberty. Rebuffing Jefferson's accusations that he was a monarchist, Hamilton argued that the real threat to American liberty came from demagogues who pretended to be faithful servants of the public. According to Hamilton, there are individuals who:

> by flattering the prejudices of the people, and exciting their jealousies and apprehensions [intend] to throw affairs into confusion, and bring on civil commotion. . . . When a man unprincipled in private life desperate in his fortune, bold in his temper, possessed of considerable talents, having the advantage of military habits—despotic in his ordinary demeanour—known to have scoffed in private at the principles of liberty—when such a man is seen to mount the hobby horse of popularity . . . to flatter and fall in with all the nonsense of the zealots of the day—It may justly be suspected that his object is to throw things into confusion that he may "ride the storm and direct the whirlwind.[37]

Whether it was in Great Britain, or ancient Rome, or the United States, the machinations of men devoid of principle, men who are averse to boundaries of any sort, men in love with themselves and with power, represent a perennial threat. The American founders, and Hamilton in particular, were fixated on the threat presented by demagogues. So much so that Hamilton began and ended his remarkable *Federalist Papers* warning of these cancerous mutations that present a constant threat to republics.[38]

Both Washington and Hamilton were, to borrow a phrase from two centuries later, revolutionaries with sober expectations. They would categorically reject Thomas Paine's famous maxim from *Common Sense* that "we have it in our power to begin the world over again."[39] And they would warn contemporary Americans to avoid selecting candidates, especially for president, through a process which puts a premium on salesmanship and flattery. In fact, the whole notion of direct popular appeals was anathema to the founding generation, particularly to the Federalists. Washington once observed that "with me . . . it has always been a maxim rather to let my designs appear from my works than by my expressions."[40] There was something intrinsically toxic to Washington, Hamilton, and Adams regarding the practice of courting public opinion. Were they to return in our time, they would be horrified at the calculated, poll-driven pandering that dominates modern American presidential campaigns as well as the process of governing itself.

A Constitutional Firewall

It was these concerns that prompted Hamilton and other framers of the Constitution to support the Electoral College, a method for choosing the American president in a manner rooted in popular consent but filtered through a firewall designed to weed out demagogues and individuals lacking in talent and integrity. The Electoral College was, for Hamilton, an ingenious device, an "excellent" method of presidential selection, which would insure that "the office of President will never fall to the lot of any man who is not in an eminent degree endowed with the requisite qualifications." Hamilton believed it to be "desirable" that "the sense of the people should operate in the choice of the person to whom so important a trust was to be confided." But it was equally important that the "immediate" choice be made by individuals "most capable of analyzing the qualities" necessary to hold the office, "acting under circumstances favorable to deliberation." Again, for Hamilton, Madison, and Washington, "deliberation" was the cornerstone of a healthy political order. The Electoral College also had the added benefit of serving as a bulwark against the "most deadly adversaries of republican government"—"cabal, intrigue, and corruption." There would be no "pre-existing" body of electors who could be targeted for corruption, but instead the "transient" and "detached" status of the electors would make them difficult targets of intrigue. No senator, congressman, or appointee of the United States government could serve as an elector, and this safeguard, coupled with the requirement of forcing the electors to meet in their respective state capitals, made it difficult for "foreign powers to gain an improper ascendant in our councils."[41]

Hamilton's concerns echoed those of his fellow jaded realists who dominated the Constitutional Convention. These delegates spent a remarkable amount of time debating the most effective way to deter foreign powers from improperly influencing American politics. It was widely assumed, rightly so, that these powers would spare no effort to infiltrate the highest levels of the United States government. As Hamilton noted in *Federalist* no. 59, as the nation grew in strength it would be subjected to "enterprises" that sometimes "originate in the intrigues of foreign powers" and were designed to "subvert" the new nation.[42]

In addition to checking foreign schemes to influence the nation's electoral process, the architects of the Electoral College were attempting to defuse the passions that were inevitably unleashed around the selection of a president. By reducing this choice to one of selecting electors, the founders again demonstrated their aversion to direct popular appeals, to the "little arts of popularity." The goal was, as Hamilton put it, to avoid "convuls[ing]" the community by maintaining some semblance of stability and order throughout the electoral process. Passions would be mitigated by selecting "several" electors throughout the nation, by dispersing the choice to each of the individual states. This was preferable to directly electing the "*one* who was himself to be the final object of the public wishes."[43] This process is far removed from the contemporary presidential selection mode, which the founders would consider conducive to selecting an unfit character for the presidency.

A very fit character, George Washington, was the unanimous choice of the Electoral College in 1789. The newly elected president was determined to create a dignified, respected presidency led by a chief executive presiding over a government of national unity. As he would later write Thomas Jefferson, "I was no party man myself and the first wish of my heart was, if parties did exist, to reconcile them." Washington was, as he told the founding father of political parties, "using my utmost exertions to establish a national character of our own."[44] Both Washington and Hamilton were committed to convincing their fellow citizens to "think continentally," as Hamilton put it in a letter to Washington in April 1783.[45] This would require the citizenry to resist the siren call of parochial interests and of what today would be known as special interest groups. As Washington put it in a letter to the Marquis de Lafayette that same year, "We now stand an independent people and have yet to learn political tactics . . . the probability, at least I fear it is, that local or state politics will interfere too much with that more liberal and extensive plan of government which wisdom and foresight, freed from the mist of prejudice, would dictate."[46] Hamilton, echoing Washington, would later observe that the point of the American experiment, as he put it in the first essay of what became known as the *Federalist Papers,* was to create a system that proved that men were capable of good government based on "reflection and choice," not on narrow interests or passionate attachments.[47]

The American government created by the founders was based on the rule of law and a rejection of participatory democracy. In that sense, this regime's harshest critics, including Howard Zinn, Noam Chomsky, and scores of progressive historians and political scientists, are right to focus on the undemocratic nature of the founders' Constitution. A few events from the early republic highlight the antipathy felt by the framers toward participatory democracy and its not so distant cousin, mob rule.

To avoid the passions and ferments of public pressure, the Constitution of the United States was drafted under conditions of absolute secrecy. The windows in that sweltering hall in Philadelphia in the summer of 1787 were nailed shut, and the heavy drapes were drawn to prevent any outsiders from eavesdropping. One of the first orders of business was the adoption of a measure "that nothing spoken in the house be printed, or otherwise published or communicated" without the consent of the convention.[48]

Secrecy prevailed both during the Constitutional Convention and long after, as James Madison's notes were not released until 1840, over fifty years after the close of the convention. During the early years of the new republic, the United States Senate met in secret, mimicking the example set by the Continental Congress, which also operated behind closed doors. The founding generation understood that secrecy fostered the best kind of decision making; one where all matters, particularly awkward or uncomfortable matters, could be discussed without fear of public retribution.[49] Secrecy allowed the delegates to frankly discuss the vital questions at hand and avoid the grandstanding that characterizes many open meetings. Public opinion would play a role in the ratification of the Constitution, but it played no role in the drafting of the document, beyond a general sense on the part of the delegates as to what might be palatable to the public.

Decision making, the founders believed, contrary to modern-day advocates of openness and transparency, was best conducted behind closed doors. Openly formulated policies are subject to the whims of the day, as Alexander Hamilton noted at the Constitutional Convention, "the people are turbulent and changing; they seldom judge or determine right."[50] Hamilton would expand on this impolitic utterance a year later at the New York Ratifying Convention when he noted that "the ancient democracies in which the people themselves deliberated never possessed one good feature of government. Their very character was tyranny; their figure deformity."[51] Those statements were the mother of all politically incorrect statements, and they would cost Hamilton dearly, although they were true.

Two other events from the early republic demonstrate how committed most of the key American founders were to the rule of law, to deliberation and reflection, and how skeptical they were of political figures and political movements promoting radical change. The first event, the French Revolution, was welcomed by almost all Americans when the news from Paris first arrived in North America, but quickly, after the revolution turned into a bloodbath, a significant number of Americans turned against it. George Washington, John Adams, and Alexander Hamilton saw important distinctions between the American and French republican movements. According to Hamilton, the American Revolution was characterized by a devotion to liberty, the French Revolution by a passion for licentiousness. Hamilton was repulsed at the ease with which Jefferson had endorsed the atrocities of the French Revolution, including his suggestion that if the revolution eliminated every man and woman save one apiece, the cost would be worth it.

President Washington feared that the French Revolution would take a destructive turn almost from the start, as could be seen in his warning to the Marquis de Lafayette that the revolutionaries should avoid "running into extremes and prejudicing your cause."[52] Hamilton believed that the rampant bloodletting that occurred in revolutionary France would provide the fuel necessary for a demagogue to capitalize on the chaos and seize dictatorial power. He noted in 1793, "After wading through seas of blood, in a furious and sanguinary civil war, France may find herself at length the slave of some victorious Sylla . . . or Caesar."[53]

Napoleon Bonaparte's rise to power would soon prove Hamilton right. Hamilton's opposition to mob rule was always linked to the idea that it would pave the way for a Caesar or a Bonaparte, and thus destroy liberty. But that kind of argument, that mob rule inevitably descends into authoritarianism, was easily twisted by the party presses of the day into a disdain for the "common man," as evidence of elitism, and of Hamilton himself being a closet authoritarian, an accusation that persists to this day in populist-inspired histories.

In the end, the French revolutionaries murdered, by a conservative estimate, well over seventeen thousand victims, including priests and nuns by the score, while churches were converted into "temples of reason" and the guillotine provided almost daily entertainment for the public. Some 85 percent of the victims of the French Revolution were commoners, foreshadowing the wholesale slaughters that successor revolutions practiced during the totalitarian upheavals of the twentieth century.[54] For Hamilton, Washington, and Adams, the French Revolution was the utterly predictable result of allowing passion to rule the affairs of men, and discarding the rule of law in favor of retribution. Hamilton, Washington, and Adam's aversion to runaway public passions and mob action set them apart from some of their contemporaries, including Thomas Jefferson, who had a comfort level with revolutionary violence that stemmed from his idealized vision of human nature, and his lack of exposure to the real fruits of revolutionary violence.

This same phenomenon of runaway violence and mob action could be seen, on a much smaller scale, during the Whiskey Rebellion, which represented in the mind of Washington and Hamilton the first domestic test of the viability of the new government. Whiskey distillers in western Pennsylvania were dismayed at an excise tax that the Washington administration had allayed on the production of whiskey. Senator William Maclay of Pennsylvania, the personification of founding-era populism, viewed the excise tax on whiskey to be "the most execrable system that was ever framed against the liberty of a people. . . . War and bloodshed are the most likely consequence of all of this."[55]

The tax was designed to help retire the debts that had accrued from the American Revolution and to pay for the constant wars with Native Americans that were frequently caused by American settlers in places like western Pennsylvania encroaching on Indian territory. Washington considered resistance to the tax, which reached its peak in the late summer and fall of 1794, to be a case of domestic insurrection. Despite concessions offered to mitigate the tax, protests had taken place since the bill was first proposed in 1791. Washington and Hamilton tried to reason with the protest leaders, and as tensions escalated the administration promised presidential pardons for those who had broken the law.

Unfortunately, it took a show of force by Washington, who led, for a time, the over twelve thousand militiamen into the field, to finally quell the rebellion. Jefferson and his followers, along with modern-day progressive historians, tend to dismiss the importance of the Whiskey Rebellion. Jefferson referred to the rebellion disparagingly as "Hamilton's Insurrection," and criticized the "inexcusable aggression" toward "people at their ploughs."

President Washington, who had cunningly named the militia force "the Army of the Constitution," considered the suppression of the rebellion to be part of his constitutional obligation to "take care that the laws be faithfully executed."[56] Washington considered the rule of law to be at stake during the Whiskey Rebellion—for the president, it came down to the question of whether an armed minority had the right to violently resist laws approved by constitutionally mandated procedures. The answer, for Washington, was clear—the United States was to be a nation that rejected mob violence and defended the rule of law against the depredations of a passionate, aggrieved minority.

Forging a Dignified Presidency

Beyond pursuing policies designed to fortify federal authority, George Washington understood the importance of symbolic acts in creating a sense of national character. This required an attention to matters of protocol that may strike modern Americans as quaint and perhaps peculiar. The "symbolic dimension" of his office, as Jeffrey Tulis has observed, was also foremost in Washington's mind, including how his "style of living should be managed so as to enhance the dignity of his office while supporting popular attachment to republicanism."[57] Much of his first term was devoted to establishing a "sovereign bond between the nation and its citizens," as historian Sandra Moats has observed. Washington knew that if the new government were to survive, "its symbolic presentation needed to be based in republican ideals, not in his popularity, because he would not live forever and the American system was not a hereditary monarchy."[58]

These matters were of utmost importance to Washington, and to Hamilton, who served as Washington's most prominent advisor, both officially and unofficially, throughout his presidency. Again, underlying these protocol decisions was the hope that the presidency would be held in high esteem by the people, and in so doing contribute to the slow process of convincing Virginians or New Yorkers to think of themselves as Americans. As Jeffrey Tulis has observed, Washington "devoted considerable time during his first year as president to decisions regarding the symbolic dimensions of his office." Washington wanted to win the respect of the people for the new Constitution and the new office of the presidency, but he was not seeking, as his progressive successors would, to establish any type of personal bond with them. Washington's relationship to the people, as Glen Thurow has rightly noted, was "not the grounds of either his powers or his duties."[59] Those grounds could be found in the Constitution of the United States.

Alexander Hamilton's advice to Washington was that creating a sense of "dignity" was essential to establishing credibility and respect for the new office. While one had to be cautious in a republic of leaning too far in that direction, "dignity" became the guiding force behind all of Washington's and Hamilton's efforts to develop respect for the office. Hamilton believed that some elements of a "high tone" demeanor would be accepted by the American public, if "extremes" were avoided. In his efforts to foster a sense of national unity, Hamilton suggested that the new president host a series of dinners to celebrate major anniversaries of the young republic, including Independence Day and the treaty which ended the war with Great Britain.[60]

This focus on "ceremony" led the populist demagogue Senator William Maclay to complain about "ceremonies. Endless ceremonies." But these events were, in the minds of the president and the secretary of the treasury, of equal importance to the president's administrative functions. The president was, in the words of historian Sandra Moats, creating a "republican political culture" by merging "republican simplicity and ceremonial dignity in a manner that no other American could."[61] Preserving the dignity of the office was at the forefront of Washington's agenda, and animated all his principles and practices while president. He noted, "the President in all matters of business and etiquette, can have no object but to demean himself in his public character, in such a manner as to maintain the dignity of office." Alexander Hamilton agreed, noting that "the public good requires as a primary object that the dignity of the office should be supported."[62] Washington was made for the role of a dignified chief executive, for almost everyone who encountered him noted his distinguished bearing. Future president, James Monroe, observed that Washington had "a deportment so firm, so dignified, but yet so modest and composed, I have never seen in any other person."[63]

The president was to be the chief of state, the personification, in a sense, of the new nation, particularly as it dealt with the rest of the world. This view was shared by most members of Congress, who, as Sandra Moats has noted, understood that "the presidency, particularly when occupied by George Washington, would epitomize the American government, both at home and abroad."[64] Washington utilized the president's head of state role more effectively than any of his successors. Part of this can be attributed to the Herculean task he confronted of unifying a nation and building respect for the presidency. Arguably, he succeeded so well that his successors did not have to take this task seriously. But they should have, particularly in times when the nation was divided. As Forrest McDonald eloquently noted, Washington "endowed the presidency with the capacity—and the awesome responsibility—to serve as the symbol of the nation, of what it is and what it can aspire to be."[65]

George Washington's appreciation for the power of symbolism in politics was superior to any of his contemporaries. Part of this stemmed from Washington's love of the theater. He seldom passed on an opportunity to attend a theatrical performance and seems to have absorbed many lessons from the stage. His dramatic actions in deflating the Newburgh Conspiracy were straight out of Shakespeare—at one point, speaking to his assembled officer corps, Washington groped for his eyeglasses and exclaimed, "Gentlemen, you will permit me to put on my spectacles, for I have not only grown gray but almost blind in the service of my country."[66] One observer noted that "there was something so natural, so unaffected, in this appeal, as rendered it superior to the most studied oratory; it forced its way to the heart, and you might see sensibility moisten every eye."[67] But Washington had spent his entire life preparing for the role of leader; what happened that day in Newburgh was the result of studied practice.

Vice President John Adams noted Washington's flair for the dramatic:

> We may say of him, if he was not the greatest President he was the best Actor of Presidency we have ever had. His Address to The States when he left the Army; His solemn Leave taken of Congress when he resigned his Commission; his Farewell Address to the People when he resigned his Presidency. These were all in a strain of Shakespearean and Garrickal [David Garrick, eighteenth-century English actor, producer, playwright] Excellence in Dramatic Exhibitions.[68]

Washington's theatrical skills served him well on his grand tours of the nation. As historian T. H. Breen has noted, each stop along the way was an occasion for "elaborate choreography," and, "like an accomplished actor," Washington devoted considerable thought to his apparel and the symbolic message that apparel would convey. On certain occasions he opted for republican simplicity, but on other occasions he wore his military uniform, conjuring up memories of his triumphal leadership of the "glorious cause."

He would frequently proceed into town "mounted [on] a great white charger," often leaving the denizens of those communities speechless. These frequent occasions of stunned silence were the result of the crowds seeing in the flesh the man they had come to view as an almost superhuman character. This pageantry had its intended effect, as one newspaper noted, for Washington's visits reaffirmed the people's confidence in the new president, and "energ[ized] . . . that government in the administration of which he has so considerable a part."[69]

Washington's flair for the dramatic helped to convince many Americans that the new federal government, and in particular the presidency, possessed greater authority than that held by state officials. When Washington traveled to New England in 1789, he was confronted with a protocol standoff between himself and Massachusetts Governor John Hancock. The latter believed he outranked Washington on Massachusetts soil, and feigned illness to force the president to pay a courtesy call on him in Boston. Washington dispatched an adeptly crafted note to Hancock that boxed the pompous governor into a corner: "The president of the United States presents his best respects to the Governor, and has the honor to inform him that he shall be at home 'till 2 o'clock. The President of the United States need not express the pleasure it will give him to see the Governor, but at the same time he most earnestly begs that the Governor will not hazard his health on the occasion." This note, coupled with the hero's welcome accorded Washington from adoring crowds throughout the Bay State, led Hancock to reconsider his position. Hancock's health suddenly "improved" and the governor left his home to pay homage to the president (Hancock was carried by servants to maintain the façade of illness). It was another small but important victory on the path to convincing the citizenry to abandon parochial loyalties and adopt an American identity.[70]

Slavery and Union

Washington was confronted with one issue which pitted his own parochial loyalties against his desire to "think continentally." The question of the status of slaves in America, both his own slaves and those owned by his many of his fellow citizens, threatened the republic he founded and potentially threatened his own personal wealth. Especially in the final years of his life,

Washington wrestled with the irreconcilable differences posed by this issue. Thoughtful citizens, and Washington was a thoughtful citizen, understood the contradiction inherent in a nation dedicated to the proposition that all men were created equal, yet that same nation kept hundreds of thousands of human beings in chains. The new nation's critics, particularly in Great Britain, could not resist taunting the "Empire of Liberty" by citing Samuel Johnson's biting observation that "the loudest yelps for liberty" came from "the drivers of negroes."[71]

When the nation's capital moved to Philadelphia in 1790, President Washington was in the awkward position of bringing his slaves into a state where the law dictated that slaves became legal residents of the Commonwealth after six months and thus free men and women. Washington chose to cycle his slaves in and out of Pennsylvania every six months, using somewhat surreptitious means to keep the ruse intact. In May 1796, one of his slaves, apparently influenced by free blacks in Philadelphia, decided to seek her freedom. Washington did not take kindly to slaves who fled from his control, and his pursuit of this slave, Ona Judge, who escaped Washington's household and fled to Portsmouth, New Hampshire, where she lived in freedom, has recently received long-overdue attention. Washington's pursuit of Ona Judge and his efforts to secure her to return is not a flattering portrait of the first president.[72]

There is, however, much to admire in Washington's growing realization that slavery was a stain on the soul of the new republic, and a blot on the record of its most prominent founder. Washington's hostility toward slavery deepened over time as he grasped that the institution of slavery threatened to rip apart the Union he had devoted his life to creating. In 1786 he wrote to an acquaintance that it was "among my first wishes to see some plan adopted, by which slavery in this country may be abolished by slow, sure, and imperceptible degrees." He also was quoted by the British actor John Bernard as saying that "no man" desired the abolition of slavery "more heartily than I do. . . . Not only do I pray for it on the score of human dignity, but I can clearly foresee that nothing but the rooting out of slavery can perpetuate the existence of our union." Unlike his fellow Virginian who succeeded him in the executive mansion, Washington freed his slaves in his will, contingent upon his wife's passing. He stipulated that they be "taught to read and write and to be brought up to some useful occupation," and his estate made payments to these freed slaves up until 1833, if not beyond. Washington never supported colonization schemes for free slaves, as this stipulation reveals, and he belatedly but firmly concluded that slavery was a threat to the health and well-being of the political order he founded.[73]

Washington's attorney general, Edmund Randolph, quoted the president as saying that if the Union broke apart over this issue, Washington would throw in his lot with the Northern antislavery states.[74] Randolph's account was probably accurate, as it is hard to imagine the author of this statement in 1783 joining in any secession effort: "Whatever measures have a tendency to dissolve the Union, or contribute to violate or lessen the Sovereign Authority, ought to be considered as Hostile to the Liberty and Independency of America, and the Authors of them treated accordingly."[75]

Washington's commitment to the Union can also be seen in an important symbolic gesture that may appear to modern sensibilities as a trivial matter, which it certainly was in comparison to slavery. But this symbolic gesture, the issuance of a Thanksgiving proclamation, was of great importance to a people unaccustomed to thinking of themselves as Americans and who were unsure of this unique new entity, the federal government. Washington's decision to issue a proclamation in the fall of 1789 was all part of his goal of convincing his fellow citizens to follow the path that he had chosen of abandoning his Virginia provincialism and become American nationalists. Sensing an opening to further this effort, Washington issued a proclamation himself rather than wait for the various state governors to issue such a proclamation. On October 3, 1789, Washington's proclamation, which was filled with references to the new nation and was specifically addressed to the "people" of the United States of America, was reprinted up and down the Atlantic seaboard.[76] As Glenn A. Phelps has noted, Washington's proclamation asked for "a special blessing for the national government and the Constitution, but *not* the states."[77] Washington's enduring commitment to nation building can also be seen in one of his final acts as a citizen, the drafting of his last will and testament, where he proclaimed his Americanism in the boldest of prose: "I George Washington of Mount Vernon—a citizen of the United States, and lately Pr[es]ident of the same."[78]

Washington's grand tours of the nation were an additional aspect of his ceremonial duties as chief of state, and one in which Washington invested a remarkable amount of time. Washington considered these tours to be an opportunity not only to cement the people's loyalty to the new nation, but also presented an opportunity for him to learn about the conditions in the states and to meet "well-informed persons who might give him useful information and advice on political subjects."[79]

The president traveled to New England from October 15 to November 13, 1789, where he was greeted by "a vast concourse of people," all of whom apparently accepted the legitimacy of his office and of the new nation. He went back to New England in August 1790, as a reward to the rogue state of Rhode Island, which had withheld ratification of the Constitution but belatedly saw the light. Washington's tour of the Southern states was a grueling slog that lasted over three months and covered over 1,900 miles. The president departed Philadelphia on March 21, 1791, and did not return to the capital until July 6th.[80] Not once during the welcoming events that greeted him along the way did Washington engage in a discussion of policy or recite anything beyond what today would be dismissed, sadly, as patriotic platitudes.

Washington and Hamilton's Model Presidency

President Washington sought to invest the executive office with enough attributes of "ceremony and pomp" as would be tolerated in a republic. These steps were designed to cause his fellow citizens to look up to the office, but of equal importance, Washington sought to impress foreign governments and visiting dignitaries. As Malcolm L. Cross has noted, Washington lived in lavish quarters first in New York City and later in Philadelphia when those cities served as the nation's capital. Whenever he traveled he rode a white horse decked out in gold bunting, and during his lengthy tours of the United States he was always transported in an elaborate coach pulled by white horses and accompanied by slaves and a small military escort. For some small towns that he visited, Washington's tour remains the greatest thing that ever happened in those locations in over 230 years. While he professed to be somewhat bothered by the "external trappings of the elevated office," he also understood that "if he behaved like an ordinary citizen he would damage the prestige needed to carry out the Presidential office."[81]

Washington was the antithesis of modern chief executives with his aversion to direct appeals to the people. These types of direct appeals to the people were "demagogic" in nature and entirely inappropriate for a constitutional republic. Washington's authority as president derived from the Constitution and his relationship with the people was indirect, as Glen Thurow has argued. Washington "refused to talk policy," as Jeffrey Tulis has noted in his groundbreaking study *The Rhetorical Presidency.* Washington was aware that he would be setting many precedents, and he was devoted to insuring that these precedents were rooted in the Constitution.[82]

Not all of Washington's precedents were adopted by his successors. His twentieth-century successors rejected many of them, including his policy of remaining quiet on many issues. Washington and most nineteenth-century American presidents frequently refrained from injecting themselves into disputes roiling the body politic. Vice President John Adams observed that Washington possessed "the gift of silence,"[83] a gift that he shared with his greatest successor, Abraham Lincoln. Washington's conception of the presidency did not carry with it the assumption that the president possessed expertise on every issue, and was duty bound to pronounce his views on topics unrelated to his position as chief of state. Silence has its virtues, as our two greatest presidents understood.

The principle that the president should not mold or inflame public opinion but rather serve as a check against it, and as a check against legislative excess, offers the most critical distinction between the Hamiltonian or Constitutional presidency and the modern presidency. Sadly, in contemporary America, the viability of a candidate for high office is frequently determined by the passion they bring into the political "arena" and the passion they unleash from their followers.

Toward the end of his life, Alexander Hamilton, operating without the influence and protection of George Washington, attempted to halt the populist slide that President Jefferson ushered in with his "Revolution of 1800." Jefferson's embrace of the idea of a government rooted in and operating on popular consent represented to Hamilton a betrayal of the Constitution and of the principle of republican government. To counter these trends, Hamilton suggested establishing a Christian Constitutional Society that would contest the leveling, populist trends in the American body politic. A controversial proposal both then and now, Hamilton's proposal for this "association" was an acknowledgment that he and his fellow Federalists had been routinely outmaneuvered at "street-level" politics by the more politically adroit Jeffersonians.

In a letter to one of his Federalist allies in April 1802, Hamilton bemoaned the fact that reason had been displaced by appeals to passion. "The present Constitution is the standard to which we are to cling," Hamilton observed to

Congressman James Bayard from Delaware, urging Federalists to march under its "banner" and rejecting changes that were not the result of amending the Constitution. He added, somewhat despairingly, that:

> Nothing is more fallacious than to expect to produce any valuable or permanent results, in political projects, by relying merely on the reason of men. Men are rather reasoning tha[n] reasonable animals for the most part governed by the impulse of passion. This is a truth well understood by our adversaries who have practiced upon it with no small benefit to their cause. For at the very moment they are eulogizing the reason of men & professing to appeal only to that faculty, they are courting the strongest & most active passion of the human heart—VANITY!

This is what led to the grim prospects of the Federalists, for as Hamilton observed, his party had not played the "passion" card and had not sought to win public approval through "the little arts of popularity." The time had come to rethink their tactics:

> It is no less true that the Federalists seem not to have attended to the fact sufficiently; and that they erred in relying so much on the rectitude & utility of their measures, as to have neglected the cultivation of popular favour by fair & justifiable expedients. The observation has been repeatedly made by me to individuals with whom I particularly conversed & expedients suggested for gaining good will which were never adopted. Unluckily however for us in the competition for the passions of the people our opponents have great advantages over us; for the plain reason, that the vicious are far more active than the good passions, and that to win the latter to our side we must renounce our principles & our objects, & unite in corrupting public opinion till it becomes fit for nothing but mischief. Yet unless we can contrive to take hold of & carry along with us some strong feelings of the mind we shall in vain calculate upon any substantial or durable results. Whatever plan we may adopt, to be successful must be founded on the truth of this proposition. And perhaps it is not very easy for us to give it full effect; especially not without some deviations from what on other occasions we have maintained to be right. But in determining upon the propriety of the deviations, we must consider whether it be possible for us to succeed without in some degree employing the weapons which have been employed against us.

Alexander Hamilton had serious moral qualms about embracing Jeffersonian tactics, and it was clear that he was not prepared to entirely abandon appeals to reason, but it would be reason bolstered by an appeal to the "positive passions" such as religious faith. Traditional religion and a new civil religion devoted to revering the American Constitution would serve as a check against passing whims of popular fancy and more importantly, visionary schemes to remake mankind. By providing a bulwark against utopianism rooted in the notion of the perfectibility of mankind and of creating a heaven on earth, the United States would avoid embarking on the path to the guillotine or the Gulag.[84]

The office of sober expectations created by Washington and Hamilton offers a model for contemporary Americans to emulate. That office possessed enough power to defend the nation from foreign and domestic threats, and in fact launched the United States on the path to becoming a superpower. But that presidency also acknowledged certain restraints and limitations on the office and the officeholder. Washington served as a unifying head of state, who was respectful of the dignity of his office, who refrained from stoking partisan divisions and becoming a captive to public opinion, always paying due regard to the Constitution.[85]

Washington's presidency serves as a reminder that a president who avoids the politics of flattery, of courting majority opinion, can perform a vital role in defense of the rights of minorities. Unfortunately, this aspect of Washington's presidency was steadily eroded by some of his nineteenth-century successors who refounded the presidency and transformed the office into the voice of the majority. Washington's letter to the Jewish Congregation of Newport, Rhode Island, on August 21, 1790, put the nation on notice that discrimination against minorities would not be tolerated. Washington wrote similar letters to Catholics, Baptists, and Quakers, but this letter to the Touro Synagogue was widely circulated in the press, in part due to the ongoing debate over the proposed Bill of Rights. The government of the United States, "which give[s] to bigotry no sanction, to persecution no assistance," requires only that those who benefit from its protection conduct themselves "as good citizens" and offer their "effectual support." The president added, "may the children of the stock of Abraham who dwell in this land continue to merit and enjoy the good will of the other inhabitants—while every one shall sit in safety under his own vine and fig tree and there shall be none to make him afraid."[86] Sadly, in service of the whims of the majority, a new type of president who considered the source of his power to be popular consent rather than the Constitution, would render ineffectual Washington's pledge to give bigotry "no sanction."

George Washington's model presidency is still within our reach. But it would require a renewed appreciation for the limits of the presidency and the limits of politics, and a renewed focus on the importance of character. The American people would also have to be weaned from the politics of passion and embrace the founders' belief that for self-government to work the citizenry must govern themselves, govern their passions.[87] At its core, it would require a reversal of trends that began during the presidency of Thomas Jefferson.

2

The Presidency of Popular Consent

Thomas Jefferson and the "Revolution of 1800"

Thomas Jefferson was the poet of the American Revolution, of the "glorious cause," the man who infused into that cause something higher than a simple crusade for American sovereignty. Jefferson's stirring rhetoric continues to inspire his fellow countrymen, for he defined the American creed, committing himself and his fellow citizens, however inadequately, to live out the ideals that "all men are created equal" and to the principle that government exists solely to secure our natural rights to "life, liberty, and the pursuit of happiness."

Jefferson was also the most adept political strategist among the key founders, repeatedly confounding his Federalist opponents and ultimately leaving them on the ash heap of history. As the nation's third president, Jefferson offered an alternative to twelve years of Federalist rule, or perhaps more accurately, an alternative to eight years of effective Federalist government under Washington, and four years of ineffective and semi-incoherent government under John Adams.

Transforming a Nation

Jefferson proclaimed his election to the presidency as the "Revolution of 1800." This "revolution," he argued, was "as real a revolution in the principles of our government as that of [17]76 was in its form; not effected indeed by the sword, as that, but by the rational and peaceable instrument of reform, the suffrage of the people."[1]

Jefferson was the early republic's foremost advocate for "expressive, participatory politics," as historian Joyce Appleby has rightly noted. By the time of Jefferson's death in 1826, as Appleby admiringly observed, "participatory politics stood at the core of American political culture," a result of Jefferson's life-long efforts to "open" doors that were previously closed by the "Federalist elite."[2]

Jefferson's election led to a fundamental transformation of the American government, upending the role of the president in the system of separation of powers and fundamentally altering the way a president would relate to the citizenry. Jefferson refounded the office of the presidency, placing it on a populist course that, in the long run, undermined the intentions of the framers of the Constitution. Ironically, considering his embrace of the notion of popular consent, Jefferson would have lost the presidency to John Adams in 1800 without the inflated electoral votes of the slave states, who could count each of their slaves as three-fifths of a person for purposes of apportioning presidential electors as well as for purposes of taxation and representation. The inflated electoral power given the slave states contributed to the lock Jefferson's party had on the nation's electoral politics for decades.

One of the more incisive analysts of Jefferson's principles and practices, Jeremy D. Bailey, has noted that the resolution of the contentious election of 1800 preserved the Constitution but "only in name." Jefferson's "informal Constitution of 1800" replaced the original Constitution, instituting a system that "placed popular presidents as leaders of the democratic system." The Constitutional presidency of Washington, Hamilton, and Madison was "transformed . . . into the democratic presidency."[3] This was the result of decades of thinking on Jefferson's part, not some aberration due to the contentious standoff with Aaron Burr and the machinations of certain Federalists to deny Jefferson the presidency. As Bailey notes, "by the time Jefferson sought the presidency, he had already devoted much of his efforts to thinking about executive power and constitutionalism."[4]

Jefferson's regard for public opinion was diametrically opposed to Hamilton's position, the latter contending that demagoguery and passion play an inordinate and dangerous role in shaping public sentiments. Jefferson argued to the contrary that public opinion served as the "best criterion of what is best," and that enlisting and engaging that opinion would "give strength to the government."[5] An electoral mandate from the people was the source of power for Jefferson's energetic executive. Free governments with leaders selected by public mandate would in fact be the "most energetic" type of government of all. Additionally, Jefferson argued that the president represented the nation's will because he was the only nationally elected figure. Jefferson was turning Alexander Hamilton's argument on its head, for the latter believed that one of the responsibilities of an energetic executive was to check popular excess, while Jefferson believed in enlisting popular opinion as the ultimate source of presidential, and constitutional, legitimacy. Jefferson made this abundantly clear in a letter he wrote to James Madison in 1787: "after all, it is my principle that the will of the Majority should always prevail."[6]

While Hamilton argued for infusing as many elements of permanence and stability in the structure of the American government, Jefferson advocated for frequent elections, term limits for the presidency, and repeated revisions of the Constitution. The notion of establishing some sort of civil religion built on worship of the Constitution was anathema to Jefferson, who endorsed the idea of allowing every generation to rewrite their Constitution, for it was inappropriate for the dead to govern the living. As Jeremy Bailey has observed, there were even occasions when Jefferson "went as far as to suggest that constitution and other forms of government were less important than the majority will," although in other instances his faith in the wisdom of the majority seemed to waver.[7]

But generally speaking, there is a consistent thread in Jefferson's majoritarianism. As he once observed, "the mother principle" of legitimate government was that "governments are republican only in proportion as they embody the will of their people, and execute it." He added that "the true foundation of republican government is the equal right of every citizen, in his person and property, and in their management."[8] While few Americans quarreled with the principle of equal rights in person or property, the idea of each citizen "managing" their government was at odds with the principle of representation so powerfully articulated by James Madison in the *Federalist Papers*.

Jefferson's belief in majority rule stemmed from his faith in the unlimited potential of mankind and of the benefits of a society constantly reinventing itself. His native optimism and boundless idealism can be seen both in his free-wheeling approach to constitutionalism, but also in his eagerness to edit the New Testament in a manner more suitable to his enlightenment tastes. His dream of an America constantly remaking itself and shedding the shackles of the past has always captured the American imagination, which explains the continuing fascination with Jefferson, although that fascination has receded somewhat in contemporary America. There were few limits to Jefferson's vision for the United States, the "world's best hope," as he put it in his first inaugural address.[9] Jefferson was the founding father of America's faith in progress, in the belief that the nation truly was a new order for the ages.

Nowhere was Jefferson's vision of reinventing America more pronounced than in his refounding of the presidency. In a passage guaranteed to render Washington and Hamilton speechless, Jefferson observed in July 1789 that "we think in America it is necessary to introduce the people into every department of government as far as they are capable of exercising it." He also seemed to suggest that direct election of the president was the preferable manner of presidential selection, noting that while the people were not qualified to "exercise themselves" the executive power, they "are qualified to name the person who shall exercise it."[10]

Jefferson's plan to revamp the presidency included amending the Constitution to recognize the existence of the party system he founded. After the awkward deadlock with Aaron Burr in the election of 1800, Jefferson was determined to avoid a repeat of that fiasco in 1804. He flirted with the idea of proposing a constitutional amendment providing for direct election of the president and the abolition of the Electoral College. He suggested this in a letter to his treasury secretary, Albert Gallatin, in September 1801, noting that "a different amendment which I know will be proposed, to wit, to have no electors, but let the people vote directly, and the ticket which has a plurality of the votes of any state, to be considered as receiving thereby the whole vote of the state."[11]

This idea was abandoned in favor of what became the Twelfth Amendment to the Constitution, although Jefferson, as was his wont, concealed his participation in the drive for that amendment. But Jefferson was, as one observer has noted, a "covert cheerleader for its ratification." This amendment ratified the existence of the party system as a key player in presidential selection and discriminated between the selection of a president and a vice president, eliminating the practice of selecting the presidential candidate who came in second as the vice president.

Beyond avoiding a repeat of the follies of 1800, the Twelfth Amendment was "part of Jefferson's larger project to transform presidential power" by making "the connection between presidential selection and public opinion . . . more explicit."[12] The framers' system of presidential selection did not announce "precisely enough the true expression of the public will," according to the nation's third president. Jefferson favored a system of presidential selection that rested on the people, not the states as represented in either the Electoral College or, in case of the inability of that body to select a winner, the House of Representatives. Jefferson believed in the ability of the people to select a sound president, for the citizenry, as he put it in his second inaugural address, possessed a "reflecting character" and "sound discretion" and thus rightly controlled the government through the "weight of public opinion."[13]

President Jefferson's second inaugural address was a discourse on the role presidential elections played in measuring public opinion and translating that opinion into policy. Jefferson's reelection was "new proof of confidence" bestowed on him by the citizenry and it was the president's task to "express the deep sense" of the public as conveyed through their electoral choice. Jefferson's faith in the public's ability to reason and to distinguish "between truth and falsehood . . . and to form a correct judgment between them" became a central tenet of Jeffersonianism.

But there was an ominous undercurrent in Jefferson's paean to the wisdom of the majority, and that was the existence of a minority, these "doubting brethren." This minority had "not yet rallied to the same point," but "facts are piercing through the veil drawn over them" and they will eventually see the light and join "the fold of their country." The "fold" of course, being "the mass of their fellow citizens." Both reason and self-interest would lead these dissenting brethren to enter "the entire union of opinion." Self-interest, of course, meant that it was in the best interest of the dissenters to ultimately go along with "the fold," "the mass," the "weight of public opinion." The "doubting brethren" who resisted the gospel of Jeffersonianism would be, in a sense, subject to the tyranny of the majority. This pressure would ultimately lead them to join "the union of sentiment."[14]

Jefferson was remarkably successful in building a presidency of popular consent and a government of majority rule. This success was partly due to a demagogic campaign directed against Federalist dissenters who were portrayed as "monarchists" or, later, as "plutocrats." Being portrayed as a "monarchist" in the early American republic was comparable to being accused of being a Communist in the 1950s. As Federalist leader Fisher Ames later observed, the accusation of "monarchist" was "a substitute for argument, and its overmatch." The Federalists rapidly declined in influence, running their last serious candidate for president in 1816. While many of their wounds were self-inflicted, the elimination of the Federalists was hastened by one of the most successful propaganda campaigns of its kind in the nation's history.

Jefferson's gracious gesture made in his first inaugural address, "we are all Republicans, we are all Federalists," was followed four days later by a private letter in which he expressed his desire to "obliterate" the Federalists. By the fall of 1802, the gloves had come off, as the president referred to Federalist office-holders as "our enemies," and added that he would cleanse the government of any remaining Federalist taint. He was "determined to remove officers who are active or open mouthed against the government" and pledged to "sink federalism into an abyss from which there shall be no resurrection for it."[15]

A Living Constitution

After leaving the White House and witnessing the realization of his dream of dispensing with the Federalists, Jefferson pursued a more ambitious goal of radically remaking the American regime. Near the end of his life he became an advocate for a "ward-republic," a scheme that would lodge governmental responsibilities at the lowest possible level of society, as close to the people as possible. There was a certain logic in Jefferson's path to the point where he embraced participatory democracy, endorsing, oddly enough, something of a New England–town meeting form of government for the entire nation (New England was the region of the country where Jefferson was the least admired). A ward-republic close to the people would require a minimal national government and would ensure that the people were the masters of their own destiny.

Jefferson defended his proposed government of ward-republics by noting that it would be as firm a polity as ever existed:

> Where every man is a sharer in the direction of his ward-republic, or of some of the higher ones, and feels that he is a participator in the government of affairs, merely at an election one day in the year, but every day; when there shall not be a man in the State who will not be a member of some one of its councils, great or small, he will let the heart be torn out of his body sooner than his power be wrested from him by a Caesar or a Bonaparte. . . . by making every citizen an acting member of the government, and in the offices nearest and most interesting to him, will attach him by his strongest feelings to the independence of his country, and its republican constitution.[16]

In addition to his commitment to minimal government locally administered, Jefferson attacked the notion of reverence for the Constitution endorsed by Washington, Hamilton, and later, Lincoln:

Some men look at constitutions with sanctimonious reverence, and deem them like the arc of the covenant, too sacred to be touched. They ascribe to the men of the preceding age a wisdom more than human, and suppose what they did to be beyond amendment. I knew that age well; I belonged to it, and labored with it. It deserved well of its country. It was very like the present, but without the experience of the present; and forty years of experience in government is worth a century of book-reading; and this they would say themselves, were they to rise from the dead. I am certainly not an advocate for frequent and untried changes in laws and constitutions. I think moderate imperfections had better be borne with; because, when once known, we accommodate ourselves to them, and find practical means of correcting their ill effects. But I know also, that laws and institutions must go hand in hand with the progress of the human mind. As that becomes more developed, more enlightened, as new discoveries are made, new truths disclosed, and manners and opinions change with the change of circumstances, institutions must advance also, and keep pace with the times.[17]

Bolstering his point that the dead should not govern the living, Jefferson added, "We might as well require a man to wear still the coat which fitted him when a boy, as civilized society to remain ever under the regimen of their barbarous ancestors." For Jefferson, true republicanism in the United States resided in the hearts and minds of the citizenry, and not in the Constitution. Republicanism could not be found in the principles of that document, nor in the system it created, but "merely in the spirit of our people."[18] That same year, 1816, Jefferson expanded his definition of republicanism even further, noting that a government meets the definition of republicanism "to the extent that its citizens engage in 'direct action.'"[19]

Since institutions should evolve with the times, Jefferson recommended that constitutional conventions be convened every nineteen or twenty years to reconstitute the political order. He bluntly noted: "The dead have no rights. They are nothing; and nothing cannot own something. . . . This corporeal globe, and everything upon it, belong[s] to its present corporeal inhabitants, during their generation. They alone have a right to direct what is the concern of themselves alone, and to declare the law of that direction; and this declaration can only be made by their majority."[20] Again, this would be done through a process like the New England town meeting, with average citizens convening to rewrite their Constitutions:

The mayor of every ward, on a question like the present, would call his ward together, take the simple yea or nay of its members, convey these to the county court, who would hand on those of all its wards to the proper general authority; and the voice of the whole people would be thus fairly, fully, and peaceably expressed, discussed, and decided by the common reason of the society.[21]

Jefferson's friend James Madison, always the more temperate of the two Virginians, was not persuaded by Jefferson's argument. Madison had once assured Jefferson that he would be at the "ready" to "receive your commands with pleasure," but in this instance he expressed his displeasure by noting that he was perhaps a mere "ordinary politician" who was unable to perceive "the sublime truths . . . seen thro' the medium of Philosophy."[22]

The idea of a civil religion, or perhaps any religion at all, was also anathema to Jefferson, who believed in progress and the advancement of the human mind. A new form of man was emerging in the United States, one capable not only of self-government but untethered from the strictures of the past. As he wrote to a young admirer in 1799, "I believe also, with Condorcet [French philosopher], as mentioned in your letter, that his [mankind's] mind is perfectible to a degree of which we cannot as yet form any conception." Jefferson was, as his biographer Dumas Malone referred to him, "a prophet of progress."[23]

For Jefferson's Federalist opponents, this notion of the march of progress of mankind was divorced from reality. Historian Linda K. Kerber has succinctly summed up the Federalist response to Jefferson's visionary musings, "All the famous Jeffersonian rhetoric about man's capacity to construct a better world from new blueprints was so much high-flown nonsense. It was given to man only to remodel his world, not to remake it, and then only with the greatest caution."[24]

Jeffersonianism paved the way for the Jacksonian populism that led to the destruction of the Bank of the United States and promoted a narrative of American history as a perpetual saga of conflict between corrupt elites and virtuous common folk. In 1816 Jefferson encouraged a citizen intent on revising the Constitution of the Commonwealth of Virginia not to retreat in the face of "the croakings of wealth against the ascendency of the people."[25] These appeals to populism, to class resentments, were effectively employed in the campaign against Hamilton and the Federalists. Through intermediaries in the press, such as Philip Freneau and James Callender, both of whom were at times on Jefferson's payroll, the message was clear: the Federalist party was intent on establishing an aristocracy of wealth and privilege, to "the exclusion of the influence of the people."[26] Thomas Jefferson and his followers were all that stood in the way of this betrayal of the spirit of 1776.

The Price of Majority Rule

The theme of Jefferson and his party as champions of the common man remained a consistent talking point throughout the entirety of Jefferson's public life and beyond. It was a potent message, and one that redounded to the benefit of the party of Jefferson and Jackson well into the twentieth century. Sadly, Jeffersonian populism also became the vehicle by which the institution of slavery further entrenched itself in American society. In the final years of his life, Jefferson began to see abolitionists as Hamilton's heirs determined to oppress the agrarian South. Consequently, Jefferson's position on the crucial issue of slavery in the American republic regressed, to the detriment of his place in the American pantheon, not to mention to the slaves he owned and to the minds he influenced.

Those who believe in the wisdom of the common man, as Jefferson did, need to confront the fact that popular wisdom among many Americans in the nineteenth century held that Africans were lesser beings not worthy of self-government. As a result, Jefferson's party led the effort to disenfranchise free blacks in the North, a development which undermines the notion that Jeffersonians championed the interests of the "common man." Free blacks in the North voted overwhelmingly Federalist, a phenomenon exploited by Jeffersonian demagogues with caustic campaign ballads such as "Federalists with blacks unite."[27] As far as promoting the interests of the common man, things looked different if you happened to be of African descent or even a Native American. Most Federalists were far more sympathetic, and at times even acted on these sympathies, in defense of those minority groups.

Populism, sadly, is frequently the vehicle by which those who run for elected office exploit the fears of those who are not quite "one of us," and seek to relegate them to second-class status, or worse. Jefferson himself was a beneficiary of, or perhaps more accurately, an enabler of this phenomenon, segueing from a proponent of the equal rights for all men, to a defender of the interests of the agrarian, slave-holding South. Jefferson was an eloquent proponent of the rights of man, but to borrow a term used by John Quincy

Adams, he was also a leading member of the Southern "slavocracy."[28] Jefferson balked at following the lead of his fellow Virginia slave owner, George Washington, who freed his slaves upon his and his wife's deaths.[29]

It was Washington's fellow "elitist" Federalists, including Hamilton, John Jay, Gouverneur Morris, Timothy Pickering, Rufus King, Thomas Fitzsimons, and others, who opposed the peculiar institution, believing that the racial animus that animated proslavery opinion on this matter was immoral and contrary to the principles of the American founding. During the War of 1812, leading New England Federalists hastened the party's demise with their involvement in the Hartford Convention, which was portrayed as a treasonous cabal intent on withdrawing New England from the war, and possibly from the Union. Yet it is often overlooked that delegates to that convention proposed a constitutional amendment to abolish the three-fifths compromise, the vehicle by which the party of Jefferson, and its slaveholding base, retained control of the presidency.[30] One of the Federalist leaders of the Hartford "cabal," Senator Harrison Gray Otis, would later note during the struggle over the Missouri Compromise in 1820 that "all persons born in Massachusetts, of free parents, were citizens," and described his state's free blacks as "legitimate co-proprietors with himself" of the United States.[31]

Only in Federalist states, which were seen then and now as bastions of "elitism," did free blacks retain the status of citizens. Maine, Massachusetts, New Hampshire, and Vermont were the only states to never disenfranchise African American voters, while Jeffersonian strongholds in the North and South increasingly restricted the African American franchise throughout the age of Jefferson and Jackson. In New York, where the governor delivered the state for Jefferson in 1800 and 1804, "most free African Americans appeared to have supported the Federalist Party, which included their former masters and some of the leaders of the Manumission Societies, including notable figures such as Alexander Hamilton," as Jason Duncan has noted. In 1799, prominent Federalist John Jay, who served as the second governor of New York, signed the Act for the Gradual Abolition of Slavery, which provided that all children born to slaves would be freed upon becoming adults, and in 1801 an amendment was added prohibiting exporting slaves out of the state. These steps, and others, were condemned by Hamilton's and Jay's Jeffersonian opponents, who "castigated their Federalist rivals for encouraging black political participation (albeit that essentially limited to the ballot box) and increasingly saw American politics as something belonging to white men alone."[32]

A government operating on the plane of "consent" during the age of Jefferson and Jackson meant a government operating to maintain racial disenfranchisement. While the franchise for white male voters expanded during this age, including the removal of property qualifications, black voters were disenfranchised in several states in the ensuing years, including in Delaware, Kentucky, New Jersey, and Maryland, and were prohibited from voting in all the states added as the nation expanded to the west.[33]

The Jefferson and Jackson revolutions epitomized the tyranny of the majority at its worst. In 1789, when the new Constitution took effect, free blacks could vote in all the states in the Union except Georgia and Virginia. In 1792, twelve of the fifteen states allowed free blacks to vote, but beginning in 1803, during Jefferson's presidency, members of his party began to constrict voting rights throughout the Union. By 1840, after the completion of the Jacksonian revolution, free blacks could only vote in four of the twenty-six states in the Union. Skin color became the discriminating factor in a nation that was slowly abandoning its founding principles and acceding to the wishes of a political party that enforced majority rule by targeting dissenting minorities.[34]

Having built a party dynasty and a Virginia dynasty through the "little arts of popularity," Jefferson's devotion to popular rule intensified in the final years of his life, to the point where he embraced the idea that foundational questions regarding the very nature of the American political order should be settled by majority vote, by "popular sovereignty," as new states were admitted to the Union. When a growing abolitionist movement threatened the political clout of slave interests within the American Union, Jefferson now argued that the best way to put slavery on the path to elimination was to expand it. Reversing himself from a stance he had taken in the 1780s, Jefferson claimed that Congress lacked the authority to ban slavery in the new state of Missouri. While continuing to pay rhetorical obeisance to the notion of the eventual extinction of slavery, Jefferson's proposals would have further entrenched the peculiar institution. As one historian of antebellum America noted, "Thomas Jefferson had virtually invented the idea of prohibiting slavery in the American West, but now, thirty-six years later, he opposed the restrictive portion of the [Missouri] Compromise, adducing the 'diffusion' argument that the expansion of slavery would ameliorate the condition of the slave."[35]

The former president saw the struggle over the Missouri Compromise as a ruse on the part of unreconstructed Federalists, led by Senator Rufus King, to resurrect themselves by fashioning a moral appeal that would move moderate Republicans into the Federalist fold.

> The Federalists, completely put down and despairing of ever rising again under the old divisions of Whig and Tory, devised a new one of slave-holding, & non-slave-holding States, which, while it had a semblance of being moral, as at the same time geographical, and calculated to give them ascendency. . . . Moral the question certainly is not, because the removal of slaves from one State to another, no more than their removal from one country to another, would never make a slave of one human being who would not be so without it.[36]

Inclined to impute the lowest possible motives to his political opponents, Jefferson dismissed the idea that those arguing for a slave-free Missouri were motivated by genuine moral concern. Jefferson believed that having failed in their effort to restore "monarchy" in the United States, Federalist reactionaries were now cynically invoking moral arguments over human bondage as a scheme to win votes.[37] While some Federalists did adopt abolitionism purely out of electoral self-interest, it is also true that many Federalists were influenced by their religious upbringing and possessed a genuine moral antipathy to slavery. One of the most famous abolitionists, William Lloyd Garrison, was steeped in New England Federalism and in the antislavery theological teachings of the Congregationalist Church.[38] As historian David Herbert Donald has noted, "virtually all [of] the parents of [nineteenth-century abolitionists] were stanch Federalists."[39] For these Federalists, ownership of human beings was contrary to the Declaration of Independence and to biblical teaching.

As Paul Finkelman has observed, the Federalists "in some ways [laid] the groundwork for what would become the abolitionist critique of American politics." From 1787 to the Missouri Compromise of 1820, Federalists "often opposed the pro-slavery racism of the Jeffersonians."[40] Many of the heirs to these antislavery Federalists would go on at first to become antislavery Whigs, and eventually form the Republican Party of the 1850s.

One of the problems with displacing the framers' Constitution and substituting a majoritarian "constitution" was that it endorsed, in essence, the idea that a majority could vote up or down on the permissibility of slavery. All matters, even those of great moral and ethical consequence, were subject to this simple, and one might say, morally neutered, manner of governing. This was part of Jefferson's legacy, one that was resisted by the "elitist" Federalists, whose fears of simple majority rule were rooted in the idea that the history of government by unbridled majorities was checkered at best.

Americans would do well to abandon the all too persistent myth that sees the Federalists as enemies of the common man. This view has distorted our understanding of the past, particularly regarding our understanding of slavery and the founding fathers, and but also our understanding of the American presidency. Federalists viewed the latter office as a bulwark of liberty, a liberty that was vulnerable to a majority intent on oppressing a minority, whether a political minority, a religious minority, a minority of wealth, and yes, a racial minority. Jefferson moved that office away from that purpose, all the while insisting, genuinely so, that he was acting in the interests of limited government and protecting the citizenry from the privileged few. But his refounding of the presidency instead set the office on an unhealthy path of kowtowing to one of the greatest sources of tyranny, that of the majority.

"The Voice of the Nation"

The reckoning for American slavery was decades away, and in the interim the Jeffersonian template for the presidency replaced that of Washington and Hamilton. The president alone represented the "national will" and was uniquely situated to see the "whole ground," as Jeremy Bailey observes. Therefore, the president served as a guiding force for the entire government, and through speeches such as Jefferson's inaugural address and through public proclamations he promoted his vision for the nation. Jefferson attempted to use his office to "direct national aspirations" and "bring the opinions of the citizens together under a single head." Jefferson's presidency was both gauging public opinion and at times shaping it and moderating it, using the presidency "to direct the public's constitutional understanding and to unify public opinion."[41] While Jefferson avoided the type of overt public appeals that would characterize twentieth-century American presidents, he did attempt to directly influence public opinion through the use of letters explaining his policies to party gatherings, state legislatures, and private citizens. In the case of his unpopular embargo of 1807–1808, Jefferson wrote some nineteen letters designed to bolster the embargo policy in the face of virulent opposition.[42]

Thomas Jefferson's elevation to the presidency was "decided by the voice of the nation," and all good citizens were now required to abide by the "will of the law" as set by that electoral mandate.[43] Jefferson's presidency was a forerunner of Andrew Jackson's and Martin Van Buren's, both of whom practiced, and to an extent, institutionalized, the "little arts of popularity." Jefferson also anticipated the Jackson presidency by rebuffing Washington's standard for government appointees, the "best available man," opting instead for "friendship" as a standard for cabinet appointments, along with programmatic loyalty to the Jeffersonian agenda. Jefferson lifted "politics over merit" and paved the way for the more significant patronage reforms instituted by Andrew Jackson.[44]

By conceiving the presidency as both a servant and shaper of public opinion, and by enhancing the role of majority consent in the government writ large, Jefferson also foretold the rise of what Alexis de Tocqueville would later describe as the "tyranny of the majority."[45] James Madison had previously warned of the dangers of majority "faction" in his famous *Federalist* no. 10 essay. Madison saw factions as a threat to popular government as they sought to convert government into a slave of its "ruling passion or interest," thereby sacrificing the common good or the rights of minorities.[46] Jefferson held that "there are two requirements for republican government, representing the majority will and executing it."[47] This was, again, contrary to the spirit and letter of the Constitution.

One formidable obstacle to Jefferson's agenda of displacing the founders' Constitution with a constitution based on popular rule was the chief justice of the United States, John Marshall. Marshall's lineage was strictly Federalist, and he was one of the last American political figures who knew, and learned from, Washington, Hamilton, and Adams. Marshall revered Alexander Hamilton and had incorporated Hamilton's legal thinking into many landmark judicial rulings, including *Marbury v. Madison* (1803) and *McCulloch v. Maryland* (1819). Marshall, a Virginian, had been appointed chief justice by President John Adams, and was President Thomas Jefferson's distant cousin, a fact which did nothing to mitigate their disdain for one another. Jefferson believed that Marshall and a Federalist-stacked judicial branch were a "subtle corps of sappers and miners constantly working under ground to undermine the foundations of our confederated fabric." Judges acted unchecked, for "they consider themselves secure for life;

they sculk from responsibility to public opinion the only remaining hold on them."[48]

More than any other man save Washington and Hamilton, John Marshall understood the threat presented by his cousin's theories. The chief justice noted in 1832 in a letter to a fellow jurist, Joseph Story, that Jefferson's doctrine of nullification had inspired South Carolina's nullification efforts in response to tariffs enacted by the federal government. Marshall observed, "We are now gathering the bitter fruits of the tree . . . planted by Mr. Jefferson, and so industriously and perseveringly cultivated by Virginia."[49]

The antimajoritarian tendencies of an unelected judiciary appointed for life ran counter to Jefferson's belief in majority rule. He noted in a Christmas Day letter to an admiring journalist that in regards to Federalist judicial usurpations, "'against this every man should raise his voice,' and more, should uplift his arm."[50] Jefferson would later add that "it should be remembered, as an axiom of eternal truth in politics, that whatever power in any government is independent, is absolute also. . . . Independence can be trusted nowhere but with the people in mass."[51] He also noted that "When the legislative or executive functionaries act unconstitutionally, they are responsible to the people in their elective capacity. The exemption of the judges from that is quite dangerous enough. I know of no safe depository of the ultimate powers of the society, but the people themselves."[52] In one of the last letters Jefferson ever wrote, he endorsed the idea of majority rule and urged a legislator to strip the courts of their jurisdiction over legislative acts. If he were to succeed in "restraining judges from usurping legislation," the legislator's reputation would be perpetually secured.[53]

Simplifying the Presidency

Another significant aspect of Jefferson's "Revolution of 1800" was his effort to depersonalize the presidency, removing the undemocratic public celebrations and "monarchical" trappings of Washington's presidency. Jefferson possessed, as he once put it to James Monroe, a "hatred of ceremony," and his presidency was one of the least ostentatious of any occupant of the executive branch.[54] But in fact, Jefferson's populist presidency relied more on personal appeal than on constitutional authority and made the fatal assumption that there would always be another Jefferson, a man of learning and proper sensibilities, on the horizon. Ironically, despite his efforts to depersonalize the presidency, the success of the Jeffersonian presidency relied to a great extent on the personal character of the president, on his integrity, on his lack of demagoguery, than Washington and Hamilton's constitutional presidency.

Jefferson's "Revolution of 1800" began on inauguration day, as Jefferson ate breakfast with thirty or so guests at a simple boarding house, after which he walked to the Capitol clad in modest plain clothes, without any trumpets blowing or fancy coaches with elaborately costumed horses.[55] After the new president completed his oath of office and delivered a brief inaugural address, he strolled back to the boarding house where he began his day, and enjoyed a meal with its relatively nondescript patrons.[56] It was democratic simplicity at its finest.

Jefferson abandoned Washington's practice of delivering an annual message to Congress, considering it too monarchical, and jettisoned the weekly levees Washington had instituted as a way of meeting the public. Those events, with their awkward bowing rituals, were also seen as an inappropriate activity in a republic. Determined to drain the swamp, or more accurately, clean out the stables, the new president quickly sold the coaches, gilded harnesses, and all the horses save one that had accumulated in the executive mansion during John Adams's presidency.[57] Jefferson also abandoned Washington's practice of touring the nation, believing such tours were an additional affront to a modest republic. The new president was "not reconciled to the idea of a chief magistrate parading himself through the several states as an object of public gaze."[58]

All these steps were designed to remove the stain of "corruption" that Jefferson believed to be the legacy of Washington, Hamilton, and Adams. His inauguration day "buried levees, birthdays, royal parades, and the arrogation of precedence in society by certain self-stiled friends of order, but truly stiled friends of privileged orders."[59] He maintained something of an open-door policy at the executive mansion and hosted frequent small dinners for members of Congress and foreign emissaries that were noted for their studied informality. He appeared to many "elitist" Europeans as ill-dressed and somewhat ill-groomed, but again, all of this was an act by a man noted for his love of fine wines and who was as comfortable in a Paris salon as the most rarefied Gaul. Portraits of the early Jefferson, and Jefferson in Europe, reveal a far more refinely coutured Jefferson than that seen in later years. Jefferson seemed to have delighted in receiving stuffy British ambassadors and "elitist" Federalist members of Congress in threadbare slippers. Senator William Plumer of New Hampshire described Jefferson in 1802 as "drest, or rather undrest, with an old brown coat, red waistcoat, old corduroy small clothes, much soiled-woolen hose-and slippers without heels."[60] Jefferson was America's first populist president, but hardly its last; he was a remote man whose private life was completely detached from the madding crowd, but whose principles and presidential practices earned him the respect and admiration of the citizenry.

A year after assuming the presidency, Jefferson noted with pride that his campaign to reverse the Federalist counterrevolution had met with great success, including the "suppress[ion] of all those public forms and ceremonies which tended to familiarise the public eye to the harbingers of another form of government."[61] Jefferson was intent on demystifying and depersonalizing the presidency, of turning it into a populist presidency where the president appeared to defer to the people's representatives in Congress, all the while acting as the puppeteer of that body whose members received directives from him frequently with instructions to "burn after reading." Jefferson believed that his presidency and his party lacked the strong-man hierarchical structure of Hamilton's Federalists, whom Jefferson believed had a penchant for "autocratic rule." In fact, Jefferson ran his party more effectively than Hamilton managed the Federalists; it was simply more difficult to see, as Jefferson's party leadership was of the hidden-hand variety.

Martin Van Buren, who would go on to become the nation's eighth president, recalled a discussion with Jefferson in 1824 in which the former president always referred to Federalist actions by saying "Hamilton" did such a thing, while his own party's actions were portrayed as the "Republicans" acted in such a way. Van Buren diagnosed the core of Jefferson's cunning leadership style: appear to be reluctant to wield power and conduct oneself with deference and in a collegial manner, seeming to obey the sentiments of the whole, all the while shaping and manipulating those sentiments in a covert manner.

Jefferson averred conflict and sought to avoid quarrels with his cabinet officers or members of Congress, governing as a president seeking consensus. This consensus of course would be achieved through the benign, oblique guidance of the president himself.[62] Jefferson was able to covertly shape congressional sentiments to a degree, and arguably shape public sentiments as well, both covertly and overtly, a skill many of his successors lacked. Although in certain cases Jefferson's Machiavellian talents eluded his successors, in other instances it seems as if these successors believed that diverting or obstructing public sentiments was an inappropriate exertion of presidential power. Truth be told, after Jefferson departed the capital for the last time and retired to his Albemarle mountaintop, there were few Jeffersons to be found.

A Passionate Revolutionary

There is an element of Jefferson's presidency of popular consent, and his deference to majority rule, that should give pause to all lovers of liberty. There was an immoderation about the man that included a disturbing tendency to embrace mob action. One sees this in repeated statements, and in some cases actions, during his remarkably lengthy public career. Jefferson seemed to have an affinity for revolution no matter what the cause or the course it took. (The Haitian slave uprising of the 1790s being a glaring exception. Jefferson feared that this successful slave uprising would inspire similar revolts in the American South). He considered Shays's Rebellion a positive event, for "the spirit of resistance to government is so valuable on certain occasions, that I wish it to be always kept alive.... I like a little rebellion now and then. It is like a storm in the atmosphere."[63] While Jefferson's reaction to Shays's Rebellion was arguably more insightful and certainly more temperate than the hysterical reaction of some of his contemporaries, the same cannot be said for his reaction to and encouragement of the French Revolution. In Jefferson's view, if that revolution destroyed half the planet and killed every man and woman save one apiece in every country (to preserve the species), it was worth it.

As he noted in an angry rebuff to William Short, a US emissary to France and a longtime acquaintance who voiced qualms about the bloody course of the revolution, "rather than it should have failed, I would have seen half the earth desolated. Were there but an Adam and an Eve left in every country, and left free, it would be better than as it now is."[64] Short would later note that Jefferson's "greatest illusions in politics have proceeded from a most amiable error on his part; having too favorable [an] opinion of the animal called Man."[65]

The same blasé attitude toward revolutionary violence permeated his response to the Whiskey Rebellion, which Jefferson labeled "Hamilton's Insurrection." Jefferson condemned the Washington administration's "inexcusable aggression" toward "people at their ploughs." While there are ample grounds to question the seriousness of both the Shays and Whiskey uprisings, hindsight always providing great clarity, Jefferson was consistently, and oddly, sanguine regarding revolutionary violence, as noted in chapter one. Beyond delighting in the fact that Alexander Hamilton was pelted with rocks and denied the right to speak by a mob during a public presentation over the Jay Treaty, Jefferson's attitude toward his opponents was borderline authoritarian. He proposed treason trials for Virginia bankers who were brazen enough to cooperate with Alexander Hamilton's hated Bank of the United States. If convicted, the bankers would be subject to execution.[66] Jefferson's hatred of the national bank had its limits, however, in that he borrowed money from both the First and Second Bank of the United States to assist in maintaining the standard of living to which he was accustomed.[67]

There was one domestic uprising that earned Jefferson's ire—the lawless and sometimes violent opposition to his various embargo acts of 1807–1808 that took place around the Lake Champlain region of Vermont and New York. President Jefferson crushed this unrest with a series of coercive acts of questionable, at best, constitutionality.[68] But the Draconian enforcement of the law regarding the Lake Champlain disorder stands out as the exception to the Jeffersonian rule of embracing popular uprisings. Jefferson was quite selective regarding invocations of the rule of law, casting the notion of obedience to law aside when revolts were directed at his political opponents.

Jefferson's immoderation was most evident in his virulent hatred for all things British, and hatred for Americans he believed to be pro-British. For Jefferson, the War of 1812 was a war against an evil empire. At the onset of the war, Jefferson wrote to President James Madison proposing that the war's opponents be targeted for lynching or the gruesome practice of tarring and feathering. Regarding dissenters in the South, the former president noted that "the Federalists . . . are open mouthed" against war and observed that "a barrel of tar to each state south of the Potomac will keep all in order." For opponents in the North, a more severe response would be required, for the Northerners "will give you more trouble. You may there have to apply the rougher drastics . . . hemp [hanging] and confiscation."[69]

As with most visionaries, Jefferson tended to see the world in black and white. His domestic opponents were rarely considered men of principle; they were corrupt courtiers of the privileged, or British agents, but most certainly not "one of us." Jefferson's zeal can also be seen in his proposal that the Madison administration burn down St. Paul's Cathedral in retaliation for the British burning of Washington, DC in August 1814. This arson could be accomplished, the former president believed, by bribing some of London's poor to act as "incendiaries" on behalf of the United States. The inconclusive end to the War of 1812, Jefferson believed, meant that the United States would be locked in an "eternal war" that would end up with the "extermination of the one or the other party."[70]

Jefferson's history of intemperate remarks is exceeded only by a few American presidents, including Andrew Jackson. There has been a successful effort on the part of some of Jefferson's admirers, both then and now, to separate Jefferson from Jackson. But while the former allegedly spoke critically of the latter in an account offered by Daniel Webster (Jackson's "passions" were difficult for him to control, Webster recorded Jefferson saying, making him a "dangerous man"),[71] attempts to draw a distinction between the two are often overdrawn, as Jefferson paved the way for Jackson and the two tended to view American politics through the same lens.

Jackson was Jefferson without the refinement, without any literary sense, a crude version of Jefferson who fought his enemies openly, and shared Jefferson's enthusiasm for majority rule. Both men played the class card to great effect, with Jefferson destroying the Federalists with this card, while Jackson dealt it to great effect against John Quincy Adams and Nicholas Biddle, the epitome of the East Coast elite. The goals of the respective plantation owners of Monticello and the Hermitage were more closely aligned than we are often led to believe. As Jefferson's biographer Dumas Malone has noted, Jefferson was on "the best of personal terms" with Jackson and had approved of Jackson's controversial invasion of Florida in 1817–1818.[72]

The Conspiracy Within

There was an additional aspect of Jefferson's public career that reveals a certain affinity between Jefferson and Jackson regarding their approach to politics. Both men assumed the worst of their opponents, adopting a conspiratorial view of their motives and quickly transforming disputes over principles and policy into personal affronts. One sees this streak in Jefferson most clearly in his combat with Alexander Hamilton during the three years and nine months they overlapped as members of President Washington's cabinet.

In the minds of most Jeffersonians, Alexander Hamilton was a British agent, a cunning immigrant who repeatedly manipulated an aging, somewhat obtuse President George Washington. Jefferson believed that Hamilton was "not only a monarchist" but an advocate "for a monarchy bottomed on corruption."[73] Jefferson suggested that Hamilton was something of a closet Caesar, and reported his concerns to President Washington, claiming that the treasury secretary sought to "prepare the way for a change of the present republican form of government to that of a monarchy."[74]

Jefferson's worst conspiratorial instincts came to the fore in his effort to oust Hamilton from Washington's cabinet. The treasury secretary had been engaged in "a tissue of machinations against the liberty of the country" from the "moment at which history can stoop to notice him," the secretary of state claimed in a letter to the president.[75] Washington dismissed these accusations as out of hand, but Jefferson never abandoned these views. At first Jefferson assumed that an innocent Washington was being manipulated by Hamilton, but over time he began to see Washington as one of Hamilton's coconspirators, as a "Solomon" who had sold his soul to the "harlot" England.[76]

Jefferson was appalled that Hamilton did not see eye to eye with him despite the latter having been "received" by Americans and "given . . . bread" and having honors "heaped . . . on his head."[77] This was one of the first of many Democrat-Republican appeals to nativism, to the notion that Hamilton was simply "not one of us." Hamilton was "bewitched and perverted by the British example" and to make matters worse, Jefferson cited in his unpublished *Anas* a report that Hamilton led a toast to King George III at a New York City dinner party. According to the report, "Hamilton started up on his feet, and insisted on a bumper and three cheers."[78]

It was Jefferson's lieutenants who tried to destroy Hamilton's reputation by leaking the story of the latter's extramarital affair with Maria Reynolds. Jefferson's underlings ensured that a Republican scandalmonger, James Callender, an operative on Jefferson's payroll, published the account of the affair which the treasury secretary engaged in from 1791 into 1792. Callender would later turn on his benefactor and publish accusations of Jefferson's alleged relationship with Sally Hemings.

Jefferson's animosity toward Hamilton ran so deep that he questioned Hamilton's courage as a soldier in the American Revolution. Jefferson accused Hamilton of cowardice in the face of a yellow fever epidemic in 1793 and dismissed reports of Hamilton's valor. The treasury secretary was in fact "timid," and his reputation for courage was simply not "genuine."[79] In addition to his dearth of courage, Hamilton was also corrupt. When Jefferson became president in 1801, he ordered his secretary of the treasury, Albert Gallatin, to comb through the records and find examples of Hamilton's corruption. None was ever found. For President Jefferson the absence of any evidence of Hamilton's corruption was only further evidence of the crafty treasury secretary's skills at deceit.[80] Sadly, Jefferson's conspiratorial interpretation of Hamilton became gospel within the ranks of many progressive historians and politicians.[81]

Part of Jefferson's genius as a partisan leader was his ability to simplify complex issues, such as the establishment of a national bank, and portray it as an attempt by elites to fashion a system designed to oppress the common man. All of Hamilton's economic and fiscal proposals were depicted in this light: a privileged few were attempting to line their own pockets and oppress the honest tillers of the land. It was a remarkably effective message, one that persists in its effectiveness. Alexander Hamilton could muster all the intellectual arguments he was capable of in defense of a national bank or assuming revolutionary war debts, but rational argument was no match for allegations of criminal conspiracy and appeals to class resentments. Those appeals will triumph every time over dispassionate economic analysis.

While the bank was signed into law in February 1791, it became *the* hot button issue to rally the Jeffersonian and Jacksonian faithful throughout much of the nation's first fifty years. This merging of a conspiratorial worldview with populist politics was seamlessly executed, although it should be noted that the hurdle was not especially high, in that the two are virtually indistinguishable. Conspiracies offer an attractive alternative to grappling with the complexities of life and provide for a concise, all-encompassing form of messaging directed at voters. This form of politics was birthed at the national level by the Jeffersonian movement of the 1790s and became routine practice during the age of Jackson.

Jeffersonian Legacies

The personalization of the presidency, direct popular appeals, the canonization of the idea of majority rule, and the decline in devotion to the rule of law, were all troubling developments for the American presidency and for the republic at large. The rule of law is intended to prevent zealots in positions of power from abusing their power and destroying the right to life and liberty. The dangers presented by immoderate visionaries render the populist presidency a threat to republican government. Jefferson was not necessarily a danger, but there were no guarantees that he would be succeeded by men of his caliber, and this was a problem now that the bulwark provided by the constitutional presidency had been breached. As his friend James Madison might have told him, "a dependence on the people is no doubt the primary control on the government; but experience has taught mankind the necessity of auxiliary precautions."[82]

When Jefferson elevated the people to a position of prominence unintended by the framers, a slow and somewhat imperceptible process began to erode those auxiliary precautions. These precautions were further undermined by Andrew Jackson, and almost obliterated by twentieth-century presidents and their academic admirers. And they were welcomed, not surprisingly, by most of the American people, who were the alleged beneficiaries of the populist presidency.

3

Andrew Jackson

"The Majority Is to Govern"

Andrew Jackson was the first president since George Washington to ride into the executive mansion due in part to his status as a war hero. "Old Hickory," the victor of the Battle of New Orleans, shared little else in common with George Washington, the personification of moderation, prudence, and magnanimity. Jackson's disdain for Washington ran deep; he was one of only twelve members of Congress to vote against a tribute to the retiring president while serving as the first member of the House of Representatives from the new state of Tennessee. In Jackson's view, Washington was a closet dictator, one who "[had] been grasping after power, and in many instances, exercised powers, that he was not constitutionally invested with."[1]

This relatively minor incident in Jackson's remarkable life is worthy of mention for the light it casts on Jackson's political views. A populist to the core, the semi-illiterate Jackson despised East Coast elites, and especially the fiscal and economic policies of the nation's first treasury secretary, Alexander Hamilton. Jackson had voted against the tribute to Washington due to the latter's support for the Jay Treaty in 1795, but he also had Hamilton's policies in mind. The Jay Treaty, as noted in chapter one, was a defining moment in the history of the early republic, drawing a line of demarcation between those professing to defend the interests of the people and those who betrayed the spirit of 1776.

Andrew Jackson agreed with Jefferson's assessment that the Jay Treaty was "an alliance between England & the Anglomen of this country against the legislature & people of the United States."[2]

Before entering the House of Representatives, Jackson suggested that Washington be impeached for his administration's sponsorship of the Jay Treaty. The treaty was "that child of aristocratic secrecy" and should "be removed, erased, and obliterated from the archives of the grand republic." Abandoning impeachment, Jackson settled for voting against the tribute resolution for George Washington.[3]

A People's President

Jackson was the personification of the American frontiersman, a rugged self-made man with a fierce sense of independence and a penchant for violence. Jackson's lengthy military and political career was animated by an impassioned disdain for those whom he believed saw themselves as his "betters." The saga of Jackson's life, and of fellow citizens like him, was a saga of being swindled by elites. These elites were to be fought with nearly the same level of ferocity he applied to the British or to Native Americans.

As a general and as a president, Jackson's leadership, as political scientist Fred Greenstein observed, "had all of the subtlety of a bludgeon."[4] In addition, Jackson's thinking verged toward the conspiratorial; in fact, it is difficult to find instances when it did not. For matters high and low, conspiracy theories were the first and frequently the last resort of his interpretation of events. One example of this can be found in his response to a bizarre rumor that circulated in 1834 where an alleged army of five thousand discontented Americans were mobilizing in Baltimore and planning to "destroy" the president. Jackson threatened to execute all five thousand members of this phantom insurgency by hanging them "as high as Haman."[5]

As with many political figures of the populist persuasion, Jackson found that conspiracy theories served as a way of making sense of a complex world he had difficulty comprehending. Conspiracy theories provided a shortcut to "understanding" without the need for intensive reading and study, and served as a substitute to exposure to a diverse world he lacked the will or the means to explore. Conspiracy theories are remarkably durable, and attractive, in that they provide the believer with a sense of control over events by attributing all their concerns, all threats to their way of life, to identifiable malevolent forces. The ability to explain the often unexplainable as somehow the result of some evil individual or cabal is oddly reassuring. These theories have always been popular with large segments of the public, and the more the presidency of popular consent bonded with the public, the greater the tendency of presidents from Andrew Jackson to Andrew Johnson to Donald Trump to use them to inspire their base.

Engaging in psychobiography is fraught with peril, but in Jackson's case his penchant for assuming that somewhere there was a cabal plotting to undermine him or his fellow frontiersmen seemed all consuming. At other times, Jackson's understanding of the world can be attributed to nothing more than a case of simple ignorance, as when he informed one of Alexander Hamilton's children, James Hamilton, that the latter's father "was not in favor of the Bank of the United States."[6]

In concert with his conspiratorial view of the world, Jackson had a penchant for violence that made him a somewhat effective but undisciplined military leader and led to an overly combative presidency. As Jackson himself once proudly noted, "I was born for a storm and calm does not suit me."[7] He was brutal in his treatment of captured runaway slaves, offering fifty dollars in a newspaper advertisement for the return of one of his slaves and "ten dollars extra for every hundred lashes any person will give him, to the amount of three hundred."[8] Jackson's advertisement amounted to a death sentence for this runaway slave.

At the risk of blaming the victim, there was something inevitable about the fact that in 1835 Jackson became the first president to be the target of an assassination. As the *New York Evening Post* observed, the assassination attempt was "a sign of the times."[9] Jackson resorted to a conspiracy theory to explain this event, claiming that it was carried out by a man hired by sitting United States Senator George Poindexter of Mississippi. At other times the Jacksonian press fantasized that Jackson's former vice president, John C. Calhoun, inspired the assassin.[10]

The age of Jackson is perhaps best known, somewhat inaccurately, as the age of democratic expansion, but it was also an age marked by a coarsening of American life and marred by frequent outbursts of violence. Jackson was comfortable with violence, as noted, and his visceral hatred for Hamilton and the Federalists led him to warmly welcome Aaron Burr in May 1805 as a guest at his plantation, less than a year after Burr shot Hamilton. Hamilton's death made Burr a hero in the eyes of all good Jeffersonians on the American frontier, as Jackson's biographer Robert V. Remini has observed.[11] Jackson killed a man in a duel the following year, and he would go on to participate in multiple duels, carrying two bullets in his body for much of his adult life.[12]

Violence permeated the age of Jackson, and its threatened employment was used by one of his surrogates to enhance the general's electoral prospects. In 1824, John Quincy Adams, Jackson's chief rival for the presidency, was the recipient of an anonymous note threatening the outbreak of civil war if Adams refused to withdraw from the race after the election was thrown into the House of Representatives. An editor of *The Papers of Andrew Jackson,* applying techniques of modern handwriting analysis, determined that the letter was written by William B. Lewis, one of Jackson's closest advisors.[13]

In 1834, halfway through Jackson's second term as president, a series of anti-abolitionist riots took place in New York City, with copycat riots occurring in other locations as well. White rioters directed their rage against free blacks or abolitionists in the streets of America's greatest city and elsewhere, while at the same time immigrants battled one another (when they were not attacking free blacks) for control of neighborhoods in those cities. This violence was something of an indicator of a perverse American vitality, the logical result of a democratizing nation paying homage to the sacrosanct notion of "power to the people." It was no coincidence that this violence coincided with Jackson's elevation to the American presidency. Less than half a century after the authors of the *Federalist Papers* warned of demagogues who fan the flames of passion, those qualities were becoming an American norm.

The Rule of the Majority vs. the Rule of Law

Jackson and his followers' penchant for violence was coupled with a disdain for the rule of law. The foremost chronicler of the age of Jackson, Daniel Walker Howe, has documented Jackson's history of "impatience with legal restraints."[14] This included the general's "creative interpretation" of executive orders that led Jackson to war with various Indian tribes in Florida, a decision that almost led the United States into war with Spain and Great Britain.[15] As a general during the War of 1812, Jackson unilaterally imposed martial law on New Orleans and arrested a civilian legislator who had questioned the propriety of the general's decision to maintain martial law after the war ended. Jackson then arrested a judge who ordered the legislator's release. A military tribunal acquitted the legislator, but Jackson refused to let the man go, and later had the judge force-marched out of town with instructions not to return.[16]

Alexander Hamilton had warned about characters such as Andrew Jackson, who achieved military glory and whose heroic status allowed them to segue into the political arena wrapped in the mantle of the people. Jackson fits this mold to an extent, and his constant appeals to class struggle and dismissiveness toward the rule of law diminished the founders' Constitution. Jackson's history suggests, as Mark A. Graber notes, "that the only common pattern in all of Jackson's legal arguments, from the War of 1812 to his farewell address, may be that all such arguments promoted the power of Andrew Jackson."[17]

Andrew Jackson was explicit in his rejection of the founding principles of the American Constitution. The foremost principle of the American experiment, as Jackson put it in his first annual message to Congress, was that "the majority is to govern." While the American framers believed in government by consent, they did not believe in government by the majority, believing instead in representation and additional checks on the tyranny of the majority. Jackson believed that impediments to majority rule, including the Electoral College, represented a perversion of the principle that "as few impediments as possible should exist to the free operation of the public will."[18]

Hamilton, Madison, and Washington created a system that allowed for the filtering effects of representation, and perhaps even allowed for the possibilities of statesmanship. Jackson's principles, building off Jefferson's, turned the presidency into the voice of the people, and diminished the prospects for statesmanship. The highest duty of the statesman, in the mind of the original founders, was to follow one's reason, reject narrow interests including one's own self-interest and the interests of a majority intent on oppressing a minority, and enrich the common good. It was not to act as a medium translating the majority's wishes into law.

Jackson's belief in majority rule was arrived at honestly, for he believed that justice demanded this, and that the history of the United States was the history of a privileged elite exploiting the majority. "Corruption in some, and, in others, a perversion of correct feelings and principles, divert Government from its legitimate ends, and make it an engine for the support of the few at the expense of the many," Jackson noted in his first annual message. It was the president's responsibility, he would later add in 1834, as the "direct representative of the American people" to prevent the privileged from taking advantage of the many.[19] In a letter written just weeks before he died, Jackson again disparaged the privileged and celebrated the "plainness of our republican citizens," the nation's repository of "true virtue." The "people, the great laboring and producing classes" formed "the bone and sinew of our confederacy."[20]

Andrew Jackson's belief in the ill intent of the privileged, along with his conspiratorial worldview, was reinforced by his loss to John Quincy Adams in the 1824 election. Jackson believed this election was stolen from him after a "corrupt bargain" was struck between Adams and Henry Clay, the speaker of the house. According to Jackson, Clay allegedly supported Adams in exchange for being appointed secretary of state. Jackson, revealing much about his self-image, then labeled Clay as "the Judas of the West," noting that Clay had received his thirty pieces of silver. "His end will be the same," Old Hickory added.[21] The furor surrounding the House's decision to award the popular vote loser the presidency propelled Jackson into the executive mansion in 1828. The lesson derived from the elections of 1824 and 1828 was clear: that Adams was elected through the constitutionally prescribed means was now seen as irrelevant due to the displacement of the constitutional presidency by Jefferson's presidency of popular consent.

Throughout the entirety of Adams's presidency, Jackson's supporters in Congress and the press deemed any action Adams undertook in the most sinister light. As historian Jeffrey L. Pasley has observed, "all of these attacks were directed at what was probably one of the least partisan administrations in U.S. history. Most of the charges were exaggerated or fictitious" but were all seen as "plausible" due to the "corrupt bargain."[22] The fact that Henry Clay shared many of the same views as Adams was dismissed as the rationale for his appointment by the Jacksonians. Adams's election to the presidency was a case of pure corruption that could only be cured by draining the swamp.

Jackson's vindictiveness was all consuming, and when he was finally elected in 1828, a major prerequisite for an individual to be awarded a cabinet post was that one had to demonstrate an appropriate level of hatred for Clay.[23] When Adams and Jackson met for their rematch in 1828, it produced one of the nastiest campaigns in American history, with the Jacksonian press claiming that Adams had acted as a pimp while serving as an American envoy to Russia, and Adams's press harping on the "illegitimacy" of Jackson's marriage.[24] This was another unfortunate but all too predictable result of the rise of the presidency of popular consent.

The coalition Jackson assembled was, at bottom, a cauldron of boiling partisan, racial, and class resentments, and in Jackson's case, all of those, plus decades of accumulated personal resentments thrown into the mix. As one newspaperman observed while discussing the lopsided race between Jackson and John Quincy Adams in 1828, the Adams campaign "dealt with man as he should be," while Jackson appealed to man "as he is."[25] Jackson played upon fears to mobilize his base, and no one understood this better than Adams, a target of Jackson's wrath and a champion of the rights of other frequent targets of those resentments, including abolitionists, African Americans, and Native Americans.

In contrast to Jackson, Adams was an inheritor of an enlightened antislavery Federalism possessed of a healthy understanding of the tyrannical instincts of the majority. Unpopular minorities bear the brunt of the populist presidency, and Adams was one of the last of a dying breed who understood the threat this presented to the American body politic. According to John Quincy Adams, Jackson was "a man governed by passion rather than reason, a demagogue."[26]

Adams diagnosed the radical change Andrew Jackson inflicted upon the presidency and the entire constitutional order. In the wake of Jackson's election, the nation would be inclined "to raise to the summit of Power a succession of Presidents the consummation of whose glory will be to growl and snarl with impotent fury against a money broker's shop, to rivet into perpetuity the clanking chain of the Slave, and to waste in boundless bribery to the west the invaluable inheritance of the Public Lands."[27]

There is considerable evidence to support Adams's diagnosis regarding Jackson's demagoguery. Jackson tended to take all policy disputes personally, as in his famous Bank War with the bank's president, Nicholas Biddle, when he told Martin Van Buren that the bank "is trying to kill me . . . but I will kill it."[28] Since this was a personal struggle for survival, the Bank War brought all of Jackson's conspiratorial fantasies to the fore. The president considered the bank to be a "monster" that sought to make "the rich richer and the potent more powerful."[29] In the early stages of his conflict with the bank, Jackson mentioned to James K. Polk that the "the hydra of corruption is only scotched not dead."

One problematic tendency found in the presidency of popular consent is that its practitioners engage in inflated rhetoric, and Andrew Jackson was one of the founding fathers of this practice. There seems to be something inevitable about this, for claiming to be the voice of the people requires a certain amount of hubris. If a person is the self-designated medium by which the voice of the people, which some believed was the voice of God, is to be propagated, one assumes a certain elevated status. Consequently, Jackson's rhetoric was boundless.

Some of Andrew Jackson's concerns regarding the Bank of the United States were not conspiratorial fantasies. There were legitimate concerns regarding the bank and its director, Nicholas Biddle, who had grown cozy with members of Congress, providing loans and hiring some members as lawyers. As with all human institutions, the bank was tarnished on occasion by corruption. The Bank of the United States had its flaws, and certainly by twenty-first-century standards operated in an ethically questionable manner. But there were also powerful arguments to be made in favor of the bank. The bank had been rechartered after the United States defaulted during the War of 1812 and had nearly lost that war by trying to win it without financing it. James Madison had reversed his position on the bank in the war's aftermath, and all those who understood economics and finance grasped the need for some federal entity that would serve as a nursery of national wealth, provide the wherewithal to conduct a war, and place the public credit on a sound footing.

But hatred of banks ran deep in the marrow of the Jefferson-Jackson coalition. Andrew Jackson was not known for subtlety, and unfortunately the notion of reforming the bank was not given serious consideration. In the minds of Jackson and his adherents, the bank was a threat to American liberty and must be destroyed.

Reasoned arguments in favor of a national bank were ineffective in the face of accusations of corruption, invoking the specter of "hydras and monsters," and passionate appeals based on class resentments. Jackson's second vice president, Martin Van Buren, eagerly endorsed the use of class warfare during the Bank War. He encouraged the president to play this card in his public messages, arguing that "this is in truth a question between Aristocracy and Democracy" and "cannot be too often or too forcibly impressed upon the minds of the people."[30] Most economic historians acknowledge that Jackson's destruction of the "monster" bank "left the country prey to violent swings of the business cycle until the present Federal Reserve System was created in 1913."[31]

Patronage, Public Relations, and the Personalized Presidency

Jackson's penchant for personalizing, and inflaming, political disputes can be seen in his holding John Quincy Adams and Henry Clay responsible for his wife's death. Rachel Jackson has passed away from a heart attack seemingly brought on from the stress of becoming First Lady and confronting accusations that she and her husband had committed adultery by marrying before her divorce from her first husband was finalized. Jackson instinctively, and incorrectly, blamed Adams and Clay for circulating reports that led to his wife's death.[32]

His tendency to personalize matters can also be seen in his handling of the Eaton Affair, a trivial matter that the president elevated into something approaching a constitutional crisis. With the shabby treatment of his wife no doubt in mind, Jackson retaliated against members of his own cabinet whose wives had ostracized Peggy Eaton, the new wife of the secretary of war, for her supposed checkered past. The "Petticoat Affair" was the height of pettiness, and indicative of Jackson's penchant for elevating personal matters into matters of state. Jackson devoted a remarkable amount of time during his first two years in office to dealing with the Eaton matter, including presenting a formal report to his cabinet. In the end, he forced his entire cabinet to resign over this matter.[33] Throughout his eight years in office, it became apparent that, unlike George Washington, Jackson never grasped that the presidency was not about him.

There was another aspect of Washington's legacy that Jackson rejected, and that involved the method of appointing federal office holders. In his quest to break the "elite" stranglehold on the American government, Jacksonian partisans were selected to fill government offices. The nation's first president, George Washington, had close to a thousand lesser offices to fill, including customs officials, lighthouse tenders, postal officials, and he insured that only those Americans who were "of known attachment" to the new Constitution received these posts. He personally supervised the selection of these officials, focusing on their integrity and character rather than on any subject matter expertise, although prior public service was a plus, as was the good standing of the individual within his community. All of this was designed to further bind the citizenry to the idea of a United States government, and to a nation rather than a locality, not to insure fidelity to a political figure or a political party.[34]

Andrew Jackson rejected that standard and gradually converted the federal government into a hiring agency for the Democratic Party. Democratizing the civil service had its merits, but the Jacksonian notion that anyone could serve in a position of responsibility had, at best, mixed results. Jackson's most prominent appointee was a close friend, Samuel Swartwout, whom he selected to be the collector of the Port of New York. After nine years on the job, Swartwout absconded to Europe with over one million dollars in his pocket.[35] This was a scandal the likes of which had never been seen under the old regime of "elite corruption."

The post office in particular became a partisan dumping ground, as George Washington's principle of political neutrality in federal hiring was discarded. As one of Jackson's political allies put it, "to the victor belong the spoils of the enemy."[36] After some awkward fits and starts, Jackson's patronage policies transformed the character of the government by granting political parties veto power over government appointments, particularly at the state and local level. Political "machines" became the order of the day, the most prominent example being New York City's Tammany Hall, which was controlled in part by Jackson's vice president, Martin Van Buren. Tammany Hall became something of a model urban machine noted for its power and corruption and its control of patronage in America's largest city.

Vice President Van Buren was a master at the game of influencing public opinion, and President Jackson quickly developed a solid grasp of these skills as well. At one point in his administration, Jackson took a page from President Washington's book and went on a tour of New England that began in the late spring of 1833, although he was not always greeted with the same amount of respect and admiration as Washington.[37]

But outside of New England, Jackson benefitted from his high name recognition and a hero status unequalled since George Washington. Jackson's larger-than-life stature allowed him to influence public opinion to a degree greater than Thomas Jefferson. Jackson did not rest either on his hero's laurels or high name recognition but instead took steps to ensure that his public messages were received in an unfiltered manner. His aides polished his frequent public statements, which appeared at a rate higher than any of his predecessors, and they expanded the practice of relying on newspapers to propagate their vision. The *United States Telegraph* became the official organ of the executive branch, subsidized by lucrative government printing contracts. When the editor of the *Telegraph* broke ranks with Jackson, the president shifted those contracts to the *Washington Globe,* which then became the administration's mouthpiece.[38]

Jackson also used the press to attack dissenters within his administration. When William Duane, one of his five secretaries of the treasury, balked at carrying out Jackson's orders regarding the Bank of the United States, the president used the *Washington Globe* as a means of disseminating stories critical of Duane. When this campaign of public shaming failed, Jackson fired Duane. The treasury secretary refused to go quietly, and instead published two insider accounts of his brief tenure in Jackson's cabinet, the first account of its kind from a former presidential appointee. Duane was determined to restore his good name in the court of public opinion, and thus inaugurated the tradition of fired executive branch officials airing their "dirty laundry" in public. This was yet another consequence of rooting the presidency in the fickle foundation of public opinion.[39]

Jackson's hand-picked successor, Martin Van Buren, engaged in the practice of media manipulation as adeptly as his predecessor. John Louis O'Sullivan, often credited with coining the phrase "Manifest Destiny," was the beneficiary of funds supplied by Van Buren, and the latter repaid the favor with pro–Van Buren pieces in his influential *Democratic Review.*[40] A presidency rooted in popular consent fostered this type of covert manipulation of public opinion.

The struggle to "control the message" led the Jackson administration to engage in a concerted campaign of censorship. Jackson endorsed a policy announced by his postmaster general prohibiting the distribution of abolitionist literature mailed to the South, and in December 1835 took the extraordinary step of urging Congress to pass a law prohibiting the mailing of "incendiary publications" dealing with slavery.[41] Jackson also urged that subscribers to abolitionist literature be "outed" by postal officials so that their fellow citizens could identify those who consumed subversive literature. Congress balked at the censorship proposal, but Jackson had revealed himself to be a proponent of the notion that a majority, at least in the South, should not be subjected to dissenting minority opinions. The majority truly was to rule.

Old Hickory on Slavery, Secession, and the Supreme Court

Andrew Jackson's stance on slavery belies his alleged championing of the common man. He was a slave trader and one of the largest slaveholders in Tennessee, making him a member of the "slaveholding aristocracy" of the Volunteer State. One of Jackson's biographers, Robert V. Remini, while sympathetic to "Old Hickory," noted that Jackson believed that "slaveholding was as American . . . as capitalism, nationalism, or democracy." Accusations of Jackson's active role as a slave trader emerged as something of a campaign issue in the election of 1828, but only solidified pre-existing positions. As president, Jackson bought and sold slaves, and would continue to do so until at least a year before he died in 1845.[42]

Jackson is applauded, rightly so, for taking a decisive stand against a budding secessionist movement in South Carolina during the Nullification Controversy of 1832–1883, but his actions against the growing abolitionist movement tends to receive less attention. Jackson despised abolitionists more than advocates of nullification, saving his greatest condemnation for them in his farewell address. The outgoing president observed that "nothing but mischief can come from these improper assaults upon the feelings and rights of others."[43] Abolitionists were Hamilton's heirs, Jackson believed, intent on restoring "the money power." As with Jefferson, Jackson believed that abolitionists, the "eastern interest" sought "political ascendancy, and power" but unlike Jefferson he believed abolitionists were determined to incite slaves to "massacre."[44]

Andrew Jackson also shared Thomas Jefferson's disdain for the judicial branch of government due to its antimajoritarian character, although in a less articulate form. Jackson's antagonism toward John Marshall ran as deep as Jefferson's, and one case captured all the antagonism Jackson and his followers felt toward John Marshall and the federal judiciary. In *Worcester v.*

Georgia (1832), Justice Marshall and the court ruled in favor of a missionary who was preaching and teaching to Cherokee Indians in the state of Georgia without a required state license.

Marshall's majority opinion ruled that the Indians were a sovereign entity and that dealings with the Indians were the responsibility of the federal government. Georgia, and Jackson himself, were intent on expelling the Cherokee and moving them to the west. Missionary "do gooders" from the North were seen as troublemakers, especially those like Samuel Worcester, who, in addition to proselytizing, helped the Cherokee develop their first newspaper. The Cherokee were in fact "a model of cultural assimilation to American norms,"[45] and Worcester defended the rights of the tribe against infringements from local settlers, earning the enmity of state officials. While Jackson likely never uttered the famous phrase "John Marshall has made his decision, now let him enforce it,"[46] there was genuine anger at the fact that the court's ruling struck at the heart of the notion of both states' rights and westward expansion, both of which were main tenets of Jacksonianism.

Andrew Jackson has been accused of genocide by contemporary critics of his Indian policy, an assessment dismissed by some scholars as hyperbole and embraced by others. Those who claim that Jackson was sympathetic to the plight of Native Americans point to his adoption of an Indian child whose family had been killed by American soldiers.[47] Without question the Jackson administration was prodded along by Georgia and other southwestern states, but it would be an overstatement to claim that the administration was forced to support Indian removal. At the same time, genocide is too strong of a term to apply to Jackson's policies, but there is no question, as his second vice president, Martin Van Buren, observed, that Indian "removal" to the west was Jackson's top first-term priority, noting that "certainly no other subject was of greater importance" to the Jackson administration.[48] Jackson proposed the act in his first annual message to Congress in December 1829, and succeeded in securing passage of the Indian Removal Act of 1830, which paved the way for the Trail of Tears.[49]

Some scholars argue that Jackson sought to care for the Indians by relocating them out of the way of predatory white settlers, but it is hard not to conclude that Jackson handled the Indian question inhumanely. If he had any moral qualms about the removal policy, he ignored a possible way out for himself provided by the judiciary. But judicial pronouncements ran counter to his principle reason for seeking the presidency: he would implement the will of the majority. As for Marshall's decision in *Worcester v. Georgia*, we do know that Jackson said, "the decision of the supreme court has fell still born, and they find they cannot coerce Georgia to yield its mandate."[50]

Jackson's Indian removal policy generated a lengthy legal and political debate for years, but ultimately culminated in the forced march to the west that led to the deaths of thousands from disease and starvation. One witness to this act of inhumanity was the French observer Alexis de Tocqueville, whose impression of this avoidable human tragedy no doubt colored his negative assessment of Andrew Jackson.[51] Senator Theodore Frelinghuysen of New Jersey, a stalwart anti-Jacksonian, condemned the president's Indian removal policies, noting that the action was a "crime" that would bring "shame" on the United States.[52]

Ironically, it is important to note that the dissenters against these inhumane policies were the same so-called conservative, antipopulist forces who defended the notion of a constitutional presidency. These forces had warned for almost forty years of the dangers presented by rule of the majority and a populist presidency. Advocates of a more humane approach to the Native American question were found at first in the Federalist Party and later among Jackson's Whig opponents (whom Jackson disparagingly referred to as "Federalists").[53] John Jay, Timothy Pickering, Henry Knox, and Alexander Hamilton all argued for national regulation of westward expansion, in part out of partisan concerns, but also out of the same religious and moral concerns that led them to an antislavery stance. Jay argued for serious penalties for American frontiersman guilty of depredations against the Indians, while Knox believed that any "civilized" man must acknowledge the justness of the Indian land claims. The Federalists, as one scholar has noted, "advocated a more just and equitable Indian policy" and "espoused some of the most enlightened views toward the American Indian of the early national period."[54] George Washington was also an advocate for somewhat humane treatment of Native Americans, but "Jacksonian democracy" put an end to these policies, just as they put an end to the notion of enfranchising free blacks.[55]

Jackson's position on race and on the place of Native Americans in the nation was a contributing factor in his antipathy toward the federal judiciary. This antagonism toward the judiciary served as a fundamental tenet of Democratic Party ideology and led Jackson to appoint Roger Taney as chief justice of the Supreme Court when John Marshall died in 1835. As Paul Finkelman has convincingly demonstrated,[56] Marshall was by no means an abolitionist, and in fact was a larger slave owner and slave trader than was previously understood, but his rulings in cases granting expanded authority to the federal government, and in cases like *Worcester v. Georgia,* did not bode well for those who sought to protect the institution of slavery and expand it westward.

The new chief justice, Roger Taney, was a member of Jackson's Kitchen Cabinet, the president's inner circle of advisors, and had also held several cabinet posts during the endless reshuffling that occurred throughout Jackson's presidency, holding the positions of attorney general, secretary of the treasury, and acting secretary of war. As attorney general, Taney drafted one of the most overtly racist accounts of the status of blacks in the history of the republic. Approving of a South Carolina provision that allowed the arrest of any free black sailor who happened to come ashore in the state, Taney noted that:

> The African race in the United States even when free, are everywhere a degraded class, and exercise no political influence. The privileges they are allowed to enjoy, are accorded them as a matter of kindness and benevolence rather than of right. ... And where they are nominally admitted by law to the privileges of citizenship ... [they] are permitted to be citizens by the sufferance of the white population and hold whatever rights they enjoy at their mercy. They were not looked upon as citizens by the contracting parties who formed the Constitution.[57]

This notion would go on to undergird Taney's infamous *Dred Scott* decision of 1857, which, in addition to offering a distorted account of American history, marked a clear refutation of the nation's founding document and helped spark the Civil War. Taney was as much a part of Jackson's legacy to his country as was Jackson's popularizing the notion of majority rule. As Daniel Walker Howe has noted, "Taney was true to Jackson's states-rights and pro-slavery bias. [Abraham] Lincoln had serious doubts about the man who put the author of the *Dred Scott v. Sanford* (1857) decision on the Supreme Court."[58] Lincoln's doubts were justified.

The Champion of Race-Based Democracy

Andrew Jackson held, until recently, a special place in the American mind, and not just with the "common man" that he championed. Countless American biographers and historians have celebrated the man, including some of the biggest names in the academic world. Historians ranging from Arthur Schlesinger Jr. to his protégé Sean Wilentz, along with Jon Meachem and H. W. Brands, have all fostered the myth of Jackson as a champion of the common man, the fighter of corrupt plutocrats. Schlesinger was one of the first to describe Jackson as a precursor to Franklin Roosevelt, with Old Hickory serving as a role model for those devoted to promoting a "usable past," in this instance, "Americanizing" the New Deal.[59]

For much of the twentieth century, progressive historians celebrated Jackson's conflict with the nation's elites and applauded his bank war or his raucous first inaugural party as symbols of the arrival to power of the virtuous silent majority. Historian Joyce Appleby, another champion of the champion of the common man, observed that "the Jeffersonian movement that became the Democratic party under Andrew Jackson held the presidency for fifty-two of the sixty years before the Civil War, stifling at the ballot box any elite pretensions to a special calling to govern."[60] Stifling "elite" pretensions and the pretensions of not-so-elite Americans as well, for Jacksonian democracy was a continuation of an exclusionary Jeffersonian ideology that stifled the voting rights of those of the wrong race. Jacksonian efforts to disenfranchise free blacks led one foreign observer to note that it was next to impossible to find a black person in the United States who was not "an anti-Jackson man."[61]

One of the architects of disenfranchising free blacks was the Jacksonian political guru and Old Hickory's second vice president, Martin Van Buren. By no means the most extreme proponent of racial exclusion, the "Red Fox of Kinderhook" nonetheless exemplified the underside of Jacksonian politics. The voting rights of free blacks were of secondary concern, at best, to the sentiments of the majority coalition assembled by the Democratic Party. The fate of that party was Van Buren's top priority, regardless of whether his party's policies were in concert with the nation's founding principles. As a member of the New York legislature, Van Buren tended to be absent when controversial votes arose regarding the issue of slavery and its expansion. Van Buren, a master politician, built a career on avoiding divisive issues. He did, however, play a crucial role in 1821 in disenfranchising free blacks through the establishment of a $250 property qualification aimed exclusively at blacks but eliminated for white voters.[62] The effect of this, of course, was to disenfranchise black voters who had voted overwhelming for the "elitist" Federalist party.

Martin Van Buren was Jackson's choice to succeed him as president, and the vice president easily won the election of 1836 with slightly over 50 percent of the popular vote, an impressive showing in a five-man field. In his inaugural address, the new president paid tribute to the majority that elected him and vowed to protect slavery in the nation's capital and beyond:

> I must go into the Presidential chair the inflexible and uncompromising opponent of every attempt on the part of Congress to abolish slavery in the District of Columbia against the wishes of the slaveholding States, and also with a determination equally decided to resist the slightest interference with it in the States where it exists. I submitted also to my fellow-citizens, with fullness and frankness, the reasons which led me to this determination. The result authorizes me to believe that they have been approved and are confided in by a majority of the people of the United States, including those whom they most immediately affect. It now only remains to add that no bill conflicting with these views can ever receive my constitutional sanction.[63]

Martin Van Buren was Jackson's acolyte, and as such, the majority was to govern on all issues. As a result of the nation's refounding, the sole principle animating the American regime became that of *vox populi.* Van Buren, as his biographer Ted Widmer notes, "saw no reason to derail his political career with intemperate objections" to slavery. Silence, fence-sitting, shifting positions, and avoiding controversial votes, were all employed by Van Buren on his path to power. But he went further than that, doing all he could to "suppress the early spread of anti-slavery materials." As he prepared to inherit the presidency from Jackson, Van Buren "ordered his cronies to take measures" against abolitionists in his home state of New York. This included disrupting their meetings and preventing them from sending abolitionist tracts through the mail. Van Buren also supported the notorious "gag rule" of 1836, which prohibited all abolitionist measures from being read on the floor of the House.[64] Antislavery views were to be suppressed at all costs in the interests of the Union, the Democratic Party, and in Martin Van Buren's run for the presidency that same year. This suppression of free speech is as much a legacy of Jackson and Van Buren as the expansion of the white male franchise.

Andrew Jackson's impact on the American presidency was equivalent to Thomas Jefferson's, as both men sought to dismantle the constitutional presidency of Washington and Hamilton. Both Jefferson and Jackson met with remarkable success, creating one of the oldest surviving political parties on the planet. Van Buren, serving as Jackson's chief strategist, was determined to revive the "Jeffersonian alliance between the 'planters of the South and plain Republicans of the North.'" It was a remarkably successful strategy, and one that would benefit the Democratic Party well into the 1960s.

As one scholar insightfully observed, after Andrew Jackson, American presidents "claimed electoral mandates to advance favored policy and no longer presented themselves as apolitical stewards of the public good."[65] Strong chief executives, so-called great presidents, would be judged on their ability to serve as partisan leaders, pushing the nation in a populist, and later, progressive, direction. There is no mystery as to why mid-twentieth-century historians such as Arthur Schlesinger Jr. and Henry Steele Commager reached back to Jackson as a precursor to Franklin Roosevelt and the New Deal. The age of Jackson and the age of Roosevelt were a century apart, but both men dominated their age as all "great" presidents should, and both men fought the elites of their day. With racism at the ballot box institutionalized first by the Jeffersonians, reinforced by the Jacksonians, reinstated by Jackson's heirs in the post–Civil War South and then by Woodrow Wilson, Franklin Roosevelt managed to patch the coalition back together by abandoning the racial component that energized the coalition, but ratcheted up the class component in his confrontation with the "malefactors of wealth." FDR was a genius at tapping into American mythology to cement his rather disparate coalition.

As Daniel Walker Howe has observed: "The Democratic Party has always maintained a certain proprietary interest in his [Jackson's] image, commemorating him as its founder in 'Jackson Day' dinners—traditionally held on January 8, the anniversary of his victory over the British at New Orleans in 1815. Franklin D. Roosevelt, an admirer of Thomas Jefferson (perhaps a more appropriate hero for a patrician), changed the name of these events to 'Jefferson-Jackson Day' dinners." While both men have fallen out of favor with contemporary party activists, for almost 150 years the party of Jefferson and Jackson won elections by exploiting racial or class antagonisms.

John Quincy Adams: The Personification of Presidential Dignity

It is unfortunate that Andrew Jackson became the presidential lodestar for many Americans, for that honor truly belongs to John Quincy Adams,

Jackson's bete noire, who upheld the dignity of the presidency in a manner like that of George Washington. Adams's respectable presidency, coming on the heels of his tenure as one of the nation's greatest secretaries of state, was stymied at every turn by resistance from Jackson's followers in Congress. But Adams's emphasis on constitutionalism and his far-sighted policy proposals for a national university, internal improvements, reforming the nation's policies toward Native Americans (Jackson's policies of "fraudulent treaties and brutal force" against the Indians was one of the "heinous sins of this nation"), and a federally sponsored astronomical observatory ("these lighthouses of the skies"), stands in stark contrast to Andrew Jackson's presidency of class conflict and conspiracy theory.[66]

Most importantly, Adams represented the best of the American aspiration for equal rights for all. Adams would not have identified as an abolitionist, for he rejected demagoguery in all its forms and believed the abolitionists' demands for immediate, uncompensated emancipation would likely destroy the nation. He was also averse to identifying with any particular movement precisely because of its particularity; he was devoted to the national interest, not to any group we would today label a "special interest group," or as Adams put it, a "partial association."[67] But later in his life he became, in the words of one of his opponents, "the acutest, the astutest, the archest enemy of Southern slavery that ever existed."[68] According to Adams, slavery, and the racism that justified its existence, was based on a "false and heartless . . . doctrine which makes the first and holiest rights of humanity . . . depend upon the color of the skin."[69]

Adams was a harsh critic of the Jefferson-Jackson doctrine of states' rights and rejected the notion of "popular sovereignty" or majority rule to settle the question of slavery. Slavery was simply contrary to the spirit of the Declaration of Independence and to the Constitution, not to mention contrary to the nation's Judeo-Christian inheritance. Regarding the Declaration, Adams claimed that "the same moral thunderbolt, which melted the chains of allegiance that bound the colonist to his sovereign, dissolved the fetters of the slave." On another occasion, the nation's sixth president noted privately that slavery was "the great and foul stain upon the North American Union." It was rhetoric such as this, which he began to publicly express during his post-presidential career as a member of the House of Representatives, that generated an endless array of death threats and two serious efforts to have Adams censured by the House.[70]

In Adams's view the 3/5ths compromise was a "national scandal," and in addition to his rhetorical and legislative efforts to secure the promises of the Declaration of Independence for all Americans, Adams became the first president to receive African Americans in the executive mansion. These facts should have caused a reconsideration long ago of the illusory claim that it was Adams's opponent who championed the rights of "the forgotten man." There was a reason why a one-term member of Congress from the frontier of Illinois, Abraham Lincoln, was appointed to a committee to handle the funeral preparations for Adams after the latter collapsed on the floor of the House and died a day later on February 23, 1848.[71]

Adams conducted his presidency in concert with the intentions of the framers, and in concert with the model set by Washington and abandoned by Jefferson and Jackson. Adams despised demagoguery, and believed that Jackson and his campaign's major-domo, Martin Van Buren, utilized that destructive tactic to secure their electoral ends. Writing in 1840, Adams acknowledged the success that Jackson had in further reconstituting the executive branch as an office rooted in popular consent. The new "direct and infallible path to the Presidency is military service coupled with demagogue policy; [and] that in the absence of military service, demagogue policy is the first and most indispensable element of success, and the art of party drilling is the second." For Adams, demagoguery was, as he put it in his own unique way, "charlatanery of popular enticement." He noted, rightly so, that the greatest champions of the downtrodden frequently enriched themselves at public expense, for these politicians were "just cunning enough to grow rich by railing against the rich, and to fatten upon the public spoils bawling Democracy."[72]

John Quincy Adams sought, as Washington had, a government of national unity, and to that end he attempted to assemble a "team of rivals" as cabinet members in his administration. He considered offering the position of secretary of war to Andrew Jackson, a remarkably magnanimous gesture considering the bad blood that developed between the two during the election of 1824. But Adams was told in no uncertain terms that the general would "take in ill-part the offer."[73] Adams was determined to use the presidency as the founders had intended, which was to serve as a unifying office, to bridge the sectional divides that existed in the nation. As Mary W. M. Hargreaves, arguably Adams's foremost presidential biographer, has noted, Adams sought to "remain aloof from partisan embroilment." He "assumed a nonpartisan stance which required that he base his appeal for popular support upon a unifying program."[74]

As with his Federalist ancestors, President Adams relied on appeals to reason in pursuit of his administration's agenda. As Hargreaves has observed, Adams's "dispassionate" appeals to reason revealed "an attachment to policy-oriented leadership that was no longer viable in the changing political context of the period." These appeals were "anachronistic as techniques for generating support." Jackson's political operatives were adept at confusing the public by proclaiming Adams's pronouncements false, producing a "cloud of doubt" that "confused popular judgment." The public response to Jackson's position on issues "were more emotional than reasoned" and tended to be rooted in parochialism and "widespread anti-intellectualism." Reason was no match for appeals to regional prejudices and to evocations of conspiratorial plotting by some distant elite.

For Jackson and his supporters in Congress and elsewhere, the showdown between Old Hickory and Adams was couched in the same demagogic way as that between Jefferson and the Federalists—this was a struggle between those determined to preserve "democracy over aristocracy," and a corrupt aristocracy at that. John Quincy Adams was one of the most honest persons ever to inhabit the executive mansion, but the constant refrain from supporters of Andrew Jackson of "corruption" eroded Adams's ability to govern. Jackson's vice president, Martin Van Buren, would admit some thirty years after the fact that Adams was "an honest man, not only incorruptible himself, but . . . an enemy to venality in every department of public service."[75]

During the age of Jackson, the "art of politics" changed rapidly, all the while Adams continued to fight the last war, if not the war before that. The "spin," the messaging, the "optics" for Adams were all holdovers from a lost world. Success in American politics was now built around the ability to communicate "cultural catchwords" and to organize those mobilized by these catchwords around a person who symbolized the "movement," in this instance Andrew Jackson. Martin Van Buren solicited support for Jackson precisely on this basis, noting to one newspaper editor that Jackson's candidacy for the presidency was based entirely on "personal popularity."[76] Jackson and Van Buren's political machine organized rallies and parades, formed local party clubs, and coordinated "a sprawling media campaign, liberally spending money, and making use of campaign paraphernalia." Adams was aware of these efforts, noting at one point the "money expended by the adversaries to the Administration . . . to vitiate the public opinion, and pay for defamation,"[77] but he felt, at least partly on principle, that he should not respond in kind.

Jackson was a war hero, the kind of rough-hewn, manly fellow you could have a hard cider with, a charismatic person, while John Quincy Adams's supporters were said to have voted for the man "from a cold sense of duty, and not upon any liking of Mr. Adams." "The element of personal charisma," as Mary W. M. Hargreaves has noted, "Adams's lack and Jackson's abundance of it," influenced voters in different ways around the nation, but its influence was profound.[78] Adams was aware of the charisma-gap that existed between himself and Jackson, wryly noting that he lacked "the powers of fascination."[79] This focus on parades, paraphernalia, and personal charisma was as far removed from the founders' hopes for presidential selection, for a system avoiding the "little arts of popularity," as one could imagine.

Andrew Jackson and his lieutenants personalized the presidency in precisely the way Hamilton and other founders had feared. Jackson's presidential campaigns took on something of a cult-like movement, as "Hickory clubs" appeared around the nation sporting hickory poles and sponsoring parades, rallies, and dances in honor of the hero of the Battle of New Orleans.[80] This personalized presidency also had consequences for governing as well, as Jackson's formal cabinet was displaced by a Kitchen Cabinet of close allies and sycophants who acted as a sympathetic sounding board for Jackson's bizarre schemes. During his eight years in office, Jackson had five secretaries of the treasury, four secretaries of state, three attorneys general, three secretaries of the navy, three postmasters general, two secretaries of war, and two vice presidents.[81] This was an administration built around Jackson, and Jackson alone.

In the thirty-six years between Thomas Jefferson's inauguration as the nation's third president and Andrew Jackson's departure from the executive mansion in March 1837, the American republic had moved from a system designed to check majority tyranny to one where the guiding precept was "the majority is to govern." And the majority did govern, using its power at the state level to disenfranchise an unpopular minority, and leveraging its powers at the state and the federal levels to remove a different but equally unpopular minority from its midst. Several American presidents, serving in an office created as a bulwark against the tyranny of the majority, either ignored or tacitly supported this campaign of disenfranchisement while simultaneously elevating the principle of majority rule into the rationale for the regime's existence.

During those thirty-six years, demagoguery, personality-based politics, populist flattery, presidential promotion of conspiracy theories, along with race-baiting and mob violence, changed the nature of the American political order, an order created to allow for reason and reflection and the possibility of statesmanship. It was a tragic, rapid, and altogether avoidable descent, hastened in good measure by the extraconstitutional transformation of the presidency engineered by Thomas Jefferson and Andrew Jackson.

4

Abraham Lincoln and the "Mobocratic Spirit"

Abraham Lincoln's stature as the nation's greatest president, challenged only by George Washington, will likely persist as long as the United States of America exists. Lincoln marshaled the English language in defense of the American experiment, and in that regard, he is unlikely to ever be surpassed, particularly considering the degradation of presidential rhetoric over the centuries. Lincoln was also the personification of magnanimity and moderation, two qualities missing in many of his successors. At the same time, Lincoln epitomized Hamilton's conception of an energetic executive and used the full powers of his office to preserve the Union and abolish slavery. And most importantly for the American Constitution, Lincoln rejected the principle of "the majority is to govern," holding that certain precepts, including the right to life and liberty, were not subject to an up or down vote. The American regime stood for more than popular sovereignty, and the American presidency had a sacred obligation to preserve the nation's founding principles.

Abraham Lincoln was a man of the people whose rough-hewn, almost primitive upbringing gave him a common touch that assisted his rise to power, but he was no common man. Despite sharing a childhood similar to Andrew Jackson, Lincoln conducted himself in a manner contrary to Jackson. Lincoln was well read, a man of reason and intellect, of moderate temperament, who did not convert policy disputes into personal affronts. He was a gentle man who did not thrive on slights; a man who grasped the dark side of human nature but appealed to our "better angels." And importantly, he was a politician who abhorred demagoguery. He was no saint, but of all the presidents in the three score and three years between Washington's departure as chief executive and his own election, Lincoln's respect for the office, his magnanimous conduct, his devotion to principle, and his near-superhuman persistence in the face of adversity, matched that of Washington.

"The Wild and Furious Passions"

Lincoln came of age politically during the Jackson era and his approach to politics was shaped by Jackson's nemesis, Henry Clay of Lincoln's native Kentucky. Clay spent a good portion of his career battling Jackson, whom he considered a dangerous demagogue. Clay was Lincoln's "beau ideal of a statesman," the proponent of the Hamiltonian "American system" of a central bank, internal improvements, and protective tariffs to help American industry.[1] Lincoln grew up surrounded by Andrew Jackson supporters, including his headstrong father, but sometime in his late teens, before he could vote, he switched his allegiance to the Whigs and became an admirer of Clay and John Quincy Adams.[2] Lincoln rejected Jacksonianism despite the fact that President Jackson had appointed him the postmaster at New Salem, Illinois.[3]

Lincoln's political thought was akin to that of the Federalists of the early republic in a variety of ways, including his antislavery stance that animated much of his career. As a young state legislator in Illinois in 1837, he took the politically risky position of opposing a resolution condemning abolitionists. Lincoln was one of five members of the House of Representatives, out of eighty-three, to vote against the resolution. Lincoln was never the favorite of committed abolitionists, nor he of them, but he was a consistent opponent of slavery who sought to halt its expansion and preserve the Union at the same time.

Lincoln's first extended speech in the Illinois House in 1837 reveals the depth of the man's aversion to Jacksonianism. He opposed the demands of a Democratic Party lawmaker, in keeping with the tenor of the times, who called for an investigation of the Illinois State Bank. Such an investigation, Lincoln argued, would foster "that lawless and mobocratic spirit . . . which is already abroad in the land."[4] As with John Quincy Adams and his Federalist forebears, Lincoln was a devoted champion of reason and feared the destructive effects of the politics of passion, a politics anchored in conspiracy theories focused on banks, immigrants, free blacks, abolitionists, "Wall Street," and various ill-defined "elites."

Lincoln was disturbed by several trends in antebellum America, including Jackson's attempted censorship of abolitionist publications. The 1830s, often portrayed as a decade of expanding democracy, was also a decade of terror for those out of step with proslavery opinion. These were years of anti-black, anti-abolitionist, anti-Irish, anti-Catholic, anti-Mormon violence, topped off by sporadic Election Day riots as well. Boston, Philadelphia, and New York City saw mobs attack abolitionist rallies. The low point was reached in 1834 when a Fourth of July celebration by African Americans in New York City led to three days of terror by roving white gangs who torched six churches and burned and looted the homes of free blacks and white abolitionists. Additionally, the subject of President Jackson's most heated vitriol, the Bank of the United States, saw one of its branch offices in New Hampshire attacked and looted by a mob in 1834.

Cincinnati was the site of multiple riots in 1836, including one directed at African Americans who also had the audacity to celebrate Independence Day. Some three weeks after the Independence Day riots, a mob destroyed the printing press of an abolitionist newspaper in Cincinnati, the *Philanthropist*, throwing the press into the Ohio River. The mob went on to invade the home of the newspaper's editor who was fortunate enough to have fled, as the Cincinnati police ignored the rampage.[5]

A devotee of reason and moderation, Lincoln was appalled by the politics of passion and the transformation of America from a republic to what he and others considered to be a mobocracy. Lincoln was twenty-eight years old when he strongly condemned the lawlessness of Jackson's America in his Lyceum Address in January 1838. The address was prompted by the murder of an Illinois abolitionist, Elijah Lovejoy, who was killed in 1837 by a proslavery mob determined to destroy his printing press. Lovejoy was one of the first journalists murdered in the United States for his unpopular views.[6] Lovejoy's murder, Congressman John Quincy Adams noted, sent "a shock as of an earthquake throughout this continent."[7]

Lincoln modeled his Lyceum Address after George Washington's Farewell Address, an address the young Lincoln knew quite well. Both speeches thematically unfolded in the same manner, and both were pleas for the rule of law, for public virtue, and warned of the ill effects of "designing men."[8] Lincoln noted that there was "something of ill-omen, amongst us," by which he meant "the increasing disregard for law" pervading the United States. This lawlessness took the form of a "growing disposition to substitute the wild and furious passions" instead of "the sober judgments of Courts." Those who administered justice had been displaced by "savage mobs," a phenomenon witnessed from Louisiana to New England. The solution to the virus of mob rule, according to Lincoln, was a renewed devotion to the rule of law, to the American founders, and to the Constitution they drafted. Every American needed to swear to "never violate . . . the laws of the country; and never tolerate their violation by others."

The nation needed a political religion, a religion of reverence for the Constitution and its laws, requiring that its citizens pledge their life, property, and "sacred honor" as signs of their devotion. "Reverence for the Constitution and laws" was needed to save the American republic, for no external foe could destroy the United States; the nation could only be destroyed from within. Harkening back to the greatest of the founders, Lincoln reminded his fellow citizens that they were George Washington's heirs, and that they must revere his name "to the last," and that Americans must never allow any "hostile foot to pass over or desecrate his resting place."[9]

One source of danger to the American republic was the designing demagogues who would not be satisfied with holding a routine political office but sought to gratify their "ruling passion" by refounding a political order and securing eternal fame. These potential Caesars disdain "the beaten path" or treading in the "footsteps" of others as they "thirst and burn" for distinction. These men, these seekers of "celebrity and fame," wish to be immortalized as founders, and they were a persistent threat to republican government. Whether Lincoln had Andrew Jackson in mind, or someone else, has been the subject of speculation to this day. But regardless of who he had in mind, Lincoln's fear of designing demagogues was deeply rooted in American political thought. His fears were shared by George Washington, Alexander Hamilton, James Madison, and John Quincy Adams. They all expressed the same concern, albeit in slightly different prose.

Lincoln's plea for a reverence for the laws and a renewed appreciation of the founders' Constitution stemmed from his devotion to reason and his suspicion, his fear, of human passions. The latter, he concluded, will in the future "be our enemy." It was "reason—cold, calculating, unimpassioned reason—[that] must furnish all the materials for our future support and defense." The "temple of liberty" could not be protected by emotion or custom, but only by "the solid quarry of sober reason." As one of his greatest biographers has noted, Lincoln was earnestly committed to "impos[ing] rationality on public life."[10] In his famous debates with Senator Stephen A. Douglas, one observer contrasted the latter's appeal to "popular prejudice and bigotry" with Lincoln's penchant for going "straight to the reason of the question."[11]

A Closet Hamiltonian

Abraham Lincoln is often cited as an unalloyed admirer of Thomas Jefferson, a man of whom the sixteenth president once proclaimed "all honor to Jefferson," the author of the principles that are "the definitions and axioms of free society."[12] Jefferson, the conventional wisdom holds, serves as Lincoln's role model. However, Lincoln's perspective on Jefferson was more complex than is generally acknowledged. Lincoln's longtime associate William H. Herndon observed that "Mr. Lincoln hated Thomas Jefferson as a man" and as "a politician." While some scholars have questioned Herndon's veracity, Herndon has proven to be a more accurate chronicler regarding all things Lincoln than was once assumed.[13]

It appears that Lincoln's preference for Jefferson over Hamilton was a tactic designed to use the South's most revered founder against them. Lincoln used Jefferson's egalitarian language against the rising tide of Southern politicians who were now questioning or dismissing the principles of the Declaration of Independence and making the case that slavery was a positive good. Additionally, Jefferson, a son of the South, was a potent weapon to employ against Stephen A. Douglas and Lincoln's other Democratic Party opponents. Lincoln's embrace of Jefferson forced some proslavery firebrands to abandon Jefferson and allowed the few antislavery voices in the South a patina of Southern respectability in the form of Jefferson's principles. This allowed antislavery Southerners to deviate from the firebrands' views while remaining "Southern."

Lincoln's support for internal improvements, his defense of tariffs, his celebration of the wage laborer in an increasingly industrialized America, and his opposition to slavery, was decidedly Hamiltonian. Yet in *The Collected Works of Abraham Lincoln*, there are only seven references to Alexander Hamilton and over forty to Thomas Jefferson, most related to the latter's role in crafting the Declaration of Independence. Lincoln did, however, mention Hamilton in one of his more notable addresses. At New York City's Cooper Union in February 1860, the presidential candidate observed that Hamilton was one of the "most noted anti-slavery men of those times." But generally, Lincoln, like Henry Clay, seldom mentioned Alexander Hamilton. Both men had to secure electoral success in regions of the country where invoking Hamilton as a role model was a surefire prescription for defeat. Any expression of affection for a dead Federalist in either Kentucky or Illinois was tantamount to committing political suicide. Nevertheless, Lincoln's repeated invocation of Jefferson and the Declaration was a masterful political tactic, but one that continues to mislead historians and biographers. Historian Allen Guelzo observed that prior to 1854 Lincoln only referred to the Declaration of Independence twice, but as the irrepressible conflict drew closer, he referred to it with greater regularity. Notably, Lincoln stopped referring to Jefferson during the Civil War, mentioning the Sage of Monticello only once after December 3, 1861, in that instance responding to a serenade that included a reference to the Declaration. And it should be noted that Lincoln was surrounded by admirers of Alexander Hamilton, including his young aide John Hay, his secretary of the treasury, Salmon P. Chase, and his secretary of state, William Seward, who considered Hamilton to be "the wisest statesman" from the state of New York and "one of the greatest and most celebrated men of America."[14]

Conspiracy Theories and the "Slave Power"

Lincoln, unlike many of his populist contemporaries, was averse to conspiracy theories. Some scholars have challenged this notion, suggesting that in the late 1850s Lincoln believed in the existence of a slaveholder conspiracy within the federal government. To some extent he did, yet he may have been partially correct. Scholars sympathetic to the myth of the "lost cause" frequently dismissed the existence of the "slave power" as conspiratorial nonsense, but recent scholarship has been more sympathetic to the charge. Lincoln believed that Stephen A. Douglas, Franklin Pierce, Roger Taney, and President James Buchanan were part of a "political dynasty" that worked in concert to erect a proslavery American regime at odds with the intentions of the framers. Lincoln qualified that claim, however, by noting that "we cannot absolutely know" that these key Democrats were part of a conspiracy.

Nevertheless, according to Lincoln, "Stephen, Franklin, Roger and James" were erecting a proslavery edifice that appeared to be drawn from the same blueprint. As he noted in his famous House Divided speech, the members of this "dynasty" might possibly expand slavery into the free states, making it even more urgent that it be "met and overthrown." However, Lincoln's rhetorical moderation can be seen in his aversion to the term "slave power"—a favorite term of abolitionists who circulated rumors of intrigue involving murder and other untoward tactics used by those intent on expanding slavery not just into the new American territories but into the existing free states.[15]

In the aftermath of the Kansas-Nebraska Act (1854) and the Supreme Court decision in *Dred Scott v. Sandford* (1857), many Americans, Lincoln included, came to believe that it was the policy of the Democratic Party to nationalize slavery.[16] The fact is that Chief Justice Roger Taney, furious at the criticism of his *Dred Scott* decision, was planning a follow-up ruling that he hoped would strike down state prohibitions against slavery, a position hinted at by Justice Samuel Nelson, who sided with the majority in *Dred Scott.*[17] While there may not have been a conspiracy between key Democratic leaders in the 1850s to preserve and expand slavery, there was collusion between President James Buchanan and Chief Justice Roger Taney, in that President Buchanan was informed of how the court would rule before the *Dred Scott* decision was released and he urged his countrymen in his inaugural address to accept it.[18] Lincoln was closer to the truth than his critics then and now have alleged.

In opposition to the spirit of Andrew Jackson, Lincoln urged his fellow citizens to obey the ruling of the court in the *Dred Scott* case, despite his deep moral objections. Lincoln's devotion to reason and to the rule of law was never tested more than during the aftermath of that notorious decision, a ruling that mortified him but did not lead him to abandon his faith in the Constitution of the United States. On June 26, 1857, Lincoln noted that he and his countrymen must obey the court's decision, but:

> We think the Dred Scott decision is erroneous. We know the court that made it, has often over-ruled its own decisions, and we shall do what we can to have it to over-rule this. We offer no resistance to it. . . . Chief Justice Taney, in delivering the opinion of the majority of the Court, insists at great length that Negroes were no part of the people who made, or for whom was made, the Declaration of Independence, or the Constitution of the United States.

On the contrary, Judge Curtis, in his dissenting opinion, shows that in five of the then thirteen states, to wit, New Hampshire, Massachusetts, New York, New Jersey and North Carolina, free negroes were voters, and, in proportion to their numbers, had the same part in making the Constitution that the white people had.[19]

Lincoln's obedience to the Constitution, and the principles of the Declaration of Independence that it affirmed, stood in contrast to many of his fellow citizens who had come to see slavery as the cornerstone of the American republic and readily abandoned those principles.

Lincoln's commitment to the rule of law, and his concern over the constitutional protections afforded minorities under the American system, were cogently stated in his first inaugural address. While Lincoln endorsed the notion of majority rule in criticizing the decision of the Southern states to secede, this endorsement was more qualified than that of Jackson. As one of his most insightful presidential chroniclers has argued, "Lincoln's polity relied on a faith in popular government. Yet Lincoln was not a Jacksonian Democrat. He stepped into politics attacking Jackson, remained loyal to a Whig party that challenged Jacksonian philosophies, [and] rebutted the political philosophy of popular sovereignty."[20] While Lincoln believed that American citizens were the ultimate sovereigns in the American polity, "he also understood that liberty as well as order demanded that they exercise their sovereignty through the political and the constitutional processes." The Constitution, as Lincoln noted in his inaugural address, guarded the rights of minorities: "If by the mere force of numbers a majority should deprive a minority of any clearly written constitutional right, it might in a moral point of view justify revolution; [it] certainly would if such right were a vital one. But such is not our case. All the vital rights of minorities and of individuals are so plainly assured to them by affirmations and negations, guarantees and prohibitions, in the Constitution."[21]

The Southern states that opted to secede had not been denied by the majority of states that elected Lincoln of any "clearly written constitutional right."[22] Lincoln believed that the secession of the Southern states constituted an act of aggression against the constitutional order long before the first shots were fired at Fort Sumter in Charleston Harbor, for those states had withdrawn for illegitimate reasons.[23]

Slaying the Little Giant

Lincoln's fidelity to the Constitution, and to its antimajoritarian provisions, was opposed by his great rival from Illinois, Stephen A. Douglas. Senator Douglas was a thoroughgoing Jacksonian who believed with his hero that the "majority is to govern." As one of Douglas's biographer notes, the senator was "dazzled by Old Hickory" and developed a "lifelong attachment" to Jacksonianism. As a young lawyer in Jacksonville, Illinois, Douglas passionately defended President Jackson's war on the Bank of the United States, claiming that he "could not remain silent when the old hero's character, public and private, was traduced, and his measures misrepresented and denounced."[24]

On another occasion, Douglas became even more animated while defending Jackson's bank war, accusing the bank of carrying on a "reign of terror" and urging Illinoisans to rally to the defense of "our venerable Chief Magistrate" who had displayed "purpose, integrity, firmness, and patriotism."[25] Douglas shared Jackson's penchant, at least as a younger man, for personalizing policy disputes and brooking no opposition to the Jacksonian agenda. When a fellow Democrat who represented Illinois in the House of Representatives broke with the president over the Bank of the United States and went on to be elected governor, Douglas labeled the man a "traitor."[26]

Douglas's maiden speech in Congress was a spirited defense in 1844 of a bill to refund Andrew Jackson for a fine he paid during the War of 1812 that had been levied against Jackson for contempt of court. The fine grew out of Jackson's implementation of martial law in New Orleans after his famous victory against the British in 1815. These events were discussed in the previous chapter and included Jackson's arrest of a journalist and a judge who challenged his invocation of martial law. Jackson's admirers considered these actions to be an example of Old Hickory's willingness to do whatever was necessary, lawful or not, in defense of American interests. Douglas condemned those who invoked the rule of law while criticizing Jackson, accusing them of undermining a true patriot: "talk not to me about rules and forms in court, when the enemy's cannon are pointed at the door, and the flames encircle the cupola."

The great champion of the rule of law, John Quincy Adams, was on the floor during Douglas's speech, and noted sarcastically in his diary, "an eloquent, sophistical speech, prodigiously admired by the slave Democracy of the House." Jackson himself, when told of Douglas's efforts on his behalf, allegedly remarked that "this speech constitutes my defense; I lay it aside as an inheritance for my grandchildren."[27]

Douglas was rewarded for his fealty to Jackson when he visited Old Hickory's plantation outside Nashville in the summer of 1844. While shaking his hero's hand "convulsively," Douglas was struck speechless. When an equestrian statue of Jackson was dedicated in 1853 in Lafayette Park next to the White House, it was Stephen A. Douglas who delivered the keynote address, hailing Jackson as the man who personified the "spirit of the age."[28]

Douglas also shared the prevailing sentiments of all good Jacksonians regarding Indian removal, seeing Native Americans as impediments to progress, or as he inelegantly put it, "barriers of barbarism."[29] The "Little Giant," as he was known to some, also shared Jackson's penchant for inflammatory rhetoric and yearned at one point in 1860 for a return to the days when Jacksonian threats seemed to quell the march toward civil war. "I wish to God we had an Old Hickory now alive, in order that he might hang Northern and Southern traitors on the same gallows," he proclaimed in 1860. Douglas considered abolitionists to be on par with secessionists, noting that he was "for burying Southern disunionists and Northern abolitionists in the same grave."[30]

Douglas's demagoguery was matched by his unique ability to sense what his audience wanted to hear and deliver a pitch-perfect message that tended to leave his listeners satisfied. He was, in many ways, a politician ahead of his time. As one observer noted, Douglas "had a popular manner, under all circumstances adapting itself exactly to his audience."[31]

In keeping with his devotion to Jacksonianism, Douglas became the leading proponent of what became known as "popular sovereignty." Douglas held that the right to self-government was *the* fundamental principle of the American experiment, and by extending this principle to the new territories white citizens could choose whether to adopt the institution of slavery. Douglas's position was an attempt to remove slavery from the national agenda and prevent the nation from tearing itself apart. His proposal seemingly offered a middle ground between those who believed that Congress possessed the power to restrict the expansion of slavery into the territories, and those who believed that neither Congress, nor any territorial or state government, could restrict slavery anywhere, anytime.

The new Republican Party, of which Douglas's Illinois rival Abraham Lincoln was emerging as a prominent member, believed that slavery could be, and should be, restricted, while Douglas argued that the federal government lacked the authority to restrict slavery. Douglas's ostensibly neutral position drew the ire of Republicans, abolitionists, and an increasing number of Southerners who argued that slavery was a positive good.

While willing to permit new territories and states to vote up or down on slavery, it is important to note that Douglas agreed with Chief Justice Roger Taney that the founding fathers had created a racially exclusive nation. The principles of the Declaration of Independence, Douglas claimed, "referred to the white race alone, and not to the African, when they declared men to have been created free and equal." The "main proposition" of the *Dred Scott* case was that "a negro descended from slave parents . . . is not and can not be a citizen of the United States."[32]

Abraham Lincoln condemned Taney's distorted interpretation of American history and considered Douglas's popular sovereignty doctrine to be fundamentally, and perniciously, flawed. By staking out a morally neutral position on slavery, Douglas was betraying the founding principles of the nation, and ignoring the fact that slavery was "a moral, social, and political evil." Douglas frequently proclaimed that he was indifferent to the choice voters made to become a free state or a slave state, any state that "wants a slave-state constitution . . . has a right to it . . . I do not care whether it is voted down or voted up." For Lincoln, slavery was a "monstrous injustice" and represented a betrayal of "our republican example." Lincoln believed that the founders, through gradual steps and indirect means, intended to put slavery on the path to extinction, but popular sovereignty threatened to reverse that course. Lincoln held that underneath the "declared indifference" of popular sovereignty lay a "covert real zeal for the spread of slavery."[33]

Abraham Lincoln considered self-government to be an important element of republicanism, but when it was used to allow one set of people to enslave another, "that is despotism." Douglas's attempt to fashion a "middle ground" on the great issue of the day and place this great moral question in the hands of public opinion was a threat to the very basis of the founders' republic. Popular sovereignty assumed that "there can be moral right in the enslaving of one man by another," a principle completely at odds with the American republic. In Lincoln's view, popular sovereignty, as historian Nicole Etcheson observed, "equated freedom with slavery."[34]

Lincoln, the Constitution, and the People

Lincoln was very much a man of the people who celebrated and commemorated them in his acclaimed Gettysburg Address. But he contended that the principles of life, liberty, and equal opportunity held a higher place in the American experiment, superior to majority rule. By dissenting from the refounding of the republic that began with Jefferson, accelerated under Jackson, and was echoed by Old Hickory's devotee Stephen A. Douglas, Lincoln was calling for a return to those founding principles which acknowledged that life, liberty, and equal opportunity were not subject to up or down votes. Lincoln's principles led him to inevitably conclude that leadership, that statesmanship, required acknowledging that majority rule presented a threat to liberty and had its limits.

In contrast to Douglas, Lincoln held that the Constitution was everything, the source of legitimate power, not "raw public will." The latter, as both the founders and Lincoln understood, was "transient," while the Constitution had a permanent, "authoritative" quality to it. All of Lincoln's principles and practices were grounded in this understanding.[35] Lincoln's reverence for the Constitution revealed itself in his first inaugural address, where the incoming president mentioned the nation's founding charter some thirty-four times.

A government of popular consent, as founded by Jefferson and Jackson, threatened to undermine the republican regime created by the American Constitution. Lincoln understood this, Douglas did not. The latter's popular sovereignty doctrine was but a passive acceptance that slavery would remain a fixture of American life, if most of the white voting public deemed it appropriate. This was one of the odious consequences of embracing the principle that elected leaders must implement the popular will. Abraham Lincoln paid all honor to Thomas Jefferson, but his conception of statesmanship, of the need to resist popular passions, of his aversion to demagoguery and his hostility to slavery, along with his conception of the proper way to conduct himself as president, was decidedly Hamiltonian.

Having said this, it is often stated that Lincoln differed dramatically with the founders, particularly Alexander Hamilton, in the esteem in which he held public opinion. This is true to an extent, but to a highly qualified extent. Both Lincoln and Hamilton believed in reason and that appeals to this faculty rather than pandering could convince the citizenry to act in their long-term interest and in obedience to the Constitution. Interestingly, their backgrounds were strikingly similar, with Lincoln and Hamilton both emerging from dysfunctional families with little to rely on to better their station in life other than their own ambition and thirst for learning. Both were self-taught men who rose to the top of a society that was remarkably fluid for its time; in a sense both men were the personification of the American dream.

Lincoln was more sympathetic to public opinion than Hamilton, but Lincoln grew up in Jefferson and Jackson's America and had absorbed elements of their refounding. But again, Lincoln's principles and practices, if examined closely, reveal that he was closer to Hamilton's understanding of the purpose of the American experiment than he was to the understanding of those who refounded the regime. It is true that one would unlikely hear Hamilton, or perhaps even Washington or Madison, claim that "public sentiment is everything. With public sentiment, nothing can fail; without it, nothing can succeed" and "our government rests in public opinion. Whoever can change public opinion, can change the government." The latter quote is frequently truncated and omits an important qualifier, that the "central idea" of American public opinion "was, and until recently has continued to be, 'the equality of men.'"[36] Yet as Lincoln demonstrated in his resistance to Douglas's drive for popular sovereignty, there was more to America than majority rule, including the non-negotiable principle of "the equality of men."

Lincoln therefore sought to educate the public, to shape public sentiment on the fundamental question of what defined the character of the American regime, and he did so as something of an educator, relying on persuasion and argument, not appeals to the "prejudices of the people," in the manner of Stephen A. Douglas. Lincoln hoped to mold public sentiment for the long term, not manipulate public opinion in the short run. It cost him politically, and arguably cost him his life in the end, but he ennobled the regime for which he died. Alexander Hamilton adopted a similar approach in terms of molding public sentiment through reasoned appeals such as his *Federalist* essays. Both men repeatedly eschewed short-term political gain for what they believed was in the enduring national interest. Both men were the very definition of statesmen.

Lincoln was also a skilled politician (far better than Hamilton) who genuflected to public opinion in terms of the timing of certain acts, including when to issue the Emancipation Proclamation. But public opinion did not dictate the content of that document or any other of Lincoln's pronouncements. The necessities of politics in a republic required a due deference to timing. An official in Lincoln's Treasury Department observed that the president's "own views were more advanced usually, than those of his party, and he waited patiently and confidently for the healthy movements of public sentiment which he well knew were in the right direction."[37] Another scholarly observer remarked that "Lincoln never attempted to propose what was more than one step ahead of the great body of political public opinion. But he always led the way."[38] And he led not by demagoguery, but by carefully crafted arguments. He once pleaded with an audience that they give "a calm and enlarged consideration" of his arguments; in other words, think broadly, dispassionately, and absent any self-interest or parochial bias.[39]

Lincoln was a man of moderation who tended to avoid inflammatory rhetoric and always urged obedience to the rule of law. But this moderation was interpreted by some of his contemporaries, and many modern critics, as symptomatic of a man lacking any moral compass; a man who did not love justice, a man who was "disgustingly well regulated" in the face of a monstrous injustice. But Lincoln's revulsion toward slavery was genuine and abiding, yet as a public figure he had to "mediate between the demands of justice and the prejudices of a democratic people." Lincoln's critics, as his famous biographer Lord Charnwood observed, "longed for a leader whose heart visibly glowed with a sacred passion." Lincoln's moderation was seen as timid, or a calculated pragmatism based on electoral concerns, but in fact he attempted to serve both justice and democracy, as Steven Kautz has noted. The kind of moderation that Lincoln displayed is frequently derided as the practice of cowardly politicians who "trim" their stance to curry favor with the public. But Lincoln believed that lashing out at slavery or any public ill by assuming a stance of moral superiority and engaging in bombastic rhetoric, "the thundering tones of anathema and denunciation," as he once put it, was ultimately ineffective. All men are sinners, and one could be more effective working to cure the ill than mounting the rostrum and acting as a "lordly judge" condemning those lacking in virtue.[40]

Lincoln was also criticized by those who believed his love of country was conditional, which in fact it was. Lincoln was devoted to his country not because of some relationship to its "blood and soil," but because it was "the last best hope" of liberty and equal opportunity. He noted in 1855 that:

> We began by declaring that "all men are created equal." We now practically read it "all men are created equal, except negroes." When the Know-Nothings get

> control, it will read "all men are created equal, except negroes, and foreigners, and Catholics. When it comes to this I should prefer emigrating to some country where they make no pretense of loving liberty—to Russia, for instance, where despotism can [be] taken pure, and without the base alloy of hypocrisy.[41]

If majority rule based on racial discrimination deepened its roots in American life, Lincoln would prefer to emigrate. The United States stood for a principle, for the idea of liberty and equal opportunity; it was more than a sovereign state governed by the whims of its current inhabitants.[42]

Part of Lincoln's greatness, as with Washington, was that he never remotely countenanced exploiting a moment of constitutional crisis to enhance his personal power—for instance canceling the election of 1864 or claiming permanent emergency powers. While he did invoke presidential prerogative powers during the Civil War, for instance suspending habeas corpus, he always made it clear these were temporary measures in force until the crisis passed. "A measure made expedient by war," he would later note, "is no precedent for times of peace."[43] And in all these instances he sought the approval of Congress, although after the fact in the case of the suspension of habeas corpus.

Lincoln was, like his hero Washington, a man of republican temperament, a man of moderation. He avoided rabble-rousing Jacksonian rhetoric, and repeatedly appealed to the "better angels" of his fellow countrymen. If any president had ample reason to weaponize his rhetoric, it was Lincoln, who faced an insurrection well out of proportion to the threat he supposedly represented, yet he chose not to do so. Lincoln's temperance, his prudence, his moderation, serve as a lesson for all American presidents, but his lesson has generally been honored more in the breach than regularly observed.

George Washington's influence on Abraham Lincoln's presidency was pronounced, as can be seen in the latter's attempt to form a government of national unity. During the transition period between his election in November 1860 and his inauguration in March 1861, Lincoln sought to recruit Southerners for his cabinet. Lincoln had nominated William Seward of New York to be his secretary of state, and Seward eventually led the search for potential Southern recruits, although in one instance Lincoln personally contacted Congressman John A. Gilmer of North Carolina in hopes of sounding him out for a cabinet post, but Gilmer refused to meet with the president-elect. It was an awkward task for the incoming president, as Lincoln noted in an anonymous editorial he wrote in December 1860, "on what terms does he [a potential Southern cabinet member] surrender to Mr. Lincoln, or Mr. Lincoln to him, on the political differences between them, or do they enter upon the administration in open opposition to each other." In the end the effort failed, but Lincoln did nominate Montgomery Blair from the slave state of Maryland as postmaster general, and Edward Bates of Missouri, another slave state, as his attorney general.[44]

Lincoln may have failed in his effort to recruit cabinet members from the deep South, but he succeeded in recruiting his political opponents, including Seward, Bates, and Salmon P. Chase, who would go on to be treasury secretary. By appointing three of his rivals, plus a forth, Simon Cameron of Pennsylvania (secretary of war), a favorite-son candidate, Lincoln had forged his "team of rivals." When asked why he had appointed his rivals, Lincoln responded "these were the very strongest men. . . . I had no right to deprive the country of their services." Lincoln also appointed Democrats for high positions in his administration, including Navy Secretary Gideon Welles from Connecticut; his second secretary of war, Edwin Stanton, a lifelong Democrat who had served briefly as Buchanan's attorney general; and his vice president, Hannibal Hamlin from Maine, a Democrat who converted to Republicanism over the slavery issue. Lincoln's political genius, as James McPherson has noted, allowed him to "herd these political cats and keep them driving toward ultimate victory," a remarkable achievement due in no small measure to his "ability to rise above personal slights."[45]

There was undoubtedly some element of partisanship in Lincoln's "team of rivals" approach, as it is always helpful to keep one's enemies inside the tent, but Lincoln's appointments also reflected the president's understanding of his office as a conciliating, mediating institution vital to the national interest. The presidency was not a tool for use in exploiting partisan divisions. Nor was the office about the individual who held it, as challenging as that has been for some of Lincoln's successors to grasp.

A Magnanimous but Resolute President

A more self-centered individual would not have been able to keep Lincoln's "team of rivals" together. The headstrong Seward proved to be a difficult cabinet member at first, but Lincoln's magnanimous character and Herculean patience led the two men to form a remarkable working relationship during the Civil War. Many presidents would have fired Seward for his Machiavellian maneuvering to enhance his own authority and for his borderline insulting behavior during the first weeks of the administration, but Lincoln never took things personally and always kept his eyes on the greater goal. Seward belatedly acknowledged this, noting that Lincoln's "magnanimity is almost superhuman." The president, he added, "is the best of us."[46] Lincoln's determination to maintain a government of national unity continued throughout his presidency, as he ran for reelection in 1864 with Democrat Andrew Johnson as his vice president on a "National Union" ticket.

Lincoln's magnanimous and moderate approach to governing can also be seen in his appeals to those Americans who chose to dissolve the Union. "We are not enemies but friends. We must not be enemies. Though passion may have strained, it must not break our bonds of affection," he proclaimed in his first inaugural address.[47] It is difficult to imagine a president such as Andrew Jackson uttering such a magnanimous statement. Lincoln's magnanimity could also be seen in his frequent use of the pardon power to spare Union soldiers from a regimen of harsh military discipline, as was his forgiving attitude regarding the treatment of captured Confederate officials as the war neared its end.

Lincoln's devotion to the Constitution and his rejection of demagoguery was powerfully expressed in his address to the 148th Ohio Regiment on August 31, 1864, on the eve of an election he assumed he would lose: "the constitutional administration of our government must be sustained, and I beg of you not to allow your minds or your hearts to be diverted from the support of all necessary measures for that purpose, by any miserable picayune arguments addressed to your pockets, or inflammatory appeals made to your passions or your prejudices."

Lincoln's aversion to demagoguery is even more remarkable considering that few leaders have been confronted with such extraordinary challenges. Despite operating under remarkable stress, Lincoln's benevolent disposition led him to avoid lashing out at his legions of detractors, both North and South. Historian Philip Paludan has noted that Lincoln practiced "positive propaganda," never referring to the Confederacy or to Jefferson Davis as the "enemy."[48] Lincoln disdained not only demagoguery but those who bullied or sought to command obedience from their fellow men, for, as he noted, "persuasion, kind, unassuming persuasion, should ever be adopted." People were more likely to be persuaded through kindness, rather than invective, for once a "drop of honey . . . catches" a man's heart, you are on "the great high road to his reason."[49]

Lincoln never personalized political disputes, whether he differed with opponents over petty politics or high matters of state. The sixteenth president always remained even-tempered, generous, and quick to acknowledge his own failings. He noted his ability to separate the personal from the political in a comment to a fellow politician, "you have more of that feeling of personal resentment than I. Perhaps I have too little of it; but I never thought it paid. A man has no time to spend half his life in quarrels. If any man ceases to attack me I never remember the past against him."[50] A colleague from Illinois once remarked that Lincoln was "a very poor hater," a quality that served him well in an arena noted then and now for its sensitive egos. He never allowed personal feelings to interfere with policies and personnel he believed would further the national interest. He noted to his Whig colleagues in the early 1850s, "stand with anybody that stands right. Stand with him while he is right and part with him when he goes wrong."[51]

Lincoln was guided by the "better angels" of his nature and conducted himself with malice toward none, to borrow a phrase. He obeyed Washington's maxim to "let your conversation be without malice or envy . . . and in all causes of passion admit reason to govern."[52] Yet he was a man of conviction who refused to alter his principles to curry favor with the public. Throughout his presidency he was under intense pressure to avoid making the abolition of slavery the centerpiece of his war aims. Politicians from both parties, newspapermen, and large segments of the public urged him to seek a negotiated settlement with the Confederacy, allowing it to preserve its institutions in exchange for rejoining the Union.

In some instances, Lincoln was urged to simply let the South go in exchange for peace. Fernando Wood, the mayor of New York City, suggested that his city secede from the Union rather than prosecute the war, while many of his fellow Democrats around the nation recoiled at the prospect of converting the war into an "abolition crusade." The Democratic-controlled legislature in Lincoln's home state of Illinois demanded that he withdraw the Emancipation Proclamation and sue for peace with the South. As always, capitalizing on racial animus provided ambitious politicians with a vehicle to enhance their electoral prospects at the cost of undermining the central precept of the American regime.

Lincoln was convinced that he would lose his bid for re-election in 1864, as he remarked to a friend, "you think I don't know I am going to be beaten, but I do and unless some great change takes place badly beaten."[53] Nonetheless, Lincoln stayed the course and defied those who urged him to modify his policies and do what was politically expedient to secure re-election. Lincoln's resistance to public pressure stands in stark contrast to his immediate predecessors, Franklin Pierce and James Buchanan, as well as to many of his successors.

Charles Dana, a journalist turned assistant secretary of war under Lincoln, dismissed the claims of those who asserted that Lincoln was a passive chief executive, a charge frequently directed at the president. Despite his disheveled appearance and lackadaisical air, Lincoln was always the master of events, for "he never gave a hair's breadth, never gave way—he always had his own way." He appeared to be utterly without guile and unassuming, not conveying any sense that he was "the boss," but "it was always his will, his order, that determined a decision." A French observer who met the president early in 1865 observed that Lincoln "dominates everyone present and maintains his exalted position without the slightest effort."[54]

Lincoln was a deliberate thinker, leading some critics to mistake his measured approach to decision making as indecisiveness. His presidency could not survive in today's culture of instant gratification and hypermedia exposure, for "he was a profound believer in his own fixity of purpose, and took pride in saying that his long deliberations made it possible for him to stand by his own acts when they were once resolved upon," one journalist noted.[55] One friend observed the president's methodical decision making and quoted Lincoln as saying "I am slow to learn and slow to forget that which I have learned—My mind is like a piece of steel, very hard to scratch any thing on it and almost impossible after you get it there to rub it out."[56]

Author Harriet Beecher Stowe also commented on Lincoln's meticulous approach to issues, noting that he was "slow and careful in coming to resolutions, willing to talk with every person who has anything to show on any side of a disputed subject, long in weighing and pondering, attached to constitutional limits and time-honored landmarks."[57] Sadly, Lincoln's devotion to deliberation, his ability to think beyond the immediate and contemplate all sides of an issue, is a virtue no longer valued in the hyperactive world of contemporary American politics.

As with his hero George Washington, Lincoln understood silence to be an important aspect of presidential leadership. There were times when silence carried more weight than a speech or proclamation. After reaching a decision through his usual deliberative process, Lincoln never said more than needed to be said.[58] On his lengthy trip from Springfield, Illinois, to Washington, DC, to assume the presidency in 1861, the president-elect refused to comment at repeated train stops as the dissolution of the Union proceeded apace. Lincoln believed that he could not deal with such complex issues in the time allotted at a train stop and was concerned that a rhetorical misstep might exacerbate the passions among the contending parties. He also observed that he was yet to assume the presidency, and perhaps did not have all the facts at his disposal.

As Jeffrey Tulis, the insightful chronicler of presidential rhetoric has noted, Lincoln's "silence thus allowed for flexibility as well as wisdom," for "hastily formed statements might engender a course of policy that was unintended." An added benefit of presidential "silence" was that a formal presidential pronouncement, once it finally appeared, generated greater public interest. Perhaps most importantly, a formal written pronouncement allowed the president to explain in greater detail the link between his actions and his constitutional mandate. Lincoln's public pronouncements were meticulously crafted; his words were chosen with care and were the antithesis of a spontaneous outburst. Lincoln's reliance on written messages also required greater use of the exercise of reason by the public, while oratory relied partly on superficial qualities, including tone of voice, appearance, and body language, for its effectiveness. Lincoln's policy of rhetorical silence complimented his belief in the merits of reason.

There is an aspect of Lincoln's presidency, and his understanding of the Constitution, that generated controversy in his time and remains a subject of dispute, and that concerns his exercise of presidential emergency power. Lincoln's actions earned him the enmity of many citizens who believed he overstepped his bounds and trampled on civil liberties in pursuit of his war ends. The president suspended habeas corpus in parts of the Union; instituted a naval blockade, which is an act of war, against the South; and expanded the military, all powers granted to Congress in Article One of the Constitution but "absorbed," at least for a time, by Lincoln. Lincoln justified these actions claiming he confronted an extraordinary situation, secession, that called for extraordinary measures. He took these steps when Congress was out of session, and while that body would eventually retroactively approve these steps, this was not how the American system was intended to function.

The arguments surrounding Lincoln's emergency measures are beyond the scope of this study.[59] In brief, Lincoln went to great lengths to embed his actions in the Constitution, noting that his constitutionally mandated oath, which was also "registered in heaven," required him to preserve, protect, and defend the Constitution. And, challenging his critics with a question of his own, he asked, "are all the laws but one to go unexecuted, and the government itself to go to pieces, lest that one be violated?"[60] Or as he more bluntly put it, comparing himself to a surgeon saving a life: "Was it possible to lose the nation, and yet preserve the constitution? By general life and limb must be protected; yet often a limb must be amputated to save a life; but a life is never wisely given to save a limb."[61]

Some scholars still consider Lincoln's precedents to be ill-founded and dangerous, ones that established a "constitutional dictatorship." For purposes of this study, Lincoln's presidency demonstrates that one can reject the excesses of the Jacksonian model and yet remain a decisive, "energetic," chief executive. Lincoln proved that decency, propriety, and magnanimity are not at odds with robustly prosecuting a war and defending the nation using extraordinary measures. A dignified presidency does not translate into a neutered presidency. This was true from 1861 to 1865 and remains true in the twenty-first century.

Abraham Lincoln was a mixture of the best of the American founding coupled with elements of nineteenth-century democratization. There were no elaborate carriages drawn by six white horses transporting President Lincoln, and in that sense, he was set apart from George Washington. But Lincoln's Farewell Address to the people of Springfield, Illinois, saw him equate his task in the spring of 1861 to that of President Washington in 1789.[62] He frequently invoked Washington's principles and practices in defense of his own actions. Additionally, the parallels between Abraham Lincoln and Alexander Hamilton, as previously noted, are also striking, in that both men came from remarkably trying backgrounds and sought to erect a body of laws that would allow the talented to rise, as they had, within a system that offered both predictability and rewards for those with an entrepreneurial spirit. Both men worshipped reason and were devoted to the law and to the preservation of the Constitution. Both men understood the dangers of a doctrine of "popular sovereignty," although Lincoln was more willing to pay homage to the people than Hamilton. But in the end, Lincoln embraced Hamiltonian policies and Hamilton's vision of an "energetic executive"—all the while keeping the man at a distance due to his toxicity in southern and western America.

As Joseph Fornieri has eloquently observed, Lincoln's presidency epitomized Hamilton's vision of a great republican statesman who "defends the public good against the momentary impulses of the people." Lincoln was precisely the type of statesman Hamilton had in mind when he noted in *Federalist* no. 71 that the "executive should be in a situation to dare to act his own opinion with vigor and decision." This meant defying majority opinion and saving "the people from the very fatal consequences of their own mistakes" with courage enough to "serve them at the peril of their displeasure." In refusing to kowtow to the demands of those who wished him to withdraw the Emancipation Proclamation and restore the proslavery status quo, and by insisting that any peaceful reunion with the Confederacy had as a prerequisite the abolition of slavery, Lincoln displayed the kind of courage, an independence from public opinion, that the founders' presidency envisioned. The majority was not to govern—the principles of liberty and equality found in the nation's seminal documents were to govern. Lincoln realized that "merely counting noses," as his great biographer Allen Guelzo has noted, was not "the last word in any political question." "Moral principle is all, or nearly all, that unites us," the future president observed in 1856.[63]

This man of remarkable talents was also a humble man, despite his likely awareness that he was the smartest man in the room. In this way, he differed from Alexander Hamilton, and a good number of his presidential successors. Evidence of his humility emerged on many occasions, but two events stand out. Once, when one of Lincoln's aides urged him to rebuke the arrogant and insulting general of the army of the Potomac, George B. McClellan, Lincoln responded, "I will hold McClellan's horse if he will only bring us success." A different general, Ulysses S. Grant, whom the president admired, was the recipient of a remarkable note from Lincoln regarding a matter of strategy: "I now wish to make the personal acknowledgment that you were right, and I was wrong."[64]

The Tragedy of Andrew Johnson

That Lincoln, this great-souled man and model president, was cut down at the war's end serves as one of the nation's foremost tragedies. Lincoln had vowed a postwar policy of "malice toward none" just a few weeks prior to his murder, and yet it is also likely that Reconstruction would have proceeded at a more robust pace than that pursued by Andrew Johnson, a man as far removed from Lincoln's character and ability as one could find. Lincoln "did not mark down the names of those who had not supported him, or nurse grudges, or hold resentments, or retaliate against 'enemies'—indeed, he tried not to have enemies, not to 'plant thorns.'"[65] In contrast, Johnson seemed to be energized by his enemies. In the tradition of his hero Andrew Jackson, a fellow Tennessean, Johnson was motivated by resentment, embraced conspiracy theories, lacked any sense of magnanimity, and practiced the politics of divisiveness. In short, Andrew Johnson was patently unfit for the job of president. Lincoln's greatest mistake as president was removing Hannibal Hamlin from the Republican ticket in 1864 and replacing him with the poorly equipped Johnson.

And yet Johnson merits a brief discussion, in part to clarify Lincoln's greatness, and to point out that Johnson was the predictable result of an overall decline in the health of the American political order. The elevation of an incompetent, slow-witted racist into the presidency was the result of an unpredictable assassination, the first successful act of its kind in the United States, but in a way Johnson's rise was utterly predictable. Johnson was, as historian Kenneth Stampp observed, the "last Jacksonian."[66] This meant, sadly, that demagoguery, class warfare, and racism contributed to his popular appeal. Despite the absence of noticeable talents, exploiting those resentments was enough to launch Johnson on a successful political career and were adequate for the presidency of popular consent. His service as a congressman, governor, senator, vice president, and president showcased the power of class and racial antagonism as a stepping stone to high office in mid-nineteenth-century America.

At his inauguration as the nation's sixteenth vice president on March 4, 1865, Johnson embarrassed himself and his office by showing up drunk. His "inaugural address" was like something out of a bad comedy; at one point the vice president acknowledged members of Lincoln's cabinet who were present, but had to pause to ask a colleague "who is the Secretary of the Navy?" The address allegedly continued with a peroration straight out of a Mark Twain novel: "I'm a going for to tell you—here today; yes, I'm a going for to tell you all, that I am plebian! I glory in it; I am a plebian! The people—yes, the people of the United States have made me what I am; and I am going to tell you here today—yes, today, in this place—that the people are everything."[67] If Abraham Lincoln ever wept in public, this would have been the day.

Johnson was a Jeffersonian and Jacksonian ideologue, proud of his lifelong commitment to "an absolute conviction of the inferiority of blacks coupled with a belief in democracy confined to whites."[68] As Annette Gordon-Reed has observed regarding politics in Johnson's Tennessee, since Andrew Jackson's time the Volunteer State was "a white man's democracy. As political rights were expanded for them, they were expressly constricted for black males."[69] Johnson's maiden speech on the floor of the House of Representatives was devoted to urging his colleagues to repay Andrew Jackson for the fine levied for the latter's lawless actions in New Orleans in the aftermath of the War of 1812 (see the previous chapter).[70]

Johnson's speeches were punctuated with attacks on America's "aristocrats," particularly its banks and bankers, and often accompanied by a firm defense of slavery.[71] Johnson was a slave owner and took a special interest in a fourteen-year-old slave girl he purchased in 1842,[72] but he had also condemned his fellow Southerners for abandoning the Union. In a speech on the floor of the Senate in December 1860, Johnson noted that "I voted against him [Lincoln]; I spoke against him; I spent my money to defeat him; but still I love my country; I love the Constitution."[73] Johnson was the only United States senator who remained loyal to the Union after his state seceded, and he had also endorsed Lincoln's emancipation policy in 1863, another act that caught the president's attention. But Johnson's Unionist stance on the Civil War had little to do with any sense of injustice regarding slavery. For him, the war was just another chapter in his lifelong struggle against "aristocracy." "Damn the negroes," he told one Union general, "I am fighting those traitorous aristocrats, their masters."[74]

Johnson's devotion to the Union was as strong and unwavering as Old Hickory's, and if slavery threatened the nation then the institution should be eliminated, but only as a by-product of a war for union. "I have lived among Negroes, all my life, and I am for the government with slavery under the Constitution as it is, if the government can be saved. . . . I am for the government of my fathers with Negroes, I am for it without negroes. Before I would see this government destroyed, I would send every Negro back to Africa, disintegrated and blotted out of space."[75] In the wake of Lincoln's murder, the new president hoped to integrate the former Confederate states back into the Union as quickly as possible, and he viewed the freed slaves as an impediment to this reunification. They were to be expended with, "disintegrated and blotted out of space," to mollify white Southerners horrified at the prospects of black voters exercising the franchise, or blacks offering their services as free-wage laborers. Johnson was lobbied in February 1866 by a delegation led by the famed abolitionist and former slave Frederick Douglass to support suffrage for the freedmen. The president later told his secretary, "those sons of bitches thought they had me in a trap. I know that damned Douglass: he's just like any nigger, & would sooner cut a white man's throat than not."[76]

It was this position that put Johnson at odds with the "Radical Republicans" and led to the first impeachment of an American president in the nation's history. The United States Senate failed by one vote to convict and remove Johnson, and his effort to win the Democratic Party's nomination for reelection as president failed in 1868. But during his short tenure in office, Johnson completed the destruction of the founders' presidency that began with his heroes, Jefferson and Jackson.

Abandoning Lincoln's practice of "rhetorical silence," Johnson, in a manner that would become conventional practice in the twentieth century, traveled the nation berating his opponents and urging the adoption of his policy prescriptions. As with many of our populist presidents, Johnson was unable to separate himself from the office he held. All policy disputes were personal, and the fate of the country rested in his hands alone. During one speech, Johnson used the first-person pronoun "I," "me," and "mine" 210 times while recounting the trials he had suffered.[77] At one point the beleaguered president compared his situation to that of Jesus Christ on the cross.

In keeping with the penchant of populist presidents to embrace conspiracy theories, Johnson accused his opponents of planning his murder. This martyr to the cause of, himself, noted that "if my blood is shed, let it be shed. . . . But let the opponents of the government remember that when it is poured out 'the blood of the martyrs shall be the seed of the Church.'" Johnson's radical Republican opponents were publicly described by the president as equivalent to Jefferson Davis and other high-ranking Confederates: they were all traitors. At one stop, when a heckler called for the hanging of former Confederate President Jefferson Davis, Johnson shot back, "Why not hang Thad Stevens [a Pennsylvania congressman calling for Johnson's impeachment] and Wendell Phillips [an abolitionist]?" In one of Johnson's public addresses, without the slightest sense of irony, the president noted that he "did not care about his dignity."[78] The dignified presidency envisioned by

George Washington and Alexander Hamilton had been destroyed less than a century after it was launched, razed with a certain amount of glee by one of Washington's unfit successors.

Ulysses S. Grant and the Johnson Legacy

Andrew Johnson was succeeded by Ulysses S. Grant, who admired Lincoln and deplored Johnson. Grant and Lincoln were fellow midwesterners who carried themselves with dignity (despite Grant's lifelong battle with alcoholism) and both kept their egos in check. Both men rejected the cheap populism that was the hallmark of Johnson's career, and both men, unlike Johnson, were cautious in their criticism of their opponents. Ulysses Grant never sought public office, unlike many of his ambitious contemporaries. As Grant told William Tecumseh Sherman regarding his elevation to the presidency, "I have been forced into it in spite of myself," noting that he could not defer without leaving the field to individuals, such as Johnson, who would lose "the results of the costly war which we have gone through."[79] Unlike Andrew Johnson, Ulysses Grant attempted, mostly in vain, to preserve those results.

Grant suppressed the Ku Klux Klan and other terror organizations in the South, and vigorously enforced, for a time, the Fourteenth and Fifteenth Amendments to the Constitution. He also held progressive views about the status of Native Americans at a time when many Americans were determined to eradicate the surviving tribes. Grant went so far as to appoint a Native American to be his commissioner of Indian affairs, a former staff officer of General Grant's named Ely Parker, a member of the Seneca tribe. Grant promised that his administration would pursue any course that would lead to "ultimate citizenship" for Native Americans. Grant described these tribes as "the original occupants of the land" in his first inaugural address, although this pledge went unfulfilled in part due to a successful effort to undermine Parker's authority.[80] Grant's attempt to alter federal policy toward Native Americans was stymied at every opportunity, but his statement in his second inaugural address that "wars of extermination . . . are demoralizing and wicked. Our superiority in strength . . . should make us lenient toward the Indian. The wrong inflicted upon him should be taken into account and the balance placed to his credit" was far ahead of his time. In 1871, Grant told a reporter "I have lived with the Indians and I know them thoroughly. . . . You can't thrash people so that they will love you." And he added, you must "make enemies friends by kindness."[81] These sentiments, while not shared by his fellow countrymen, stand as a testament to Grant's magnanimity and judiciousness.

Andrew Johnson's limitations are heightened by the fact that his presidency was bracketed by Lincoln's and Grant's. While the latter's administration had more than its share of scandals, Grant himself is a figure worthy of admiration. In contrast to Lincoln and Grant, Johnson was a man motivated by pettiness and malice. His principles were grounded firmly in white supremacy. Johnson endorsed this doctrine in no uncertain terms in his third annual message to Congress on December 3, 1867, in one of the most disturbing documents ever produced by an American president. It is important to cite his views at some length, since Johnson's message was a seminal statement of racial supremacy, and a seminal statement in the history of American demagoguery:

> The subjugation of the [former Confederate] States to Negro domination would be worse than the military despotism under which they are now suffering. It was believed beforehand that the people would endure any amount of military oppression for any length of time rather than degrade themselves by subjection to the Negro race. Therefore they have been left without a choice. Negro suffrage was established by [an] act of Congress, and the military officers were commanded to superintend the process of clothing the Negro race with the political privileges torn from white men.
>
> It is not proposed merely that they shall govern themselves, but that they shall rule the white race, make and administer State laws, elect Presidents and members of Congress, and shape to a greater or less extent the future destiny of the whole country. Would such a trust and power be safe in such hands?
>
> It is the glory of white men to know that they have had these qualities [the ability to manage public affairs] in sufficient measure to build upon this continent a great political fabric and to preserve its stability for more than ninety years, while in every other part of the world all similar experiments have failed. . . . it must be acknowledged that in the progress of nations Negroes have shown less capacity for government than any other race of people. No independent government of any form has ever been successful in their hands. On the contrary, wherever they have been left to their own devices they have shown a constant tendency to relapse into barbarism.
>
> The great difference between the two races in physical, mental, and moral characteristics will prevent an amalgamation or fusion of them together in one homogeneous mass. If the inferior obtains the ascendency over the other, it will govern with reference only to its own interests for it will recognize no common interest—and create such a tyranny as this continent has never yet witnessed.

Already the Negroes are influenced by promises of confiscation and plunder. They are taught to regard as an enemy every white man who has any respect for the rights of his own race. If this continues it must become worse and worse, until all order will be subverted, all industry cease, and the fertile fields of the South grow up into a wilderness. Of all the dangers which our nation has yet encountered, none are equal to those which must result from the success of the effort now making to Africanize the half of our country.[82]

In populist and progressive circles, the celebration of an American political figure frequently hinges on the extent to which that figure challenged the "elites" of their time. But far too often this populism was accompanied by the vilification of minority groups, be they racial, political, economic, or religious. Andrew Johnson practiced this kind of politics, targeting the wealthy for their "crooked" ways while attacking freed slaves for their "barbaric" ways.

Johnson frequently, and deservedly, comes in near last in those perennial polls of presidential greatness, and while his standing in the American pantheon is currently quite low, this has not always been the case. Many early twentieth-century historians alleged that the policies of Reconstruction were foisted upon the country by an elite cabal of northeastern Republicans intent on helping their industrialist friends and enriching themselves. These accounts often portrayed Johnson as the noble common man battling elitists of all stripes, both North and South. Claude Bowers and William E. Dodd, and members of the so-called Dunning School affiliated with Columbia University, were fond of recounting the horrors of Reconstruction, with lurid tales of newly freed black men deflowering white women. One scholar who endorsed this view was the nation's twenty-eighth president, Woodrow Wilson. As we will see in our next chapter, Wilson believed that the Ku Klux Klan was the savior of white civilization in the South, a flawed but well-intentioned entity that repulsed the unholy alliance of Radical Republicans and rapacious free blacks.

Andrew Johnson was a fitting heir to the presidency of popular consent and of the principle that "the majority is to govern," a principle that paved the way for the politics of demagoguery and racism. Ironically, many of the so-called elitists disparaged by Andrew Jackson and Andrew Johnson remained true to the founders' presidency and recoiled at this type of politics, a politics which degraded the office ennobled by Abraham Lincoln.

5

Woodrow Wilson

"To Be as Big a Man as He Can"

Woodrow Wilson was one of the most significant chief executives in the history of the American presidency. Impressed by the activist presidency of Theodore Roosevelt (while dismissing the presidency of his immediate predecessor, William Howard Taft), Wilson built on Roosevelt's activism and bestowed it with an intellectual imprimatur that influenced the thinking of presidential practitioners as well as scholarly observers for decades to come. While Roosevelt's activism was rejected by some of his twentieth-century Republican successors, Wilson's interpretation of presidential power became gospel within the ranks of his Democratic Party. Thus, Wilson deserves recognition as *the* president who launched the activist presidency of the twentieth century, which persists to this day.

The Banal Presidency

Woodrow Wilson is one of the few American presidents who thought deeply and at length about the nature of the office he came to hold. One of the major works on the American government to appear during Wilson's formative years, and one that influenced the future president's thinking, was James Bryce's *The American Commonwealth* (1888). The book's author was a member of the British Parliament and a professor at Oxford University, and his chapter "Why Great Men Are Not Chosen Presidents" captured the late nineteenth-century scholarly assessment of the banality of the American presidency. Wilson agreed with Bryce's conclusion that "the trivial and mechanical parts of his [the president's] work leave too little leisure for framing large schemes of policy," and shared Bryce's view that presidential weakness was compounded by separation of powers. A president may promote large policy schemes but "he needs the cooperation of Congress, which may be jealous, or indifferent, or hostile."

In addition to frustrating presidential designs, Congress was also something of a dead end for those seeking a noble kind of fame, for "the methods and habits of Congress, and indeed of political life generally," frustrated those ambitions. In the United States, talented individuals were drawn into the business world, partly due to the lucrative rewards offered in the private sector. In contrast, the public sphere in Europe offered those with noble ambition the prospect of dealing with "burning" or fundamental questions of the nature of the regime, questions that were settled in the United States. Additionally, one could make a career of politics in these regimes but not in the United States, partly due to a tradition of rotation in office.

Compounding the American situation was the fact that the "ordinary American voter does not object to mediocrity. . . . Who now knows or cares to know anything about the personality of James K. Polk or Franklin Pierce? . . . The only thing remarkable about them is that being so common place, they should have climbed so high." Finally, the exposure one was subjected to in the American republic discouraged those with noble ambitions and encouraged parties to search for nondescript mediocrities. "Fiercer far than the light which beats upon a throne is the light which beats upon a presidential candidate, searching out all the recesses of his past," Bryce observed. "Hence, when the choice lies between a brilliant man and a safe man, the safe man is preferred."

Bryce's seminal chapter was seen by many, accurately or not, as a symbol of the frustration felt toward an American regime that lacked dynamic leadership. Bryce's work has perhaps been given more attention than it deserves and has been subjected to an inordinate number of distorted interpretations, for he was not entirely criticizing the American regime or the presidency—great leaders were a rarity, and "they are not, in quiet times, absolutely needed."[1] Presidential mediocrity was to some extent a symbol of American strength and stability. But regardless of whether Bryce has been misinterpreted or not, and over time his position on presidential greatness and mediocrity evolved, Wilson would later review Bryce's book for *Political Science Quarterly*, calling it a "great work, worthy of the heartiest praise."

Wilson's link to the work and its author was not inconsequential, for the professor had been solicited by Bryce to submit a chapter for the book, but he deferred. Wilson later described himself as "captivated" by Bryce's "strength and dash and mastery."[2]

As a young professor, Woodrow Wilson was searching for ways to inject dynamism into the American political system and considered the absence of avenues for public fame to be a serious shortcoming. At first Wilson yearned for the dynamism that he believed existed in the British parliamentary system and he argued for the incorporation of elements of that system into the United States. Separation of powers was consistently described by Wilson as a deterrent to vitality and the source of gridlock, denying the possibility for statesmen to emerge.

Woodrow Wilson believed the Gilded Age presidency was a symptom of this unhealthy American regime. He was critical of the "mediocrities" who inhabited the White House between Lincoln and Teddy Roosevelt. Yet while their images are unlikely ever to be engraved on the face of Mount Rushmore, these presidents avoided the bombast and theatrics of Andrew Johnson's presidency and were more in accord with the founders' understanding of the role of the office. Nonetheless, they were not charismatic leaders of the kind Wilson believed were necessary for the salvation of the nation.

A Darwinian Constitution

Wilson's disdain for the mediocrity of American politics was exceeded only by his contempt for the adoration Americans held for their Constitution. Wilson and many of his fellow scholars found this blind faith in the founders a formidable obstacle to progress. This worshipful attitude prevented the American government from dealing with the complex problems of the twentieth century. Wilson's goals were remarkably ambitious, for he sought not only to democratize the presidency but also the entire American constitutional order. With the help of progressive scholars and journalists, Wilson succeeded, in part, in undermining the reverence Americans felt for the Constitution and its architects.

One of the reasons the American regime needed to be reconstituted, and why Americans needed to be disenthralled from their habitual veneration of the Constitution, was to break the gridlock caused by the separation of powers and confront corporate America. Both Professor Wilson and President Wilson believed that Hamilton and Madison's antiquated Constitution was an obstacle to creating an activist government capable of checking this corporate power. In a nod to his conspiratorially inclined populist predecessors, Wilson claimed during the election of 1912 that "an invisible empire has been setup above the forms of democracy."[3] This was in keeping with the stance of William Jennings Bryan who would go on to join Wilson's cabinet and who repeatedly warned of the ill intent of the "invisible empire." This conspiratorial strand ran deep in populist circles and to a lesser extent in progressive circles, with the former frequently exclaiming their fears of Jews, immigrants, and "the Rothschilds," all the while embracing white supremacy.[4] Progressives and populists alike agreed that the existence of this "invisible empire" required the overthrow of the old order and the establishment of an activist federal government to combat corporate power. The times were changing, and the Constitution needed to change with it.

Wilson claimed that the founders' Constitution was one of Newtonian checks and balances, and in the mind of Western intellectuals like Wilson, Newton had been supplanted by Charles Darwin's theory of evolution. Those influenced by Darwin's work and other scientific thinkers believed that a Constitution had to evolve with the times just as a living organism must adapt to changing circumstances. The mechanical, Newtonian approach of the founders gave the American government a static, "machine-like" quality, yet government should be "accountable to Darwin, not to Newton," Wilson argued. Government should be "modified by its environment, necessitated by its tasks, shaped to its functions by the sheer pressure of life."[5] The Constitution, which had a tendency to be seen in biblical terms—strictly observed and not to be tinkered with—was in fact "not merely a lawyers' document: it is a vehicle of life, and its spirit is always the spirit of the age." "Living political constitutions," Wilson emphasized, "must be Darwinian in structure and practice."[6]

Early in his career Wilson, as mentioned, favored importing elements of a parliamentary system into the American government. Wilson had an affinity for all things British, and his late nineteenth-century assessment of the presidency led him to conclude that it would be best for the president to be more of a prime minister. This way, the chief executive could serve as both a party and a legislative leader, thereby bridging the antiquated and obstructionist system of separation of powers. However, Wilson's position evolved over time, especially after William McKinley's forceful conduct of the

Spanish-American War, when he began to see the president as uniquely situated to revitalize the American polity and displace the sclerotic Constitution.[7]

In 1908, while serving as president of Princeton University, Wilson published *Constitutional Government in the United States,* which contained a plea for energizing the American presidency, an office he hoped someday to win. The American presidency is "the vital place of action in the system" and the office takes the measure of the man who holds it, gauging his "wisdom as well as his force." Wilson sought not only to energize the presidency but to make the entire federal government more efficient by freeing it from the "friction" of separation of powers. A "friction-free" government, as we shall see, led Wilson to sanction some of his administration's most onerous policies.

The Constitution "bids him [the president] speak" particularly in times of "stress and change" and "thrust[s] upon him the attitude of originator of policies." The latter was contrary to the Constitution and to over one hundred years of tradition, but Wilson was not inclined to look to the past. A new era had dawned, and the Constitution and American political traditions had to keep up with the times. "The Constitution," Wilson argued, "was not meant to hold the government back to the time of horses and wagons." American reverence for the Constitution, and the founders, was misplaced, for this document was created when "there were no railways, there was no telegraph, there was no telephone."[8]

Predictably, the Princeton professor was one of the first to argue that the American presidency was an almost superhuman task. Wilson observed that the president is the "most heavily burdened officer in the world" and its inhabitant must possess "an inexhaustible vitality." "Men of ordinary physique and discretion, cannot be Presidents and live, if the strain be not somehow relieved. We shall be obliged always to be picking our chief magistrate from among wise and prudent athletes—a small class." Wilson may well have had the obese William Howard Taft in mind when he wrote this; Taft's girth, in the minds of most progressives, was only surpassed by his sloth-like, lethargic approach to the presidency. Wilson was an early contributor to the mythology of the activist presidency, an office requiring near Herculean qualities. The president as superman would become gospel for those who would go on to celebrate the merits of "presidential government." The notion that the burdens of the American presidency are only capable of being dealt with by a select few animates the writing of journalists, scholars, and many of the memoirs of those who worked for various twentieth-century presidents.

Wilson also argued that presidents needed to abandon the cramped, archaic view that the primary task of the presidency was to administer the federal government. It was imperative that twentieth-century presidents recognize that as the nation grew in influence and power, they are "more and more directors of affairs and leaders of the nation"—they must be men of enlightened "action."

Additionally, the president must possess the willpower to force disparate elements to cooperate, for "their cooperation is indispensable, their warfare fatal. There can be no successful government without leadership," without coordination of "the organs of life and action." The president was "the unifying force in our complex system, the leader both of his party and of the nation," and he alone could overcome the debilitating gridlock of constitutional government by serving as *the* leader. Wilson's constitutional reforms were coupled with equally important policy considerations: the president would preside over an executive branch composed of experts who would regulate the economy in the interest of the common man. This would be accomplished by unleashing the power of the federal government to check corporate power.

Along with presiding over this regulatory state, the president would serve as an educator and visionary who would lead the nation through his oratorical skills. Again, only the president can provide this leadership, for his status as the lone nationally elected figure means that he serves as the spokesman of the people. Wilson argued that "his [the president's] is the only voice in affairs" and once he wins the confidence of the people, "no other single force can withstand him, no combination of forces will easily overpower him." If he adopts the mantle of true leadership, his presidency "is anything he has the sagacity and force to make it." The president is "the representative of no constituency, but of the whole people. . . . If he rightly interpret[s] the national thought and boldly insist[s] upon it, he is irresistible." The American people would welcome this bold leadership which brings a "zest" to public life, for the nation's "instinct is for unified action, and it craves a single leader" who possesses the "insight and caliber" to lead.[9]

Teacher and Preacher in Chief

During his time at Princeton, Wilson was impressed by Theodore Roosevelt's expansive interpretation of executive power and his willingness to pressure

Congress by mobilizing public opinion. Wilson held that the essence of statesmanship was the molding of that opinion. "Policy—where there is no arbitrary ruler to do the choosing for the whole nation—means massed opinion, and the forming of the masses is the whole art and mastery of politics."[10] Wilson had always been driven, as he put it as a young man, "to impel them [the people] to great political achievements."[11]

According to Wilson, the president needed to act as an educator instructing the public on the proper course of action required to address contemporary issues. Considering this, Wilson began holding regular press conferences and restored the practice halted by Thomas Jefferson of delivering his State of the Union messages in person, laying out his agenda for the nation. "The forming of the masses," as Wilson put it, required effective packaging, exemplified in Wilson's case with his New Freedom tag line for his administration. Theodore Roosevelt had begun the practice of presidents branding their administrations with a catchy slogan; in Roosevelt's case, it was the Square Deal.[12]

Woodrow Wilson also believed that presidents must possess the rhetorical skills necessary to mobilize the nation to meet the demands of the day. As James Ceaser observed, the public good could only be realized by a president forming a "life" relationship with the people. Wilson believed that a "popular leader" or "popular statesman"' had to "overcome the inertia of institutional rule and 'interpret' for the people the truly progressive principles of the era." Wilson's refounding, as with Jefferson's and Jackson's, called for presidential leadership based not on the powers granted in Article Two but "by reason of their [the leaders'] contact and amenability to public opinion." As Ceaser observed, the Wilsonian definition of statesmanship was reduced to the "art of guiding public sentiment."[13]

Wilson believed that the fears of Washington, Hamilton, Madison, and other founders regarding the ascension of a demagogue into the presidency, were no longer a legitimate concern for twentieth-century Americans. The nation had reached a stage of development where it was simply unimaginable that this could happen, in part due to the wise, moderate temperament of the citizenry. The difference between a visionary president and a demagogue was, according to Wilson, that the former was "obedient to the permanent purposes of the public mind" while the latter was "trimming to the inclination of the moment."[14] While Wilson offered a somewhat ill-defined distinction between a responsible president and a demagogue, he offered little reassurance that the American public would rebuff a "self-interested" "trimmer."

The Taft Alternative

One of Woodrow Wilson's opponents in the 1912 presidential election was deeply concerned about the election of "self-interested" "trimmer[s]." William Howard Taft was the anti-Wilson and anti–Teddy Roosevelt compressed into one large frame. A brief discussion of Taft's presidency is in order because he stands as a twentieth-century exemplar of a chief executive who respected the framers' Constitution and rejected the presidency of popular consent. Taft is an underestimated president, due in good measure to his alleged conservatism in contrast to the two progressive titans who bookended his presidency. The American political order would benefit from a deeper understanding of Taft's presidency, but the prospects of that are slim considering the scholarly bias in favor of activist presidents like Roosevelt and Wilson.

Taft was, as his biographer Jeffrey Rosen noted, a believer in the idea that public opinion must be "filtered through constitutional structures and enlightened representation." Representative government, separation of powers, individual rights, and the rule of law were central to Taft's thinking as a president and as chief justice of the Supreme Court. [15] Taft, unlike Roosevelt and Wilson, recoiled at the progressive drive for direct primaries, recall provisions, and referendums on matters of public policy. Roosevelt had gone so far as to claim that it was the responsibility of elected officials to resign if their conscience led them to resist the people's desires. In that case, the official "should not try to continue in office against their [the public's] will."[16] Taft was also repulsed by Roosevelt's attacks on judges and with the former president's proposal to allow for judicial decisions to be overturned by popular vote.[17] Taft noted disdainfully that Roosevelt's attacks on the judiciary echoed that of Andrew Jackson: "There is a decided similarity between Andrew Jackson and Roosevelt. He had the same disrespect for law when he felt the law stood between him and what he thought was right to do."[18]

Taft, echoing Alexander Hamilton, whom he greatly admired, argued that the Constitution was intended to check "every temporary wind of passion." He added "we are not a pure democracy governing by direct action, and the great men who framed our fundamental law did not intend that we should be."[19] Taft rejected Andrew Jackson's claim, embraced by both Roosevelt and Wilson, that the president was the "tribune of the people." This claim was rooted in hubris and was a threat to constitutional government. The people,

Taft asserted, had not given to any one person "the mandate to speak for them as peculiarly the people's representatives." The idea that any American president would see himself acting in this manner, of playing "the part of a Universal Providence and set[ting] all things right," was completely contrary to the principles of republican government.[20] Taft was one of the last American presidents committed to abiding by the founders' conception of the presidency.

President Taft's rejection of the presidency of popular consent was known by all who worked for him in the White House. He once told his military aide that "I will not play a part for popularity." He would later add, "the truth is that it is not the height of my ambition to be popular."[21] Taft believed that Roosevelt was excessively focused on his public image and in maintaining good relations with the press. His predecessor "talked with correspondents a great deal" and believed that he "must communicate his feelings."[22] Through his contacts in the press, and through his larger-than-life personality, Roosevelt kept both his policy preferences and his personality, along with his family, a constant subject of media attention.[23] Communicating presidential "feelings" and showcasing the chief executive's private life was an element of the personalized presidency that both Roosevelt and Wilson, and most of their successors, employed to forge a bond with the public.

Taft spurned these tactics and suffered accordingly. "I don't want any forced or manufactured sentiment in my favor," he noted in 1910. As one of his chroniclers, Lewis L. Gould, observes, "the notion of the chief executive as a celebrity who made news through the force of his personality was anathema to Taft. He did not wish to entertain the public."[24] Looking back on his presidency, Taft wrote his wife that his time in office was "humdrum" and "uninteresting."[25] That was due in good measure to Taft's reluctance to pander to public opinion and engage in presidential theatrics.

But Taft's presidency was hardly "humdrum." He had a remarkably impressive record, and a progressive one at that, on issues related to conservation and antitrust. Taft protected more land than Teddy Roosevelt and did so in one term as opposed to Roosevelt's almost two terms in office.[26] At one point in Taft's presidency, Roosevelt argued that Taft's antitrust policies were too aggressive; in the end, Taft brought close to seventy antitrust cases in one term, while Roosevelt oversaw forty-four cases.[27] Taft's presidency demonstrates that one can be an assertive president and still abide by the letter and spirit of the framers' Constitution.

The Wilsonian Era

William Howard Taft suffered one of the most ignominious defeats for an incumbent president in the nation's history. Woodrow Wilson won the 1912 election in a divided field of four contenders: Taft, former President Theodore Roosevelt, and socialist candidate Eugene Debs. Taft came in third in the four-man field. Wilson won with 41.8 percent of the popular vote, and the incoming president made it clear that he categorically rejected everything Taft represented. Wilson believed his conception of presidential power would provide more effective leadership for a complex, industrialized world, unlike the founders' presidency which was a vestige of a simpler, lost world. Wilson's presidency would dominate not only domestic American politics, but it would stand astride the entire world. "The President can never again be the mere domestic figure he has been throughout so large a part of our history. . . . Our president must always, henceforth, be one of the great powers of the world," Wilson wrote four years prior to his race for the White House. He went on to note that "the President is at liberty, both in law and conscience, to be as big a man as he can."[28]

Wilson's oversized assessment of the potential of the American presidency was exceeded only by his oversized ego. As historian Forrest McDonald has noted, Wilson's conception of himself "was little short of messianic."[29] A sixteen-year-old Woodrow Wilson pointed to a painting of British Prime Minister William Gladstone and murmured "Gladstone, the greatest statesman that ever lived. . . . I intend to be a statesman too." He informed a classmate at Princeton that after taking voice lessons he would practice speaking in his father's church "in order to prepare for the future" and that he could "almost see the benches smile at some of [his] opinions and deliverances."[30] The day after winning the presidency, the chairman of the Democratic National Committee paid the new president a visit to discuss possible appointments. Wilson immediately put the chairman on notice that "before we proceed, I wish it clearly understood that I owe you nothing. Remember that God ordained that I should be the next president of the United States."[31]

Wilson's self-identification as a savior was evident in his frequent public pronouncements elevating every issue to a matter of deep moral import. French President George Clemenceau said of Wilson, "He thinks he is another Jesus Christ come upon the earth to reform men."[32] In urging the American people to back the League of Nations, Wilson claimed that "the facts are marching and God is marching with them. You cannot resist them."[33] When he presented his plans for the league to the United States Senate, the president claimed that he was merely a servant of a higher power: "the stage is set, the destiny disclosed. It has come about by no plan of our conceiving, but by the hand of God who led us into this way. We cannot turn back."[34]

Wilson, a lifelong educator, saw himself as the nation's chief visionary. Wilson's approach was in significant accord with Thomas Jefferson's understanding of the presidency, but less so with Andrew Jackson, the anti-intellectual president. Jefferson saw the presidency as partly a teaching office, and Wilson more than any other president relished this role. Furthermore, Woodrow Wilson and Thomas Jefferson were the nation's most idealistic presidents, and both men suffered from a Quixotic tendency to try to force reality to bend to their respective ideologies. Despite their checkered human rights records at home, both men believed that the United States was the last, best hope of mankind, and sought to bring the blessings of liberty to the world, albeit through dramatically different means. Both men rejected the cold, calculating rationale of a foreign policy based on national interests, believing, particularly in Wilson's case, that the concerns of humanity should prevail over the national interest. The United States, Wilson believed, along with many of his fellow progressives, had a providential duty to teach the world. Campaigning for president in 1912, "We are chosen," he said, "to show the way to the nations of the world how they shall walk in the paths of liberty." The United States was to play the role of the world's preacher, for America "lies at the center of modern history."[35]

The preacher's son saw himself both as a moral leader of the United States and a moral leader of the world, and this heightened sense of importance served as an impediment to compromise. When the press reported that the president was considering a compromise on a piece of legislation, an angry Wilson scolded reporters and told them, "when you get a chance, just say that I am not the kind that considers compromises when I once take my position. Just note that down so that there will be nothing more of that sort transmitted to the press."[36] Wilson's reluctance to compromise contributed to the downfall of his beloved League of Nations; had he accepted the proposals of the Senate Foreign Relations Committee for relatively minor changes to the league, he may have prevailed. This reluctance to compromise also translated into a tendency, which is an abiding feature of the presidency of popular consent, to view every opponent as the personification of evil. Opponents of the

League of Nations were compared to Russian Bolsheviks and were accused of aiding the enemy.[37]

Labeling one's opponents as "enemies" is a hallmark of the presidency of popular consent. This practice undermines the vital role envisioned by the framers of the president as a force for unity. The president was to act as the nation's chief of state, not as a partisan cheerleader. Woodrow Wilson completed the project begun by Jefferson and Jackson of severing the presidency from this vision and from its constitutional restraints. As the authority of Wilson's refounded presidency derived from the personal relationship between the president and the people, and his ability to channel that popularity into achieving concrete results, then the president was free to be as big a man as he wanted to be, and to tar those out of step with his "mandate." Technological advances unheard of in Jefferson's and Jackson's time contributed to Wilson's success in establishing a personal bond between the president and the public and in tarnishing his opponents.

This personal bond led him, a remarkably proud and conceited man, to claim that he was, during the divisive debate over the League of Nations, "simply an instrument of the people's will."[38] Wilson may have believed this, but regardless of whether he did or not it was good politics, at least in the short run. But by publicly proclaiming he was a mere "instrument" of the people, the president was as far removed from the framers' conception of executive power as you can get—even from those framers such as Alexander Hamilton who were advocates of an energetic executive. Hamilton, suffice it to say, held "the little arts of popularity" in contempt and believed that one of the president's primary responsibilities was to protect an overbearing majority from trampling on the rights of unpopular minorities, including those possessed of property.[39] Most of the founders, as noted, considered the concept of "popular leadership" to be a danger to liberty, and that a republican leader should never identify themselves as "an instrument of the people's will."

Wilson and the Tyranny of the Majority

A disturbing feature of the presidency of popular consent is the tendency of presidents who embrace this concept to claim they are simply following the public's will, and the League of Nations is a perfect example of this phenomenon. Wilson's claim to the contrary, there was no American majority demanding the creation of such an entity. The presidency of popular consent temps those presidents with expansive agendas, or expansive egos, to manufacture public support through media manipulation and other public relations techniques. These techniques undermine not just the credibility of the presidency, but of republican government itself. Wilson, as we will see, heartily adopted such tactics during World War I.

The idea that the president serves as the voice of the people was clearly on display during the Wilson years, as were the dangers associated with that model. This presidency aids and abets in the formation of tyrannical majoritarianism. Woodrow Wilson's record on civil liberties was one of the worst in the nation's history, particularly during the period in and around the American entry into World War I. In 1916, as the nation considered intervening in the Great War, Wilson led a patriotic parade through the streets of Washington, DC, and concluded the festivities with a speech at the Washington Monument. The president harangued the crowd with a plea that a certain unnamed group "must absolutely be crushed" to prevent it from subverting America, and laid down a marker that "loyalty to this [American] flag is the first test of tolerance in the United States." Wilson added that the Democratic Party should include a plank in its platform noting that all real Americans would endorse his actions on the domestic and foreign fronts.[40]

When the United States entered the war, dissenters were routinely arrested, harassed, or deported, in some cases for simply speaking out against American involvement in the conflict. Some 2,168 Americans were prosecuted under the controversial sedition and espionage acts that Wilson signed into law in 1917 and 1918, including Eugene V. Debs, the Socialist Party's presidential candidate who ran against Wilson for president in 1912. Debs was convicted and sentenced to ten years in prison for speaking out in favor of draft resisters.

Throughout the war, and in its immediate aftermath, the United States Postal Service routinely opened mail and sometimes confiscated it, while newspapers and magazines with an antiwar perspective were harassed or shut down. Foreign periodicals had to submit their publications to the United States government for prepublication review. Wilson's two attorneys general, Thomas W. Gregory and A. Mitchell Palmer, ran the most Draconian Department of Justice in the nation's history. While some of Wilson's defenders have blamed Gregory or Palmer for the department's excesses, for the most part Wilson either encouraged or remained silent while his Justice Department ran roughshod over the rights of dissenting minorities. The infamous "Palmer raids" of 1919–1920 witnessed wholesale violations of civil liberties; in Detroit over eight hundred people were imprisoned for up to six days in a windowless corridor of a federal building equipped with one toilet.[41]

In another instance, Wilson urged Attorney General Gregory to indict the editor of the *Kansas City Star* in 1918 for his antiwar stance. Only once did Wilson overrule his censoriously inclined postmaster general, Albert S. Burleson, and that was when the latter tried to ban the magazine the *Nation* from using the US mail.[42] It is rather fitting that Wilson's record on civil liberties was so checkered, for he believed that "men as communities are supreme over men as individuals."[43]

Some of Wilson's emergency measures fit within the principles and practices of his wartime predecessors and were justifiable. There were legitimate governmental concerns regarding spying and sabotage on the home front. But what made Wilson's actions especially problematic was his enlisting of thousands of American citizens as government informers, as sources who would surveil one another and report any suspicious activities. German Americans, for obvious reasons, were especially suspect. Wilson fueled the majority's paranoia about the enemy's wily plots to undermine America in his message to Congress asking for a declaration of war: "From the very outset of the present war, [Germany] has filled our unsuspecting communities and even our offices of government with spies and set criminal intrigues everywhere afoot against our national unity of counsel, our peace within and without, our industries and our commerce." There were millions of German Americans in the United States at the time, which posed a challenge for a suspicious administration. Most of "them" were loyal, according to Wilson, and "they will be prompt to stand with us in rebuking and restraining the few who may be of a different mind and purpose."

If there should be disloyalty, it would be dealt with "a firm hand of stern repression." A major element of that "firm hand of stern repression" was the American Protective League (APL) which worked in concert with the Department of Justice to inform on various "disloyal" Americans. The APL, which grew to 250,000 members, was designated as an "officially recognized auxiliary" under the control of the United States attorneys throughout the nation. Wilson expressed some concerns about the APL but never curtailed its operations. At one point in 1917, Attorney General Thomas Gregory boasted that "those disloyal persons and moral and physical degenerates who believe nothing is worth fighting for" would face the wrath of an "avenging government." Gregory would later ominously add, "It is safe to say that never in its history has this country been so thoroughly policed."[44]

Wilson remained largely silent throughout the months of a nationwide loyalty dragnet. But the presidency of popular consent had always remained silent or tacitly encouraged this type of majority tyranny throughout the nation's history. The APL was simply the latest embodiment of the tyranny of the majority, which the founders' presidency was intended to resist. A prominent historian of Wilson's civil liberties record noted that the nation's twenty-eighth president "was frequently harshly critical of the groups accused of disloyalty when he referred to them in his public addresses. . . . His abdication of personal responsibility left the fate of civil liberties to subordinate officials . . . and the public, at a time when few were inclined to be moderate." Predictably, abuses began to occur in this atmosphere of suspicion, including the lynching of Robert Prager, an Illinois coal miner who also happened to be German American, in 1918.[45] But Woodrow Wilson made a career out of ignoring the problem of lynching, as we shall see. The majority was not only to govern, they were to define the rule of law.

Wilson lacked the quality of magnanimity so pronounced in George Washington and Abraham Lincoln. As with his populist predecessors, Wilson tended to personalize policy disputes and had difficulty distinguishing between his interests and that of the office he temporarily held. The president was remarkably stingy with applications for clemency from those who were dragooned in his administration's disloyalty dragnet. Hardliners such as Attorney General A. Mitchell Palmer urged him to pardon numerous individuals convicted under the espionage and sedition acts, but Wilson stubbornly refused.

Wilson was especially vindictive toward Eugene Debs, the former presidential candidate turned antiwar activist. Palmer and other members of Wilson's New Freedom coalition, including prominent labor leaders, urged Wilson to pardon Debs. When Palmer submitted a formal pardon request in January 1921, over two years after the end of the war, the embittered president wrote across it, "Denied. W. W." As the noted iconoclast H. L. Mencken said of Wilson and the Debs case, "Magnanimity was simply beyond him." Mencken added, astutely, that in a similar situation Washington or Lincoln would have pardoned Debs.[46]

It would fall to Wilson's successor, the lowly Warren G. Harding, to pardon Debs. Harding was far more progressive than Wilson on matters of civil liberties and civil rights, although it would be difficult to discern this fact from many scholarly accounts of the era. Wilson's regulatory agenda and his commitment to an activist presidency have won applause from scholars who put a premium on those presidential accomplishments. Harding simply did not meet that standard, and that, coupled with a series of high-profile scandals, led to his ranking as one of the nation's worst chief executives.

Wilson and Race

While President Wilson's record on civil liberties is disturbing, his record on racial matters is even worse and has only belatedly received its due. He was the standard bearer of a party whose base, and leadership, had been hostile to African Americans since its founding. The Democratic Party had broadened suffrage to white male voters throughout the nineteenth century while at the same time depriving the vote to free blacks. The Thirteenth, Fourteenth, and Fifteenth Amendments to the Constitution, which had abolished slavery and granted citizenship to former slaves, at least in theory, had been adopted in the aftermath of the Civil War. The Civil Rights Act of 1866 had also passed over President Andrew Johnson's veto, while other Reconstruction initiatives became the law of the land, at least for a time. But a ten-year experiment at reconstructing the South ultimately collapsed when a tired white majority opted to reunite and put the divisiveness of the war behind it. The majority was intent on "moving on," on seeking "closure," to borrow modern clichés, and the price for that closure was paid by the newly freed slaves.

One of those interested in "moving on" was Woodrow Wilson, a son of the South who was born in 1856 and spent his youth in Virginia, Georgia, and South Carolina. When he was eight years old, Wilson saw Confederate President Jefferson Davis in chains on his way to a Union prison.[47] He absorbed all the tales of the perfidy of Reconstruction that would come to animate the chroniclers of the "lost cause" mythology, a mythology which focused on the "horrors" of Yankee carpetbaggers and the rapacious freedmen they manipulated. Wilson wrote about Reconstruction in a remarkably blunt manner in his *A History of the American People* (1902): "The white men of the South were aroused by the mere instinct of self-preservation to rid themselves, by fair means or foul, of the intolerable burden of governments sustained by the votes of ignorant Negroes and conducted in the interests of adventurers."

Wilson decried the policies of the Radical Republicans, who sought the "veritable overthrow of civilization in the South" by "put[ting] the white South under the heel of the black South." He praised those freedmen who "stayed quietly by their old masters and gave no trouble," but was disappointed that those cases were the exceptions. Wilson referred to the Ku Klux Klan as "men half outlawed, denied the suffrage, without hope of justice in the courts, who meant to take this means [actions against the freedmen and Northern "adventurers"] to make their will felt."

During the "disorder and social upheaval" of Reconstruction, "every countryside wished to have its own Ku Klux . . . until at last" arose a "great Ku Klux Klan, bound together in loose organization to protect the southern country from some of the ugliest hazards from a time of revolution." The Klan found that "the negroes were generally easy enough to deal with: a thorough fright usually disposed them to make utter submission." Wilson criticized the Klan for its transformation from an organization dedicated to "mischievous frolic" and "extravagant prank[s]" to one that sought to "right a disordered society through the power of fear." But the actions of these "knights errant" was attributable, and excused, as the actions of copycats, "malicious fellows of the baser sort," who lacked the original Klan's "compulsions of honor." The entire Klan itself eventually degenerated into a brutal outfit which enforced a "reign of terror." This new version of the Klan did not distinguish between men of principle and those with oppressive designs, Wilson argued.

The future president claimed that some of the white targets of the Klan were Northern school teachers who "taught lessons of self-assertion against whites" and trained their students to be "aggressive Republican politicians and mischief-makers between the races." While some of the teachers came on an "errand of mercy and humanity," many others came "with bitter thoughts and intolerant purpose against the white people of the South." These teachers were accompanied by Northern political figures who came as a "predatory horde," although Wilson noted that some of these political figures were men of integrity.

The oppression of white Southerners halted only when Reconstruction ended, which marked the termination of "Negro rule under unscrupulous adventurers." The end of Reconstruction witnessed the "natural, inevitable ascendancy of the whites, the responsible class." Or as Wilson curtly added, "the supremacy of the white people was henceforth assured in the administration of the Southern states."[48] The end of Reconstruction marked the end of a reign of terror against whites from "insolent and aggressive" freedmen, who were "sick of work, covetous of pleasure." The freedmen were like a "host of dusky children untimely put out of school. . . . They were a danger to themselves as well as those whom they had once served."[49] The majority in the South was finally permitted to govern.

Many of the quotes cited above were featured in one of the most famous, and notorious, films in the history of American cinema, D. W. Griffith's *The Birth of a Nation.* Griffith's film was an innovative cinematic celebration of the Ku Klux Klan written by the president's friend Thomas Dixon, a graduate school classmate of Wilson's at John Hopkins University. *The Birth of a Nation* was based on Dixon's play *The Clansman* and became the first film in American history screened in the White House. Wilson's daughter, Ellen, who was married to Treasury Secretary William McAdoo, served as the hostess for the invitation-only screening. While some of Wilson's sympathetic biographers have gone to great lengths to distance Wilson from the film, the president never repudiated his friend's motion picture, and in fact after viewing the film he congratulated D. W. Griffith for his "splendid production" and noted that he would happily assist him with any future "historical and political" films he had in mind.[50] As we shall see in regards to political propaganda, Wilson was somewhat ahead of his time in appreciating the power of film to influence public opinion.

Wilson's racism influenced his decision making throughout his life. While serving as president of Princeton University, Wilson rejected proposals to admit black students, while other Ivy League schools such as Harvard, Columbia, and the University of Pennsylvania accepted African Americans. Wilson considered Princeton to be something of an intellectual Valhalla and claimed that "the whole temper and tradition of the place are such that no Negro has ever applied for admission." An African American student who applied directly to Wilson was met with a response from the future American president that "it is altogether inadvisable for a colored man to enter Princeton."[51] As a private citizen and academic, Wilson opposed Teddy Roosevelt's more progressive stance on race, objecting in one instance to TR's selection of an African American to be the collector of the Port of Charleston, South Carolina. President Roosevelt's action was "an unwise piece of bravado" because the collector would exercise authority over white merchants. This was, according to Wilson, simply "too much . . . to stand." During his two years as governor of New Jersey, from 1911–1913, Wilson did not appoint a single African American to a position in his administration.[52]

Wilson's election in 1912 was seen by some elements of his coalition as an opportunity to reverse the minimal progress made by some African Americans under decades of post–Civil War Republican rule. One somewhat limited avenue of advancement had come about with the reform of the old Jacksonian "spoils system," which had allowed the incoming administration to stock the federal bureaucracy with loyal party adherents. The 1883 Pendleton Act had partially restrained this practice by establishing the United States Civil Service, which had allowed some African Americans, particularly in the nation's capital, to secure federal employment. This was particularly true in the treasury and post office departments, where some blacks had risen to management positions and had managed to enter the middle class.[53] At the time of Wilson's election in 1912, the federal government employed thousands of African Americans, including approximately four hundred employees who held white-collar clerk positions and other middle-management posts. While those numbers are dwarfed by the entirety of the American population, these African American federal officials emerged as prominent figures, as historian Eric S. Yellin notes, especially in the African American community.[54]

Some of Wilson's cabinet members were offended by this, and apparently Wilson was as well, as he supported their efforts to segregate the federal workforce. Postmaster General Albert Burleson, the son of an officer in the Confederate army, was repulsed by the practice on nation's postal trains of blacks and whites using the same bathroom facilities, linens, and glassware, and ordered an end to this practice. Burleson also transferred all the black employees of the Post Office Department, save one, to the "dead-letter office," which was a dead end in the postal bureaucracy. The one employee who was spared this indignity was the subject of an even more undignified slight—he was forced to work surrounded by screens so that white employees would not have to see him.[55] Secretary of the Treasury William McAdoo, who became the president's son-in-law in 1914, defended his actions at the Treasury Department by noting "I am not going to argue the justification of the separate toilets orders, beyond saying that it is difficult to disregard certain feelings and sentiments of white people in a matter of this sort."[56] Applicants for civil service jobs were required to submit photographs, which facilitated the process of eliminating minorities from the pool of potential candidates.[57]

Wilson's segregationist policies were partly the result of his unalloyed racism, but there was also an element of "principle" in this approach to governing. Wilson considered himself something of an expert in the new field of public administration, and the notion of "friction" was all the rage among the scholarly promoters of this new school of thought. In Wilson's view, racial antagonism in the workplace was a source of friction, or inefficiency, and thus steps designed to reduce this type of bureaucratic impediment were entirely proper. As Eric S. Yellin has observed, "In 1887, as a young political scientist, Wilson had proposed a rational 'study of administration' that sought the means to 'destroy all wearing friction' in the management of government. . . . Progressives clung to notions of dissolving 'friction' and promoting bureaucratic efficiency as essential to government reform." In the face of criticism from organizations like the National Association for the Advancement of Colored People (NAACP): "Wilson retreated to bureaucratic speak, with its comforting assurances that anything that increased efficiency was in the interest of all Americans. . . . This creed was integral to Wilson's approach to government. . . . As president of the United States and an articulate spokesman for administrative reform, Wilson made a powerful case for ignoring the demands of black Americans in the service of efficient government."[58]

Oddly, Wilson's devotion to making the nation "efficient" extended to the spiritual lives of the people as well. He noted in 1916 that he had "great enthusiasm for rendering America spiritually efficient," which meant abandoning America's historic emphasis on individualism for higher, communal purposes, although a racially restricted community to be sure.[59]

President Wilson's record on lynching, a practice which expanded under his watch, was equally troubling. There were thirty-eight lynchings in the United States in 1917, fifty-eight in 1918, and over seventy in 1919. Wilson's advisors were concerned that these acts of terrorism could disrupt the war effort but showed little concern for the African American victims. Wilson was slow to respond but eventually did issue a proclamation condemning lynching in July 1918 in a remarkably antiseptic statement devoid of any reference to the racist foundations of this practice.[60]

Race riots like those that had occurred under Andrew Jackson's watch occurred throughout the nation during Wilson's second term. A riot in East Saint Louis, Illinois, in July 1917, saw rampaging whites attack blacks who were accused of taking jobs from whites and of acting as strikebreakers. Despite pleas from African American leaders for federal troops to intervene and stop the violence against blacks, Wilson refused.[61] Casualty counts from the East Saint Louis violence vary but seem to be in the range of forty to well over one hundred deaths. The situation worsened as large numbers of returning African American veterans of World War I rejected the notion that they revert to second-class citizens. As W. E. B. Dubois put it, "we return from fighting. We return fighting. Make way for Democracy! We saved it in France, and by the Great Jehovah, we will save it in the United States of America, or know the reason why."

Close to 370,000 African Americans had served in the war, and many had embraced Wilson's notion of making the world safe for democracy, including at home. Yet within weeks of the armistice of November 1918 the United States seemed to embrace its status as a separate and unequal society with renewed vigor. From January 1919 to May 1919 there were more than twenty cases of white mobs lynching blacks, including one black veteran who was lynched after he balked at demands that he remove his uniform. Race riots broke out in Washington, DC, Knoxville, Tennessee, Omaha, Nebraska, and in Chicago, where thirty-eight people were killed.[62] Wilson's repeated response to these racial rampages was one of studied silence.

Woodrow Wilson's record regarding Native Americans was equally troubled, as his administration moved vigorously to open more Indian territory for use by white farmers and cattlemen. Wilson's policy, pursued under the guise of increasing self-sufficiency of individual Native Americans, contributed to the loss of millions of acres of land taken from various tribes. As one of the leading historians of the Wilson presidency has noted, his administration ignored "protests from a small number of citizens appalled by this policy of reducing Native Americans to beggary in the name of progress."[63]

As was always the case with the presidency of popular consent, minorities were the frequent targets of the majority's exploitation. The president, defying the intent of the framers, facilitated these majoritarian encroachments. One of the enduring features of the presidency of popular consent was that the president's constitutional obligation to "take care that the laws be faithfully executed" was simply ignored in favor of the whims of the majority.

Wilson's patronizing, condescending attitude toward American minority groups was matched by a similar attitude toward the nation's Latin American neighbors. He approached them as he did all lesser orders, with a mix of disdain coupled with a desire to uplift them. "We are," he noted in 1913, "in spite of ourselves, the guardians of order and justice and decency on this Continent. We are, providentially, naturally, and unescapably charged with the maintenance of humanity's interest here."[64] That same year, Wilson noted that "I am going to teach the South American republics to elect good men."[65] Wilson's condescension was echoed by his secretary of state, William Jennings Bryan, who observed that "those Latin republics are our political children, so to speak."[66] Wilson judged a successful foreign policy on the basis of its altruism; any action that was not taken in the "selfish" interests of the United States was by its nature inherently good.

Wilson's expansive ego, and his deep religious faith, produced a toxic combination that saw the president dispatch American troops to Haiti, Cuba, Panama, Mexico, and the Dominican Republic, all in the name of a foreign policy of uplift. This was done, Wilson reassured the world and his fellow citizens, in the absence of any selfish motives. "Such a time has come," Wilson observed, due to the "providence of God" where "America will once more have an opportunity to show to the world that she was born to serve mankind."[67]

"Molding the Minds of the Masses"

Woodrow Wilson's efforts to rally the nation after the American entry into World War I reveals the extent to which the president believed in the power of public opinion, and in the lengths to which he would go to manipulate that opinion through government-sponsored propaganda and censorship. The breadth of Woodrow Wilson's "information" campaign has few parallels in American history. Wilson faced the daunting task of persuading a divided American public to support the war; after all, he too was a reluctant convert to entering the struggle. During his campaign for reelection in 1916, the president observed, "so far as I can remember, this is a government of the people, and this people is not going to choose war."[68] But German assaults on American shipping and the exposure of the "Zimmerman telegram" where Germany proposed that Mexico enter the war on its behalf in return for the territory seized by the United States in the 1840s, led the president and large numbers of Americans to embrace war. The United States Congress declared war on Germany on April 6, 1917, although substantial numbers of Americans were still opposed, including fifty members of the House of Representatives and six United States senators.

The president wasted little time in creating a propaganda arm of the government to bolster support for the war, creating the Committee on Public Information (CPI) on April 13th. The committee was headed by George Creel, a progressive journalist turned supporter of the war. Creel's committee was charged with publicizing the "absolute justice of America's cause, the absolute selflessness of America's aims," and to "arouse ardor and enthusiasm" among the public. Filmmakers, writers, teachers, psychologists, advertising gurus, and cartoonists were all hired by the committee to influence public opinion.[69] One of the CPI's employees was Edward Bernays, Sigmund Freud's nephew, who is considered the father of public relations. Bernays, after his service with CPI, chillingly observed "ours must be a leadership democracy administered by the intelligent minority who know how to regiment and guide the masses."[70] He also noted that propaganda was a remarkable tool to manipulate public opinion: "it has been found possible so to mold the mind of the masses that they will throw their newly gained strength in the desired direction. In the present structure of society, this practice is inevitable."[71] Bernays and other members of Creel's team engaged in an "enlightened" form of demagoguery, in other words, demagoguery rooted in the new science of psychology and sociology.

Aaron Delwiche, a student of the committee's work, observed that "the CPI blended advertising techniques with a sophisticated understanding of human psychology, and its efforts represent the first time that a modern government disseminated propaganda on such a large scale. It is fascinating that this phenomenon, often linked with totalitarian regimes, emerged in a democratic state."[72] All regimes have found it necessary to control information related to the conduct of war, including troop movements, operational plans, and other military matters. Secrecy is essential to any military effort, as is the gathering of foreign intelligence and the use of covert operations abroad, including covert propaganda. These operations have been used by American leaders since George Washington's time, and this is perfectly appropriate conduct for a republican government. But a domestic propaganda effort stoking hatred and implying disloyalty on the part of war opponents is another matter altogether. German Americans, Socialists, antiwar activists, labor organizers, all felt the brunt of the CPI's campaign to celebrate "Americanism."[73] The CPI sought, as George Creel put it, to fan the "anger of an aroused people," and by so doing contributed to the oppression of dissent on the home front.[74]

Creel and Wilson have their defenders who insist that the two resisted censorship and generally avoided the practice of other groups that circulated false stories of German atrocities and presented "the Hun" as an ape-like creature led by the "Beast of Berlin," Kaiser Wilhelm. Nevertheless, CPI propaganda repeatedly referred to the Hun, and one of its popular posters noted that "such a civilization [Germany] is not fit to live." Others note Creel's pledge to engage only in "positive propaganda," but the fact is that the CPI manipulated the news by either sanitizing bad news or suppressing it at times. As Creel noted, the "news itself must be given a new definition."[75]

Stories written by the CPI were routinely published in the nation's newspapers and not identified as a CPI product. The agency's manipulation of public opinion was quite shrewd, as the CPI would alter the rationale for the war to suit a particular audience. For instance, it would tell business groups that the war was designed to destroy German industries; labor unions were told that the war was designed to protect cheap labor from undermining American wages; religious groups were told it was a war for democracy and the rights of small nations; educators were told it was a war to check the importation of dangerous German ideas into the academy.[76] The latter campaign was quite successful, as schools dropped the German language from their curriculum, cut any positive references to Germany out of textbooks, and orchestras stopped playing any German music, including Beethoven.[77]

As one student of Wilson's presidency noted, the CPI's "manipulation of public opinion was just as dangerous as the methods it sought to avoid."[78] While the Wilson administration eschewed the more Draconian practices of its European counterparts, its practices remain troubling. In venerating public opinion by grounding a presidency in something as fickle as that opinion, the allure of manufacturing "correct opinions" becomes an attractive option. Wilson's domestic propaganda campaign demonstrates that the presidency of popular consent is far more of a threat to liberty than a presidency that abides by the framers' presidency. If a president can manufacture public opinion, then public opinion offers a flimsier boundary to presidential ambition than the "parchment barriers" of the Constitution.

A Disturbing Legacy

Woodrow Wilson's presidency was the epitome of the presidency of popular consent in its dismissal of the Constitution, its manufactured support for the war, its pervasive disregard for the rights of wartime dissenters, and its racial policies designed to afflict the minority and comfort the "feelings and sentiments" of the majority. Wilson embraced Jefferson and Jackson's celebration of popular sovereignty. The president asked and answered his own question regarding America's purpose in a speech in January 1916: "Do you never stop to reflect just what it is that America stands for? If she stands for one thing more than another, it is for the sovereignty of self-governing peoples."[79] This was not the answer one would have received from most of the nation's founders or from Abraham Lincoln.

Woodrow Wilson deserves all the notoriety he has received for transforming the American government. Pulitzer Prize–winning author David Kennedy observed that "Woodrow Wilson matters because he is one of the shapers of the modern presidency," and noted that Wilson understood "that the president, as he put it himself, is free to be as big a man as he can be." Columbia Professor Ira Katznelson echoed David Kennedy by noting that Wilson's presidency was a time of "extraordinary new assertion of governmental capacity . . . as well as presidential ambition." Katznelson added that Woodrow Wilson matters "as the first modern president. . . . Wilson matters as someone who followed a progressive political agenda and who established a model for subsequent possibilities, some of which had to wait a long time to come back."[80] His use of the presidency to check the power of the "invisible empire" of corporations, his creation of the Federal Reserve system, his support for the Sixteenth Amendment's progressive income tax and the Seventeenth Amendment's direct election of senators made Wilson a hero to twentieth-century progressives.

There is no question that Gilded Age excesses motivated both Theodore Roosevelt and Woodrow Wilson to press for necessary reforms, including child labor provisions, to ameliorate the injustices of the era. Yet one can celebrate these reforms and at the same time acknowledge the damage Wilson inflicted on the American presidency and the Constitutional order. Any impartial examination of Wilson's public record must reckon with this aspect of Wilson's legacy. Wilson's "anti-constitutionalist repudiation of institutions," indeed, "his entire theory of U.S. politics and the presidency," Paul Carrese rightly notes, "was so hubristic as to repudiate the Constitution and the political science upon which it rested." Indeed, while Wilson was not the leader of the movement to adopt the Seventeenth Amendment, he supported it, and its damage to the founders' design, coupled with his democratization of the presidency, permanently harmed the American political order.

Despite the failure of his ambitious proposal for American participation in the League of Nations, Woodrow Wilson successfully upended the Hamiltonian, or constitutional, understanding of the role of the presidency and overturned the sense of what a president should be expected to accomplish. Unfortunately, the Wilsonian conception of the presidency, adopted wholeheartedly by Democrats and eventually by Republicans, produced a massive expectations gap—a long train of heightened expectations followed by dashed hopes.[81]

Wilson's efforts to popularize the presidency was aided and abetted by many of his fellow academics who believed that a document designed in horse-and-buggy days had little to offer twentieth-century Americans. A new metric for determining presidential "greatness" emerged, one that defined greatness as activist presidents pursuing progressive policies. Far too many scholars have a predilection for presidents such as Woodrow Wilson, Franklin Roosevelt, John F. Kennedy, and Lyndon Johnson, while "caretaker" presidents, like William Howard Taft or Gerald Ford, are slighted in such polls because of their unwillingness to remake American society. This bias toward progressive presidencies is part of Woodrow Wilson's legacy, for the Princeton professor changed the way political practitioners and his fellow academics thought about the presidency.

One of Woodrow Wilson's most significant legacies involves his reforming the process of presidential selection. Wilson envisioned a process whereby successful presidential candidates would no longer be indebted to a political party for their selection, for presidential nominees would be chosen through primaries and the nominee would then impose his will on his party, rather than be subject to the party's dictates. Presidential selection would hinge on a candidate's personal attributes, his "charisma," his ability to win votes in open primaries. And the power of the presidency itself would rest in good measure on these same personal attributes, not in any formal grant of constitutional authority.

Wilson devoted himself to democratizing the presidential selection process as a means of "extend[ing] the power of the people." He believed that selecting a nominee through party conventions dominated by bosses operating behind closed doors and content to ignore public opinion was an outmoded system for a modern, industrialized nation like the United States. In December 1913, Wilson urged Congress to pass legislation establishing the direct primary as the method for selecting presidential nominees.[82] Wilson's proposal failed, but his call to democratize the presidential selection process would resonate throughout the twentieth and twenty-first centuries, coming to fruition with John F. Kennedy's insurgent candidacy in 1960, and the insurgent candidacies of George McGovern, Jimmy Carter, Barack Obama, and Bernie Sanders, the latter being a true insurgent who did not belong to the party whose nomination he sought.

More than a century later, we continue to live under Woodrow Wilson's regime, as scholars judge Wilson's successors by the standards he set. Wilson was a worthy successor to Jefferson and Jackson in terms of continuing the process of refounding the presidency. More than any of his predecessors, Wilson altered the nation's expectations of what a president could be expected to achieve. For this reason, and for his heinous record on race and civil liberties, it is long past the point where Wilson's place in the American pantheon needs to be seriously reconsidered. It is time for a sober assessment of those presidents whose populist politics and paeans to majoritarianism came at a remarkably steep price, both in terms of damage inflicted on the presidency and on the rights of those out of step with the majority.

6

FDR and Harry Truman
"Give 'Em Hell"

The mid-twentieth century witnessed the full flowering of the presidency of popular consent. Arguments made in favor of the framers' or Constitutional presidency were often dismissed as quaint but reactionary musings of those refusing to evolve with the times. This was understandable considering Franklin Roosevelt's command of the office in a remarkably trying time. Roosevelt demonstrated the potentialities of the popular presidency by restoring the nation's confidence amid a great depression and leading the nation to superpower status in World War II. Roosevelt's impact on the office was so great that almost every president since FDR sought to match the hold he had on the American imagination and to achieve all that he did in his first hundred days in office. This standard, inapplicable to most situations modern presidents find themselves in, nonetheless tempted many of Roosevelt's successors to try to equal his accomplishments.

While there is much to praise in Roosevelt's presidency, including a compelling case that he saved American capitalism and assembled a remarkable national security team to prosecute World War II, there were troubling aspects to Roosevelt's presidency. These included his tendency to undermine existing institutions, in keeping with the legacy of his former boss, Woodrow Wilson. There was the same brittleness toward political opponents and a tendency to equate dissent with disloyalty, as well as a disregard for the rule of law, which is a permanent feature of the personalized presidency. FDR had difficulty distinguishing between the office he held and his personal well-being, which is perhaps to be expected considering he spent over twelve years in the White House.

Founding Fascists

Franklin Roosevelt was no intellectual, but he absorbed the prevailing scholarly thought of the early twentieth century, which, ideas always having consequences, influenced his thinking and those of many of his peers. That thinking tended frequently to disparage the drafters of the nation's founding documents, and arguably the content of the documents themselves. Scholars such as J. Allen Smith and Charles A. Beard were the "public intellectuals" of their day who shifted academic thinking on the American founding and the Constitution in an entirely new direction. These men, and other progressive scholars, provided the intellectual underpinnings of the New Deal. Their ideas seeped down into mainstream thinking, as they always do, and were welcomed by populist and progressive forces frustrated with judicial objections and the cumbersome nature of separation of powers.

J. Allen Smith held that the Constitution was "framed and secured" by a conspiracy of "the property-owning class." This counterrevolutionary Constitution was designed to frustrate the popular will and check what should be the essence of any legitimate government, "the unhampered expression and prompt enforcement of public opinion." The founders, including Alexander Hamilton, were concerned with protecting plutocrats, and thus "perverted" the principle that "public officials are agents of the people."[1]

One of Smith's admirers was Professor Charles A. Beard of Columbia University, who built on Smith's thesis and converted it into one of the most influential works in the history of American political science, *An Economic Interpretation of the Constitution of the United States* (1913). No scholar had a greater impact on American political thought during the first half of the twentieth century than Charles A. Beard. The release of *An Economic Interpretation* could not have been better timed, as it coincided with Woodrow Wilson's assumption of the presidency. Beard contended that the Constitution was "an economic document drawn with superb skill" by a group of men whose personal wealth was "immediately at stake." The Constitution "placed the dollar before the man," as the *New York Times* put it in a review of Beard's book; self-interest lay at the heart of the American founding, and institutions like the Supreme Court were designed to protect the self-interested few in perpetuity.

By diminishing the reputation of the framers, Smith, Beard, and other progressive scholars sought to pave the way for a more adaptable, living Constitution. Beard supported the initiative, referendum, and recall provisions backed by progressives, and strongly objected to the Supreme Court's tendency to overturn progressive legislation. The blame for this, Beard believed, lay with the framers, who were committed to "safeguard[ing] the rights of private property against any leveling tendencies on the part of the propertyless masses." In fact, the American founders were not that far removed from Fascists like Benito Mussolini in terms of condemning democracy. "The fathers of the American republic," Beard noted in 1929, "notably Hamilton, Madison, and John Adams, were as voluminous and vehement as any Fascist could desire."

Unlike some progressives who occasionally genuflected to the Constitution out of political calculation, Beard candidly argued that the Constitution blocked the ability of social movements to engineer change, and thus had to go. According to Beard, the solution was to bring the Constitution "under the control of the people" by adopting Thomas Jefferson's proposal of holding a Constitutional Convention every twenty years if the public so desired. Opponents of this perpetual constitutional change were derided by Beard as cultists, religious fanatics who resisted "lay[ing] profane hands on the Ark of the Covenant" and who blindly defended "gods, the sacred oracles . . . the fathers and the separation of powers."[2]

Franklin Roosevelt adopted much of the Smith-Beardian condemnation of the selfish founding plutocrats, although he tended to confine his critique to the Federalists, Alexander Hamilton in particular, and wrapped himself in the mantle of Thomas Jefferson and Andrew Jackson. This was smart politics on several levels, in that most Americans were not comfortable cutting their ties with all the founders, plus it had the added benefit of allowing a Northern patrician with a Harvard degree to identify with Jefferson and Jackson and appeal to Southern voters. In 1924, Roosevelt wrote that the America of the 1920s resembled the period of 1790 to 1800, "when Alexander Hamilton ran the federal government for the primary good of the chambers of commerce, the speculators," and other insiders. Hamilton was a "fundamental believer in an aristocracy of wealth and power," and the question for the nation, and for the Democratic Party of the 1920s, was whether, as FDR put it, there was "another Jefferson on the horizon." There was, of course, and it was the Sage of Hyde Park.[3]

President Herbert Hoover, FDR's opponent in 1932, was the new Hamilton in that Hoover believed "popular government was essentially dangerous and essentially unworkable." Hamilton, according to FDR, believed in "autocratic strength" and so did, apparently, Hoover and his party. The election of 1932 was a referendum on which tradition in American politics would prevail: the Hamiltonian tradition of elitism backed by autocratic government, or the Jeffersonian tradition which defended the toiling majority from "control by the few," as Roosevelt put it. The winner made it clear that Jeffersonianism, at least as interpreted by FDR, was back in control of the federal government after a twelve-year reign of Hamiltonian-style Republican rule.[4]

"The Three-Horse Team"

The new president pursued an ambitious agenda designed to restore the confidence of the American public that was "ill housed, ill clad, ill nourished," as Roosevelt would later note. A variety of federal agencies were created to ameliorate the excesses of the free market and create a social safety net, as well as generating jobs for the well over 25 percent of the public that was unemployed. The president faced an extraordinary challenge, one of the worst in the nation's history. Much to his dismay, FDR's ambitious agenda ran into one of the constitutional anachronisms that progressives had been criticizing for years: the federal judiciary. Charles A. Beard and other progressive actors and academics had been critical of the courts for their tendency to strike down progressive legislation and for their inclination to ignore the explicit link between economics and the motives of political actors, including jurists. Beard would go on to endorse Franklin Roosevelt's court-packing plan, delivering a nationwide radio address where he claimed this plan would bring the Supreme Court "back within the Constitution."[5]

It was this effort on Roosevelt's part, to bring the Supreme Court in line with New Deal policies, that was the most damaging and irresponsible event of his presidency. Yet it was utterly predictable, in that FDR saw himself as the heir to Jefferson and Jackson, and in no arena was this comparison more relevant than in his war with the judiciary. Roosevelt was simply continuing the conflict which began in 1801 and continued intermittently until the

1930s. Remarkably, FDR engaged in a more strident battle with the court than either Jefferson or Jackson and went well beyond that of Abraham Lincoln.

As Robert Scigliano has observed, Roosevelt was the only president of the four to publicly attack the Supreme Court, "several times." FDR sought a Supreme Court that was not "so independent that it can deny the existence of facts universally recognized." Universally recognized by whom, and how that universality was measured, was left unmentioned. In March 1937, the president proposed the addition of up to six justices to the nine-member court for every justice over the age of seventy. By infusing young blood into the court, FDR sought to fulfill the wishes of progressives to convert the Constitution into a "living" document that kept abreast with the times. Roosevelt's "court-packing plan" would permit the court to reach the "right kind" of decisions regarding the "social and economic problems" confronting the nation, as younger justices would have a deeper understanding of problems from "personal experience and contact with modern facts and circumstances" which confronted "average men."[6]

Roosevelt believed that the failure of the Supreme Court to uphold his New Deal agenda represented a failure of democracy. The "success and survival" of democracy was at stake because one member of the "three-horse team," the Supreme Court, was refusing to pull together with the legislative and executive branches. As FDR put it in his folksy way, due to the intransigence of one of the horses, the "field" was not being "ploughed."[7] A few days later, Roosevelt added, "it is the American people who want the furrow plowed. It is the American people themselves who expect the third horse to pull in unison with the other two."[8] The wishes of the majority of the public, as expressed through voting, should guide the decisions of the Supreme Court, not the Constitution.

Roosevelt's frustration with the deliberative, or some would say cumbersome, nature of the American system had frustrated and continues to frustrate American presidents. But Roosevelt's public claims that the failure of the Supreme Court to ratify his policies broke with tradition and threatened to undermine the rule of law. "Every delay," the president argued on March 4, 1937, made it more unlikely that the federal government could reach an "intelligent, speedy, and democratic solution of our difficulties."[9] The American system was never intended to be speedy, which is why the founders created a republic, not a pure democracy.

It is worth repeating that much of what Roosevelt did helped conserve American capitalism and is worthy of acclaim. He resisted the demagoguery of Senator Huey Long of Louisiana, of Father Charles Coughlin, the "radio priest," and Congressman William Lemke of North Dakota, all of whom would have entirely reshaped the American political order. And it should also be noted that FDR's reaction to a crippling worldwide depression stands in stark contrast to the Fascist "solution" pursued by some of his European contemporaries.

Nonetheless, with his attacks on the court, Franklin Roosevelt crossed a line that no president should ever cross. His demagogic attacks on the independence of the judiciary, urging them to abide by his landslide win in the election of 1936, is contrary to the essence of a constitutional republic. It was demagoguery in the service of the notion that "the majority is to govern," always and everywhere, including when it came to judicial decisions. FDR's "court-packing proposal" and its accompanying demagoguery was the nadir of his presidency, and was arguably one of many low points for those concerned with the rights of political minorities. Thankfully, Roosevelt's attacks on the court backfired, or more precisely, his proposal to pack the court failed, due to bipartisan resistance in Congress.

But in the long run, FDR won his battle with the Supreme Court, due to the decision of one justice to shift his vote upholding the constitutionality of New Deal initiatives. Roosevelt's attitude toward the court stemmed from his flawed view that the president held of the nation's founding. As is often the case, bad history makes for bad constitutional interpretation. Roosevelt's view of the founding was inspired by Jefferson and his biographers, whose account of the founding portrayed the Sage of Monticello as the only man who stood between the American people and Alexander Hamilton's desire to create an American autocracy.

"A Jefferson on the Horizon"

This distorted view of American history found its way into the only book review Franklin Roosevelt ever wrote. The book's author was a Democratic Party activist and part-time popular historian, Claude Bowers. Bowers saw American history as an endless class struggle between the "upper classes" and "the masses." The upper class took its marching orders from Wall Street while the lower class was perpetually victimized by this East Coast cabal. Alexander Hamilton was the founder of this corrupt system, a "dictatorial" leader who "thought of himself of the race of military masters." This portrayal of Hamilton animated the pages of Bowers's *Jefferson and Hamilton: The Struggle for Democracy in America* (1925).

Roosevelt's review was entitled "Is There a Jefferson on the Horizon?" The answer to that question was that the "Jefferson on the horizon" was Roosevelt himself. FDR enthused over Bowers's book and noted that he "longed to write this very book." Hamilton's fondness for chambers of commerce and his "contempt for the opinion of the masses" meant that if Hamilton had triumphed, darkness would have descended over America. Due to the heroic exertions of Thomas Jefferson, who directed "escape after escape" from this authoritarian nightmare, the United States eventually lived up to the spirit of 1776.[10] FDR would go on to elevate Thomas Jefferson into the pantheon of American immortals, placing him on the United States nickel, on the most commonly used postage stamp of the day, and erecting the beautiful Tidal Basin memorial to the Sage of Monticello and helping to select the truncated quotes that adorn its walls.[11]

Claude Bowers was such a prominent figure within the Democratic Party that he was selected as keynote speaker at the party's 1928 convention and was asked to nominate FDR at the 1932 convention. Bowers's overtly racist account of Reconstruction, *The Tragic Era* (1929) ("then came the scum of Northern society . . . inflaming the negroes' egotism, and soon the lustful assaults began. Rape is the foul daughter of Reconstruction. . . . It was not until the original Klan began to ride that white women felt some sense of security.") caught the attention of FDR, who praised it, observing that "the period from 1865 to 1876 should be known as America's Dark Ages." Roosevelt urged that Bowers's book be widely circulated throughout the South; one associate of the president later equated Bowers's attraction to Democrats with Harriet Beecher Stowe's attraction to abolitionists. As a reward for his service to FDR and to the Democratic Party, Bowers served as a United States ambassador to Spain, and then to Chile, for the duration of FDR's and Harry Truman's presidencies.[12]

Bowers's caricatured, populist accounts of American history influenced many of FDR's most important speeches, including his address to the Commonwealth Club of San Francisco in 1932. In that address Roosevelt claimed that Hamilton believed that America's well-being "lay in the autocratic strength of its government," while Jefferson guarded the interests of the toiling common man.[13] Andrew Jackson, FDR would later note, continued the fight against "the same evil Jefferson fought—the control of government by a small minority instead of by popular opinion duly heeded by the Congress, the Courts, and the President."[14] The modern Supreme Court, in FDR's view, was part of a cabal that kept the common man under the control of a new Hamiltonian elite.

Franklin Roosevelt to the contrary, the framers created the federal judiciary with the explicit intent that they were not to heed public opinion. Federal judges were given lifetime tenure and were not to be selected by the public. Additionally, the notion that the courts were to ally themselves with the other branches of government was not part of the founders' plan. Yet this was a constant theme of FDR's presidency: that public opinion, not the Constitution, should dominate and guide the nation's public affairs. According to Roosevelt, "a government can be no better than the public opinion which sustains it."[15] The founders believed that the essence of statesmanship was to rise above the conventional wisdom, to be better than popular opinion, and to resist that opinion at times.

Without the slightest touch of irony, Roosevelt claimed that one of his favorite predecessors, Andrew Jackson, fought for "social justice" and "human rights."[16] As with Jackson, FDR viewed his domestic political opponents as un-American, as "enemies," a term he frequently employed. Jackson gave no quarter to his enemies, and Roosevelt committed himself to do the same. The people of Jackson's time loved him for "the enemies he made," Roosevelt noted in 1936, and as Jackson fought for the people against "autocratic or oligarchic aggression," so too would FDR.[17] Now, in the 1930s, those "autocratic" few who controlled industry and the banks had again met their match. "With this handful it is going to be a fight—a cheerful fight on my part, but a fight in which there will be no compromise with evil."[18]

The Enemy Within

Franklin Roosevelt captured the hearts of millions of Americans through his buoyant rhetoric and his role as commander in chief during World War II. But he also inflamed partisan divisions through his tendency to view his domestic opponents as the enemy and purveyors of evil. He lacked George

Washington's understanding of the power that accrued to a president who acted as a chief of state and lacked both Washington's and Lincoln's sense of magnanimity. While campaigning for reelection in 1936, Roosevelt delivered a speech that Washington or Lincoln would never have delivered. The president argued that "never before in all our history have these forces [business monopolies, 'reckless bankers'], been so united against one candidate as they stand today. They are unanimous in their hate for me—and I welcome their hatred." More ominously, Roosevelt promised to get even with these malefactors of great wealth: "I should like to have it said of my first Administration that in it the forces of selfishness and of lust for power met their match. I should like to have it said of my second Administration that in it these forces met their master."[19] And FDR repeated his pledge to "master" the forces of selfishness in his second inaugural address, when he noted, "we have begun to bring private autocratic powers into their proper subordination to the public's government. . . . They have been challenged and beaten."[20]

Even during a great war, President Roosevelt could not resist labeling his domestic opponents as un-American; in fact, some were Fascists. In his State of the Union message in 1944, Roosevelt warned of the consequences if conservatives succeeded in blocking his "economic bill of rights": "If such reaction should develop—if history were to repeat itself and we were to return to the so-called normalcy of the 1920's—then it is certain that even though we shall have conquered our enemies on the battlefields abroad, we shall have yielded to the spirit of Fascism here at home."[21] This divisive, highly charged language amid a war demonstrates that Franklin Roosevelt was not in the same league as Abraham Lincoln in terms of appealing to "the better angels of our nature." The presidency of popular consent debases everyone who embraces it, even those like Roosevelt who was often described as having a "first-class temperament."[22] In order to constantly mobilize public support, presidents resort to appeals to base motives, to the lowest passions. If public opinion is seen as the foundation of presidential power and implementing that opinion is seen as the end state of the American regime, then constitutional government ceases to exist.

The ugly side of Franklin Roosevelt's majoritarianism is also revealed in his checkered record on civil liberties. Second-guessing presidents who preside over difficult armed conflicts is something that should be done with caution and a great amount of deference. But more than any of his immediate predecessors, as well as his immediate successor, Roosevelt used the Federal

Bureau of Investigation (FBI) as his private detective agency. This practice began before the nation's entry into World War II and fell well outside the bounds of a legitimate national security initiative.

A large FBI surveillance program begun in 1936 transformed the bureau into "the intelligence arm of the White House," according to one historian. FBI Director J. Edgar Hoover fed an eager president reams of political intelligence while Roosevelt brought his domestic critics to Hoover's attention, including some who wrote letters to the White House critical of his "fireside chats." A frequent target of the FBI were news organizations that promoted isolationism, all of this encouraged by a president who urged Hoover to move "against publishers of seditious matter."[23] The *Washington Times-Herald,* a voice of isolationism in the nation's capital, was the target not only of electronic surveillance, but the planting of informers as well. All of this was done, as historian Allen Weinstein suggests, with "only the shallowest (if any) national security justification."[24] As we have seen before, the presidency of popular consent, with all its personalized elements, leads the office holders to blur, if not outright eliminate, the distinction between the office and themselves.

Roosevelt's surveillance of his political opponents pales in comparison to his Executive Order 9066 of February 1942, which led to the internment of 120,000 people of Japanese ancestry, of whom 80,000 were American citizens. The president's order prohibited any avenues of appeal even though no criminal charges were leveled against the internees. First Lady Eleanor Roosevelt, FBI Director Hoover, and Attorney General Francis Biddle all opposed the president's order, with Biddle describing it as "ill-advised, unnecessary, and unnecessarily cruel." Again, the cruel underside of majoritarianism reared its ugly head in this case, as there was no similar order issued targeting German Americans or Italian Americans on the East Coast, despite the fact there was far greater military and intelligence activity occurring in that area. As Biddle noted, "the decisions were made not on the logic of events or on the weight of the evidence, but on racial prejudice that seemed to be influencing everyone."[25]

The army general in charge of enforcing the interment policy bluntly noted the racial component at work in FDR's order: "the Japanese race is an enemy race. . . . And while many second- and third-generation Japanese born on United States soil, possessed of United States citizenship, have become 'Americanized,' the racial strains are undiluted." Roosevelt himself seems to have had qualms about the very presence of Japanese in the United States, writing in the 1920s that "the mingling of Asiatic blood with European or American blood produces, in nine cases out of ten, the most unfortunate results. . . . Japanese immigrants are not capable of assimilation into the American population, thus their right to purchase property in the United States should be limited."[26]

In addition to his concerns over Japanese immigration and intermarriage, Roosevelt used the term "racial purity" while supporting laws designed to restrict the rights of Japanese immigrants to the United States. As the most insightful chronicler of FDR's internment policies, Greg Robinson, has observed, there was a continuity of thought regarding FDR and Japanese Americans that long predated Executive Order 9066. After the attack on Pearl Harbor, there was, needless to say, no reconsideration of his attitude: "These words and actions point to Roosevelt's continued acceptance, in the months after Pearl harbor, of the idea that Japanese-Americans, whether citizens or longtime residents, were essentially Japanese and unable to transform themselves into true Americans. Therefore, in a time of conflict between the United States and Japan, they could be presumed to be supportive of their Japanese brethren."[27]

In addition to racial animus, conspiracy theories also contributed to oppressive government action against minority groups. These theories have been a consistent factor in shaping the policies of presidents who govern based on public opinion. Roosevelt himself circulated one of the more peculiar theories making the rounds after the attack on Pearl Harbor, telling his cabinet that "friends of his" had recently traveled to the Baja region of Mexico and came upon secret Japanese air bases that were to be used in attacks against California.[28] Rumors such as these circulated from the very top of American society to the bottom, and contributed to the imprisonment of eighty thousand of their fellow citizens without due process.

Despite this bleak record on civil liberties, Roosevelt broke with the popular presidency's historic animus against African Americans, often at the behest of the First Lady, Eleanor Roosevelt. But the process was halting and uneven, as one episode illustrated. While FDR began to speak out earlier than many Western leaders regarding the rise of Nazism, he missed an opportunity to condemn Nazi racial politics and America's own checkered racial past. In 1936, eighteen African American athletes won fourteen medals, a quarter of the total medal haul for the United States Olympic team in Berlin. When track star Jesse Owens returned home with four gold medals from the Berlin games, the president never congratulated him or invited him to the White House. As Owens bitterly noted later, "Hitler didn't snub me—it was our president who snubbed me. The president didn't even send a telegram." Owens's snub was partially rectified when President Gerald Ford presented him with the Presidential Medal of Freedom in 1976, forty years after the fact. The remaining minority members of the 1936 team were commemorated in a White House ceremony eighty years later in 2016 by the first African American president, Barack Obama.[29]

FDR's hesitant approach to Jesse Owens and to civil rights writ large, including his aversion to anti-lynching legislation, was designed to avoid alienating Southern elements of his New Deal coalition. To compound matters, the polling results that Roosevelt devoured essentially ignored African American voters and thus slighted issues of their concern. An American population that was approximately 10 percent African American was reflected, at most, as 2 percent in any Gallup survey outside of the Southern states, and not reflected at all in the South, due to their disenfranchised status in that region of the nation. Nonetheless, one pollster said that Roosevelt was "the most alert responsible official I have ever known to be concerned about public opinion systematically." As historian Jill Lepore observed, "with FDR, polling entered the White House and the American political process. And there it remained." This despite the fact that "instead of representing public opinion, polling essentially silenced the voices of African-Americans."[30]

Public Opinion and the Holocaust

The sensibilities of American public opinion also played into FDR's response to the Holocaust, and according to some scholars, so did his own anti-Semitism. A presidency grounded in public opinion is inclined to avoid those deeds that history and political philosophy consider acts of statesmanship. Regarding the worst case of genocide in world history, the American public chose to look away, and this contributed to the excessively cautious approach Roosevelt's administration took to the question of accepting Jewish refugees from Europe who might have been spared the death camps.

Most citizens of Western nations were aware of Nazi atrocities by 1938 at the latest, when the events of "Kristallnacht," a savage nationwide assault on Jewish businesses, homes, and synagogues, occurred that November in Germany. The Gallup polling organization surveyed the American public in the wake of Kristallnacht, asking "Do you approve or disapprove of the Nazi treatment of Jews in Germany," with 94 percent claiming they disapproved (leaving, remarkably, 6 percent who approved). That very same week, Gallup asked the public "Should we allow a larger number of Jewish exiles from Germany to come to the United States to live?" Seventy-two percent of the American public said "no," while only 21 percent said "yes." The rest were undecided. In April 1938, prior to the Kristallnacht pogrom, 54 percent of the American public agreed with the statement that "the persecution of Jews in Europe has been partly their own fault," while 11 percent of Americans saw it as "entirely" the fault of the Jews of Europe. Two months after Kristallnacht, 67 percent of Americans opposed a bill in Congress that would have allowed children from Germany to come to the United States.[31]

The shock of the German invasion of Poland in September 1939 did little to change these attitudes, with 48 percent of Americans saying the United States should not get involved in the war even if Britain and France were in danger of collapsing. FDR, the consummate politician, delivered a "fireside chat" shortly after this poll pledging that the nation would "remain a neutral nation." Within months prior to Pearl Harbor, 80 percent of the public persisted in opposing United States' entry into the war.[32]

As the antislavery forces of the nineteenth century were aware, a presidency grounded in public opinion is a presidency destined to trim its positions on some of the most pressing moral issues of the day. And Franklin Roosevelt trimmed. Public opinion, treated worshipfully by politicians and pundits alike, can be so horrifically misguided at times, as it was in the years leading up to and through the deadliest war in world history. The United States admitted a paltry 180,000 to 220,000 Jewish refuges between 1933 and 1945, a number far lower than immigration laws allowed.[33] Only once during Roosevelt's twelve years in office did his administration allow the legally permitted number of immigrants from Germany (approximately 26,000 annually) to enter the United States. For the bulk of his presidency, this quota was less than 25 percent filled.[34] The Roosevelt administration chose to "slow roll" the immigration of those, including children, seeking refuge from Nazi persecution.

In fairness to Roosevelt, he understood the threat Hitler presented long before many others in the West, and he took the initiative by using his powers as commander in chief to provide a lifeline to Great Britain during its most trying hours. Roosevelt sought, as he put it, to provide Britain with all aid "short of war." The two nations negotiated an arrangement whereby the United States loaned the British fifty mothballed destroyers in exchange for the rights to eight British military bases. In March 1941, FDR convinced Congress to pass his Lend-Lease program (a $7 billion expenditure) that allowed the British and other allies access to the American "arsenal of democracy."[35] The president paid a political price for doing so and was forced during his unprecedented quest for a third term to kowtow to public opinion and reassure the American people. He noted in 1940, perhaps with an element of frustration, that "I shall say it again and again and again: your boys are not going to be sent into any foreign wars."[36]

But Roosevelt was not willing to pay the political price, which he might well have been able to sustain, of admitting more European Jews to the United States. Some scholars have cited anti-Semitism as the rationale for FDR's reluctance to allow more refugees. As Holocaust scholar Rafael Medoff has discovered, Roosevelt shared the prejudices of his day regarding Jewry. At various points in his life, FDR privately complained about

> Jews "overcrowding" certain professions in Germany, North Africa, and even in Oregon. He was one of the initiators of a quota on the admission of Jews to Harvard. He boasted to one friend—a U.S. senator—that "we have no Jewish blood in our veins." He claimed antisemitism in Poland was a reaction to Jews dominating the local economy. And he embraced an adviser's proposal to "spread the Jews thin" around the world, in order to prevent them from dominating their host countries.[37]

The president's defenders frequently lay the blame for his callous immigration policies on his assistant secretary of state, Breckinridge Long, who directed the nation's visa program from 1940 to 1944. Eleanor Roosevelt was a fierce critic of Long's, but her husband refused to remove him. While Eleanor Roosevelt successfully convinced FDR to overrule State Department objections to admitting British children to the United States, he rejected her proposal to expand the program to include Jewish children.[38]

Congressional opposition, rooted in public opposition, led Roosevelt to defer to anti-immigrant sentiment. Even pragmatic proposals to allow the admittance of experts with skills essential for the war effort were defeated in Congress. Breckenridge Long sought to sanitize news about the Holocaust and offered misleading testimony to Congress about the number of Jewish refugees admitted to the United States. In the end, as George McJimsey, a chronicler of FDR's presidency has observed, "saving the Jews languished because Roosevelt chose not to press the issue and followed instead a passive policy of small efforts, gestures, tokenism, and inattention."[39]

Franklin Roosevelt's attitude toward Japanese Americans and European Jews were shared by most of his fellow Americans at the time. In that sense, FDR was a representative man of his era. But leaders, statesmen, are supposed to appeal to the "better angels" of their fellow citizens and reject the prejudices of their time. Eleanor Roosevelt understood this, her husband did not. FDR did not hesitate to use his impressive rhetorical skills to condemn the "evil" practices of bankers and industrialists, but he could never find the wherewithal to condemn the evil prejudices of his fellow citizens. On that count, the majority was simply not to be challenged.

"It Almost Seemed . . . That You Were across the Room from Me"

Franklin Roosevelt's ability to appeal to the common man is considered one of the hallmarks of his presidency. He stands out as the nation's first mass-media president, and his ability to forge a personal relationship with "the masses" was key to his success. As a candidate for the presidency, FDR pledged in 1932 to pursue policies that were faithful to "the forgotten man at the bottom of the economic pyramid."[40] Roosevelt delivered his first "fireside chat" on March 12, 1933, and would persist in this practice for the next twelve years, delivering thirty-one "chats" over the course of his presidency. While Calvin Coolidge and Herbert Hoover had used radio to make formal, some would say stiff, pronouncements, FDR abandoned this mode of communication, opting instead for a relaxed approach that made it seem as if the president had dropped by for a chat.[41] The purpose of these chats was to allow the president to develop a bond with average Americans, a type of bond that was beyond the wildest dreams of Jefferson, Jackson, and even Woodrow Wilson to an extent.

Roosevelt's "fireside chats" were a remarkable success in creating a personal bond with voters. One letter writer to the president noted, "when your radio talk began everyone seemed to become hypnotized, because there wasn't a word spoken by anyone until you had finished and as if one voice were speaking all spoke in unison 'we are saved.'" Another writer observed, "you have a marvelous radio voice, distinct and clear. It almost seemed the other night, sitting in my easy chair in the library, that you were across the room from me. A great many of my friends have said the same thing." Another exclaimed, "Your voice radiates so much human sympathy and tenderness, and Oh, how the public does love that."[42]

On April 30, 1939, 150 years to the day when George Washington became the nation's first president, Franklin Roosevelt became the first president to appear on television when he opened the World's Fair in New York City.[43] A little over two decades later, television would completely transform American politics, altering expectations of the presidency and removing the last vestiges of distance and dignity, and personalizing the presidency in a way not envisioned by the framers of the Constitution. The triumph of the popular presidency was complete, and with it came the notion of presidential government, hailed by its proponents as a way of circumventing the separation of powers and making the federal government more efficient.

Roosevelt's deft use of electronic media was central to his vision to remake the American polity. He used the new avenue provided by technology and married it to a more traditional American style, that of a religious proselytizer. While Woodrow Wilson may have been the nation's first progressive-preacher president, Roosevelt refined the technique. Ronald Isetti has rightly observed that "few presidents have employed biblical symbols, religious language, and moral injunctions in their public addresses more often than Roosevelt did." Roosevelt's speeches were, as another scholar noted, "essentially sermons rather than speeches."[44]

A War against Evil-Doers

The president's first two inaugural addresses focused on forcing the moneychangers from the temple and the returning of the people to the promised land. In his second inaugural address, FDR recalled his first inauguration by noting that the nation pledged itself to "drive from the temple of our ancient faith those who had profaned it." Roosevelt continued to emphasize the crusading nature of his presidency in other speeches as well, noting "in the place of the palace of privilege we seek to build a temple out of faith and hope and charity." The American people were assured that "your government is still on the same side of the street with the Good Samaritan and not with those who pass by on the other side." And it was not a leap to read into these Depression-era speeches that Roosevelt saw himself as the new Moses leading his people to salvation. "Shall we pause now," he asked after four years in office, "and turn our back upon the road that lies ahead? Shall we call this the promised land? Or shall we continue on our way?"[45]

Almost every president since George Washington had invoked God and religious metaphors partly to create an American civil religion, and to pay due respect to the religiosity of the American people. But Abraham Lincoln, for instance, did not pretend to know which political party, which policies, God supported. Confederates and those who remained loyal to the Union, Lincoln observed in his second inaugural address, "both read the same Bible and pray to the same God, and each invokes His aid against the other. . . . let us judge not, that we be not judged. . . . The Almighty has His own purposes."[46] FDR knew which side God was on, and who walked on the other side of the street: his Republican opponents. Prior to his presidency, his opponents had subjected the country to "nine mocking years with the golden calf and three long years of the scourge."[47]

In light of this thinking, it was a small leap for FDR to see his opponents as the personification of evil. These opponents, "the privileged princes of these new economic dynasties, thirsting for power," were intent on creating "a new despotism" which was "wrapped . . . in the robes of legal sanction." The common man of the 1930s confronted a problem like that facing the "minuteman" of the 1770s. Both men simply wanted to control their life, and this desire was stifled in the 1930s by the despots of the "new industrial dictatorship."[48]

Nonetheless, it must be conceded that Franklin Roosevelt's optimistic oratory helped sustain the nation through economic depression and world war. Unfortunately, while there is much to celebrate regarding FDR's presidency, there is also much to lament. This same stirring oratory led to inflated expectations as to what could be expected of the American presidency. Roosevelt's second inaugural address in 1937 contained some of the most extravagant claims made by any American chief executive. The president was not only remaking the morals of American society, he was setting the stage for a morally improved world where "evil" was in retreat:

> We are beginning to wipe out the line that divides the practical from the ideal; and in so doing we are fashioning an instrument of unimagined power for the establishment of a morally better world. . . . In this process evil things formerly accepted will not be so easily condoned. Hard-headedness will not so easily excuse hardheartedness. We are moving toward an era of good feeling. But we realize that here can be no era of good feeling save among men of good will. For these reasons I am justified in believing that the greatest change we have witnessed has been the change in the moral climate of America.[49]

This was Roosevelt at his visionary worst, celebrating a vaguely defined "unimagined power" that was transforming the morals of the nation and the world, a world about to plunge into an orgy of war and genocide. This was a presidency, rhetorically speaking, that was out of control, but would nevertheless serve as a lodestar for many of FDR's successors.

Plain-Spoken Demagoguery

When Franklin Roosevelt died on April 12, 1945, most of his fellow countrymen knew little about his successor, Harry S. Truman, who had been vice president for less than three months. Fortunately for the fate of the nation, Democratic Party leaders had forced former Vice President Henry Wallace off the party ticket in 1944 and replaced him with the more stable Truman. This is a notable example of the vital role party leaders played in blocking erratic presidential and vice-presidential nominees. Wallace was a devotee of a bizarre Russian mystic he referred to as his "guru," and was also something of a devotee of all things Soviet. He was also fond of astrology and had relationships with other "mystics," including one who addressed the eccentric Iowan as "Cornplanter" or "Chief Standing Corn."[50] Harry Truman had been a relatively nondescript senator from Missouri, a beneficiary of Kansas City's somewhat notorious "Pendergast Machine," who supported the World War I veteran's bid to become a county court judge and launched him on an extraordinary political career.

President Truman built on the somewhat halting steps of Franklin Roosevelt to begin to fulfill the promises of the Thirteenth, Fourteenth, and Fifteenth Amendments, which proclaimed that the United States was a nation of equal justice under law. Defying some of the precedents of his more cowardly predecessors, Truman took a stand for racial justice that almost cost him his presidency. Truman's record on civil rights is remarkably impressive, considering that he came from a border state with family ties to the Confederacy and from a party noted for its 145-year history of opposition to civil rights. Truman was the first president to address the NAACP, delivered from the steps of the Lincoln Memorial, and established the first presidential commission on civil rights in the nation's history.[51]

Truman was also the first American president to send a civil rights message to Congress, urging the enactment of measures that would close the gap between "our ideals and some of our practices." Noting the founders' commitment to the principle that "all men are created equal," Truman went on to cite "flagrant examples" of discrimination "which are utterly contrary to our ideals." The president urged the abolition of the poll tax, the adoption of federal antilynching laws, the creation of a civil rights division at the Department of Justice, voting rights for residents of Washington, DC, and an end to segregated facilities in interstate commerce and to discriminatory practices in federal employment and in the armed forces. It was an expansive agenda, followed by action, including an executive order desegregating the armed services on July 26, 1948.[52]

In January 1949, Harry Truman became the first president to prohibit segregation during his inaugural festivities. But Truman's inauguration almost did not happen, due to a revolt in the Democratic Party against his civil rights initiatives and the party's adoption of an even more assertive civil rights plank at its national convention. Strom Thurmond, Richard Russell, and other Southern Democrats made a last-ditch effort to stop Truman and defeat the civil rights plank, but to no avail. Thurmond and his supporters refused to make Truman's nomination unanimous and bolted the party to form their own States' Rights or "Dixiecrat" party. Truman was forced to run in a four-man field in 1948, against Republican nominee Governor Thomas E. Dewey of New York, Strom Thurmond, and former Vice President Henry Wallace.[53]

Truman's "whistle-stop" campaign became the stuff of legends, as the beleaguered incumbent came from behind to defeat Dewey, the favorite as the fall campaign began. But as much as Truman's commitment to civil rights was the stuff of magnanimity and statesmanship, his 1948 campaign for president was the epitome of demagoguery, a campaign that degraded the office of the presidency. This campaign has been oddly romanticized, despite its ugly content and its far-reaching, ugly implications. There is a direct line between Truman's demagoguery in 1948 and the rise of another demagogue,

Senator Joseph McCarthy of Wisconsin. Both men appreciated the rewards that accrued to political figures tarring their opponents with a broad, ill-defined brush. A close examination of Truman's conduct in 1948 reveals that the campaign of beatification of the Missourian that began in 1992 with the publication of David McCullough's *Truman* needs a healthy corrective.[54]

Truman's whistle-stop campaign involved 352 speeches spread out over three separate trips, in a seventeen-car train that covered thirty-one thousand miles in thirty-three days.[55] It was a seventeen-car train that carried a cargo of half-truths and misrepresentations and loads of demagoguery. On some occasions the president made as many as sixteen different stops, traveling long into the night defending his Fair Deal policies and urging voters to support him come November. The opposition, the president reminded voters, were Fascists who were not any better than Adolf Hitler and Benito Mussolini. On October 26, 1948, Truman claimed that the parallels were obvious between Dewey and his supporters and Hitler and his backers: "when a few men get control of the economy of this nation, they find a front man to run the country for them. Before Hitler came to power, control over the German economy passed into the hands of a small group of rich manufacturers. . . . So they put money and influence behind Adolph Hitler." This same threat confronted the United States in 1948, with Dewey serving as the Hitlerian puppet of these nefarious interests. Dewey would take the nation down the same path as Germany in the 1930s. Truman added: "that's what the Republican candidate calls 'delivering for the future.' Is that the kind of future you want?"[56]

This was not "the little arts of popularity" but rather the art of slander. Truman's crude populism worked, as he barnstormed the country accusing his opponents of being "gluttons of privilege" and "cold men . . . cunning men. And it is their constant aim to put the government of the United States under control of men like themselves. They want a return of the Wall Street economic dictatorship." These men had a "dangerous lust for power and privilege" and they would pave the way for "big business" so they could "take the country over, lock, stock and barrel."[57]

As one chronicler of the campaign of 1948 has put it, in order to achieve victory Truman was "willing to sow dissension, stir up fear, and slander his opponents." The closet Fascists he opposed were instruments of "powerful reactionary forces" intent on reducing the Bill of Rights to a "scrap of paper." Echoing the rhetoric of Senator Joseph McCarthy, Truman accused Dewey of working in concert with Communists. "The Republicans," the president claimed, "have joined up with this Communist-inspired Third Party to beat the Democrats."[58]

The Truman of the 1948 campaign was a remarkably small and petty demagogue, who, in keeping with his populist forebears, seemed unable to distinguish between his political fortunes, his party's political fortunes, and the office he held and all that it represented. Truman's principal opponent, Thomas Dewey, ran a somewhat bland and issue-free campaign, which is frequently the tact taken by front runners, but he also ran on character, presenting himself as a man of principle who would avoid factional appeals and govern in the national interest. He lost as a result.

In a way, Dewey's campaign harkened back to the conception of presidential selection from the early republic, but it was no match for a candidate prepared to use "brass knuckles," as one of Dewey's supporters put it, who added that "it is poor judgment to defend oneself with a powder-puff." The supporter presciently added that Truman was "creating hatred between citizen and citizen and class against class."[59] These tactics had been employed by advocates of the popular presidency since Jefferson's time, and had generally worked. The price was the degradation of the presidency, at times the degradation of certain minorities, and of the entire American political order.

One advisor to a future president who was inspired by Truman's whistle-stop campaign was Roger Stone, an occasional advisor to Donald Trump, who rightly noted the frenetic pace and scorched-earth tactics of Truman and Trump in the closing days of their respective campaigns for president. Trump, as Stone observed, "was copying the playbook of peppery and determined Harry Truman," and both campaigns were "a campaign of us and them, of anger, and bitterness, of the haves and the have-nots."[60]

Harry Truman deserves all the praise he belatedly received for his handling of an endless series of crises, from the Berlin Blockade, to the Korean War, to the founding of America's Cold War doctrine and infrastructure, and as mentioned, his courageous pursuit of civil rights. On all these issues, the former haberdasher repeatedly rose to the occasion. Unfortunately, in order to win his own term of office out of the shadow of FDR, he sank to depths of demagoguery equaled only by Andrew Jackson, Andrew Johnson, and Donald Trump.

7

Ike and Jack

A Study in Contrasting Presidencies

The nation's historians and political scientists routinely rank Dwight Eisenhower as one of the greatest presidents in American history, ensconced amid luminaries such as Abraham Lincoln, George Washington, and Thomas Jefferson.[1] Eisenhower's impressive standing is somewhat remarkable in that prior to his election as the nation's thirty-fourth president, he never ran for any public office in the United States. "Ike," as the American people affectionately knew him, lacked the grassroots political experience that honed the skills of many of his presidential predecessors and assisted their rise to the top of the American government. And yet Eisenhower's experience as the architect of Operation Overlord, or perhaps more accurately, the man who kept a fragile coalition together and secured allied victory on the western front, uniquely prepared him for the demands of governing in a pluralistic, contentious society such as the United States.

In leadership both at home and abroad, Eisenhower demonstrated remarkable skill at coalition building and soothing the hurt egos of assorted prima donnas. British General Sir Alan Brooke observed that Ike "possessed an exceptional ability to handle Allied forces, to treat them with strict impartiality, and to get the best out of an inter-Allied force."[2] Eisenhower's talents as a coalition builder would be tested throughout his presidency, as the chief executive faced a Congress controlled by the opposition party for six of his eight years in office.

"The Hidden Hand"

Dwight Eisenhower was a rarity among incoming American presidents in that he devoted considerable thought as to how to best structure his White House, as well as the executive branch writ large. According to one of his White House aides, Eisenhower, "more than any President in recent history . . . was an organization man."[3] Eisenhower favored a hierarchical organization in terms of managing the executive office, and he granted a considerable amount of authority to the White House chief of staff. It seems to be something of an iron law that Republican presidents, perhaps due to their affinity for the business community, have tended to lean toward strong chiefs of staff presiding over a hierarchical structure, while Democratic presidents, with more of an affinity for the academic world, tend to favor a less-hierarchical, more free-wheeling approach.

Dwight Eisenhower was, in some ways, a natural born administrator, a skill he had honed during his lengthy military career. Unfortunately, many of Eisenhower's successors, and a fair number of his predecessors, devoted little attention to this aspect of their presidencies in favor of playing the role of national visionary. A sergeant major who served with Eisenhower in the army in 1918 noted that "despite his youth" Ike "possessed a high understanding of organization, the ability to place an estimate on a man and fit him into a position where he would 'click.'" Eisenhower brought this same skill with him into his presidency. He was determined to allow his cabinet officers to run their departments as they saw fit; the cabinet heads were, as biographer Jean Edward Smith has noted, "the equivalent of his Army commanders."[4]

The most astute observer of Eisenhower's leadership style, political scientist Fred Greenstein, argued that Eisenhower's "subtle" approach to delegating authority was the result of his "experience of commanding a vast intricate organization and his extensive staff experience in the army." He understood that leaders must avoid being overwhelmed by details, while at the same time avoiding delegating so much authority that he "would dilute his own ability to keep the actions of his associates in line with his own policies." Eisenhower understood something that many of his successors seemed unable to grasp, that "the government of the United States has become too big, too complex . . . for one individual to pretend to direct the details of its important and critical programming."[5]

President Eisenhower's propensity to delegate led to criticism of his leadership style, with many pundits claiming that Eisenhower was passive and detached. The president expected his cabinet officers and agency heads to manage the day-to-day affairs of their departments, while he focused on the critical policy decisions that provided the overall guidance for his administration.[6] But this was seen in some quarters as a negligent method of governing. Ike's critics contended that he was ill-equipped to understand the complexities of the issues he confronted, and he was often accused by his political opponents of focusing on his golf game to the detriment of governing.

Massachusetts Senator John F. Kennedy believed that Eisenhower's stodgy Rotary Club presidency was simply not suited for the challenges of the "revolutionary" twentieth century—what was needed was a robust presidency to replace Ike's "detached, limited concept of the Presidency." Most Democrats accepted Kennedy's description of a torpid Eisenhower presidency; the Eisenhower years were, according to Kennedy, "eight years of drugged and fitful sleep."[7] One of Eisenhower's harshest critics was his immediate predecessor, Harry Truman, who observed "He'll [Eisenhower will] sit right here and he'll say, 'do this, do that'! And nothing will happen. Poor Ike—it won't be a bit like the Army. He'll find it very frustrating."[8]

Harry Truman was right that Eisenhower (along with Truman) found the American presidency to be frustrating, but he was wrong to assume that Ike thought he could simply issue orders and expect to get things done. Eisenhower was in fact a Machiavellian leader who, according to Vice President Richard Nixon, "usually preferred the indirect approach where it would serve him better than the direct attack on a problem."[9] Out of public view, Eisenhower was, in the words of Fred Greenstein, the "hidden-hand" president. The president who appeared to be detached and at times uninformed was "exercising power quietly, behind the scenes, without issuing public declarations, indeed without doing anything to reveal his role."[10]

As Chester Pach and Elmo Richardson have observed, Eisenhower frequently left the impression that he was not involved with the decisions of his subordinates, when they were in fact carrying out his decisions. His alleged detachment had the added political benefit of protecting the president should these policies fail. As Pach and Richardson note, "by deflecting any criticism toward his associates, [Eisenhower] would remain above the battle, thus preserving his popularity and his freedom to maneuver."[11] Throughout his presidency, Eisenhower followed what former aide William Ewald described as an "arm's-length" strategy "on missions great and small, trivial and grave."[12]

Fred Greenstein first broached the notion of Eisenhower as the "hidden-hand" president with the publication of his book *The Hidden-Hand Presidency: Eisenhower as Leader* in 1982. Taking advantage of recently declassified materials, Greenstein upended the dominant narrative in academic circles of Eisenhower as a passive and detached president. Greenstein's book was truly a path-breaking work of scholarship that challenged caricatured notions (some of which were rooted in ideological hostility) regarding the nation's thirty-fourth president. According to Greenstein, Eisenhower, despite cultivating "the reputation of being above political machination," was in fact an "activist" president.[13] His activism was sometime designed to curb what he viewed as excessive or expansive government initiatives, which helped to further confuse his critics who had a knee-jerk tendency to view "activist" presidents as those favoring an expanded role for the federal government.

Greenstein presented a compelling case that Eisenhower, unlike many twentieth-century American presidents, understood the contradiction inherent in the office of the presidency between the chief executive's role as head of state, a ceremonial role but one of great importance in terms of generating public respect for the office and for cultivating national pride, and the president's role as "prime minister," responsible for governing and shaping public policy and for leading his political party. The ability to deftly blend those very divergent tasks has eluded many American presidents. Eisenhower managed this blending far better than many presidents before or since his time. As Greenstein observed, due to Eisenhower's appreciation of the role of president as head of state, "public confidence in and respect for the presidency was widespread." By cultivating this ceremonial role, Ike "conveyed to his countrymen that their president was worthy of respect." Ike operated "on the assumption that a president who is predominately viewed in terms of his political prowess will lose public support by not appearing to be a proper chief of state." As such, "Eisenhower went to great lengths to conceal the political side of his leadership." [14] It is important to note that since Eisenhower's time, respect for the office of the presidency has declined precipitously.

Eisenhower was the last American president, apart from Ronald Reagan, who understood that power and influence accrues to a president who embraces his role as head of state, and that the American political order is healthier when a president assumes this unifying role. Eisenhower, like

Washington before him, conducted himself in a dignified manner as president. As he noted in 1960, "among the qualities American government must exhibit is dignity. In turn the principal government spokesman must strive to display it. In war and in peace I've had no respect for the desk-pounder and the loud and slick talker."[15]

Eisenhower also broke with his populist predecessors and successors who frequently resorted to personal attacks against their opponents. Ike's commitment to a "no personalities policy" was a major factor in his success as a leader. In this regard Eisenhower was similar to Lincoln, whom he admired because "you can find no instances when he stood up in public and excoriated another American."[16] Eisenhower presents an alternative style of presidential leadership than that offered by Andrew Jackson, Andrew Johnson, Harry Truman, Richard Nixon, and Donald Trump.

Ike's ability to withstand insults and avoid personal attacks was also coupled with an appreciation for the virtue of humility, which, as Eisenhower observed in 1965, was a "quality I have observed in every leader whom I have deeply admired." Additionally, unlike some of his successors, including Lyndon Johnson, Richard Nixon, and Donald Trump, Eisenhower was willing to take the blame for mistakes and give credit to subordinates for successes. This too was related to his sense of humility, for it was "[his] own conviction that every leader should have enough humility to accept, publicly, the responsibility for the mistakes of the subordinates" he had appointed and likewise "give them credit, publicly, for their triumphs."[17]

Ike's refusal to publicly speak ill of someone, which explains his reluctance to openly challenge Senator Joseph McCarthy, worked to the president's favor in that it kept contentious policy debates from devolving into mudslinging contests. Eisenhower succinctly described his approach to leadership in a comment he once made to his personal secretary: "always leave a line of retreat open to your antagonist, and the most important one you can leave is never to challenge his motives."[18] Eisenhower admonished one of his White House aides by editing a statement that had been prepared for him by noting, "this is an attack on a person. When you said it was deliberate . . . you were attacking his motives. Never, ever, attack a person's motives."

As the president once observed, "I do not engage in personalities." Eisenhower claimed in a private letter that he had "never violated" the precept of "avoid[ing] public mention of any name unless it can be done with favorable intent and connotation," and that he "reserve[d] all criticism for the private conference." In case the point was missed, he added, "speak only good in public."[19] "A leader's job," according to Eisenhower, "is to get others to go along with him in the promotion of something. To do this he needs their good will. To destroy good will, it is only necessary to criticize publicly."[20] Eisenhower projected the image of the common man and urged that his speeches be accessible to a "Kansas ditch digger," and he conducted himself in a nonpartisan manner devoted to "an ecumenical commitment to all categories of Americans." Ike was determined, unlike his two partisan predecessors, to "establish links across the nation's party and social divisions."[21] Modern presidents have much to learn from Eisenhower, which would require a rejection of the FDR, the Truman, and most egregiously, the Trump model.

Eisenhower also understood the need for presidential silence, as Lincoln did, and did not overexpose the office by bombarding the public with an endless litany of pronouncements. When his advisors would press him to go on television, Ike responded:

> I keep telling you fellows I don't like to do this sort of thing. I can think of nothing more boring, for the American public, than to have to sit in their living rooms for a whole half hour looking at my face on their television screens. . . . I don't think the people want to be listening to a Roosevelt, sounding as if he were one of the Apostles, or the partisan yipping of a Truman.[22]

Eisenhower did not adopt a catchy slogan to brand his administration, and as such acted as a kind of a throwback to the pre-twentieth-century presidency.[23] There was a kind of colorless administrative focus to the Eisenhower presidency that led critics to accuse him of lacking a "vision."

It comes as no surprise that Eisenhower's rejection of elements of the popular presidency cost him in the short run in terms of scholarly assessments of his presidency. Ike was dismissed as a figurehead, a leader who failed to personalize the presidency and take advantage of television, to maximize all the advantages technology provided to the modern presidency. In 1962, shortly after leaving the presidency, Eisenhower, was ranked twenty-first in a poll of scholars, tied with Chester Alan Arthur.[24] This was during the heyday of the New Frontier when the notion that the president should be as big a man as he wanted to be was much in vogue. Another important element of Eisenhower's hidden-hand presidency was his public communications strategy. The president kept the press and the public confused about his intentions and the depth of his involvement in decision making by his unfathomable press conferences that were notable for Ike's butchered syntax and metaphysical meanderings. Eisenhower also frequently deflected questions about controversial matters by proclaiming "I'll have to look that up." When his worried press secretary warned him about a potentially sensitive matter likely to be raised at an upcoming press conference, the president responded, "Don't worry Jim. . . . If that question comes up, I'll just confuse them."[25]

As Fred Greenstein has observed, Eisenhower used language to "create smoke screens for his actions" and to convey "deliberately ambiguous messages that left him freedom of action." This tactic, as Greenstein notes, was not limited to Eisenhower, but what set him apart from other political figures was Ike's ability to "leave the impression that such utterances were guileless."[26] Ike's "aw-shucks" grin and his Rotary Club affability were critical factors in his successful employment of oratorical feints.

The Limits of the Hidden-Hand Presidency

Eisenhower was arguably one of the most effective chief executives of the twentieth century, leaving the presidency after two consecutive terms in office as a remarkably popular figure. But his leadership style had its critics. Leading from behind, or utilizing a hidden-hand approach, was arguably of limited effectiveness in dealing with some of the most vexing political problems confronting the nation. In two critical areas, President Eisenhower refused to invoke the moral authority of the presidency (which was a potent force in 1950s America, and still exists in a considerably diminished form today) to deal with high matters of state. Abraham Lincoln, for instance, utilizing his formidable pen, proclaimed a new birth of freedom for the United States.

But visionary pronouncements were not Eisenhower's style, and his reluctance to exercise this unofficial presidential power tarnished his record in office. This book is critical of the excessive use of these pronouncements in the service of a partisan policy agenda. But there are occasions when the president, as head of state, should exercise this authority and speak out in the cause of binding the nation's wounds. Eisenhower missed two such opportunities.

The first issue where Eisenhower was arguably negligent concerned his reluctance to vigorously condemn the demagoguery of a fellow Republican, Senator Joseph McCarthy of Wisconsin. As with all good demagogues,

McCarthy promoted a conspiracy theory, this one claiming that the American government was riddled with Communists from top to bottom and that these "moles" were responsible for losing China and for making concessions to the Soviet Union at the Yalta Conference and elsewhere. (There were communist agents in the Roosevelt administration who deserved to be uncovered and prosecuted. McCarthy took this legitimate security concern and embellished it to serve his own ends). This was a "conspiracy so immense" it came to include Eisenhower's mentor General George C. Marshall, and in the minds of some, even Eisenhower himself. Eisenhower employed his usual stealthy approach to these issues, which, while arguably somewhat effective, deprived the American citizenry of a valuable educative opportunity. In other words, condemning a demagogue like McCarthy in 1952, when Eisenhower had the opportunity to do so, would likely have cut the scurrilous senator's crusade short. The general, however, chose to bide his time, and let McCarthy hang himself, with Eisenhower covertly providing the rope.

Eisenhower believed that "nothing will be so effective in combating his [McCarthy's] particular kind of troublemaking as to ignore him."[27] Eisenhower ultimately undermined the Wisconsin senator, in part by using his vice president, Richard Nixon, whose anti-Communist credentials were impeccable, to publicly and privately undercut McCarthy's support in the Senate and beyond. In the end, sixty-seven of McCarthy's senatorial colleagues voted to censure him for "conduct unbecoming a senator" on December 2, 1954.[28]

Eisenhower defended his indirect approach in dealing with McCarthy as "common sense." Ike observed at the time that "I am quite sure that the people who want me to stand up and publicly label McCarthy with derogatory titles are the most mistaken people that are dealing with this whole problem."[29] In fairness, it should be noted that a number of recent studies of Eisenhower's presidency applaud the president's covert undermining of Senator McCarthy, but it remains an open question in the minds of some observers whether a more public challenge from the respected Eisenhower would have hastened McCarthy's demise. Sadly, McCarthy's chief advisor, New York attorney Roy Cohn, a professional demagogue, would go on to school future president Donald Trump on matters of "public relations." Cohn was, in Trump's words, a "vicious protector."[30]

The second great issue, and a far greater one than the threat of McCarthyism, concerned the American system of apartheid, or Jim Crow, still firmly entrenched almost a century after the end of the Civil War. On civil rights, the president's actions were equally cautious and opaque. Once again, Eisenhower refused to throw the full weight of his office, and more importantly, the full weight of his stature as a national hero, into the debate over desegregating American society. The legacy of "separate but equal" laws in the United States, which the Supreme Court in 1954 ruled were inherently unequal, struck many Americans as a case of justice deferred, and a test of the nation's moral character. But the president never issued a clarion call to end these odious practices, although he did send one thousand paratroopers from the 101st airborne division to Arkansas in 1957 to enforce a desegregation order in the face of violent opposition to admitting African American students at Little Rock's Central High School.[31] Additionally, two of his Supreme Court appointees, Chief Justice Earl Warren and Justice William Brennan, were key players in the major civil rights decisions emanating from the court in the 1950s and 1960s.

Ike also signed into law the Civil Rights Act of 1957, the first such act since the days of Reconstruction. But Eisenhower severely damaged prospects for the legislation and bolstered Southern segregationists when he blurted out at a press conference that "there were certain phrases I didn't completely understand."[32] The Civil Rights Act eventually passed, but not until it was watered down by powerful Southern Democrats who controlled key committees in the House and Senate. Nonetheless, the Civil Rights Act of 1957 represented something of a small step on the road to securing equal rights for African Americans.

It is important to note that Eisenhower never made a bold public statement of the type that President John F. Kennedy made in June 1963, that "we are confronted primarily with a moral issue. It is as old as the scriptures and is as clear as the American Constitution. . . . The heart of the question is whether all Americans are to be afforded equal rights and equal opportunities, whether we are going to treat our fellow Americans as we want to be treated."[33] To the extent that Eisenhower defended his actions in Little Rock, for instance, it was always in a legalistic sense of enforcing the law as interpreted by the Supreme Court. Ike never suggested that this was a case of simple justice, of equal treatment under the law, a principle enshrined in the nation's founding document.

Eisenhower's biographer Jean Edward Smith considers Ike's "moderation" in these matters as an attribute, for Ike was "determined to enforce the court order, but with as little bluster as possible. . . . Eisenhower took the most divisive issue to confront American society since the Civil War and moved it toward a solution with as little rancor as possible."[34] But the truth is, as Ike's biographers Pach and Richardson have observed, "Eisenhower simply hoped that the issue of civil rights would simply vanish. . . . Because of his reluctance to take sides in partisan conflicts, he did not know how to provide the moral leadership that would hasten popular acceptance of desegregation."[35] This caution was disappointing, because Ike's bona fides as an American hero presented him with an opportunity to influence public opinion to a far greater extent than other political figures of his time, and thus secure his place as a successor to the principles and practices of Abraham Lincoln, whose party he led.

Dwight Eisenhower's place in the pantheon of American military and political heroes will likely endure as long as the nation endures. His administration kept the peace between the two nuclear superpowers, ended the Korean War, strove to maintain a balanced federal budget, oversaw a relatively prosperous economy, conducted itself toward its political opponents in a civil manner, and bolstered respect for the office of the presidency. Unlike many of his successors, Eisenhower championed the rule of law, arguing that "the clearest way to show what the rule of law means to us in everyday life is to recall what has happened when there is no rule of law." The general who visited the Nazi death camps at the end of World War II and noted that "the things I saw beggar description," spoke from experience.[36]

In contrast to the marked partisanship that characterizes American politics today, the Eisenhower years offer an alternative vision of American society where the politics of personal destruction is the exception not the rule. Nevertheless, Eisenhower's cautious and concealed approach to Joseph McCarthy and to civil rights for African Americans raises legitimate questions about the efficacy and appropriateness of leading from behind on matters one would deem central to the regime: equal justice for a long-oppressed minority, and the defense of the norms of civility that allow a republic to function.

The New Frontier

John F. Kennedy was the anti-Eisenhower in many respects and was the epitome of the visionary president promoted by Woodrow Wilson and other avatars of twentieth-century American progressivism. Kennedy's charisma allowed him to form the type of bond that Wilson and other progressive thinkers considered *the* critical element of effective popular leadership. While one could argue that Franklin Roosevelt was the archetype of the progressive presidency, the rise of television allowed Kennedy to forge a bond with the public that was far greater than he otherwise might have made in his two years, ten months, and two days in office. Because of his mastery of television and public relations writ large, the abbreviated Kennedy presidency became the benchmark by which many progressive politicians and scholars measured presidential success.

As previously discussed, Woodrow Wilson believed that the president (assisted by the best and brightest administrators) was to serve as a visionary and lead the nation into the promised land, or, in Kennedy's case, into the "new frontier." Kennedy's oratory, crafted with a considerable assist from speechwriter Ted Sorensen, was as soaring and as visionary as any twentieth-century progressive. Kennedy claimed that "man can be as big as he wants. No problem of human destiny is beyond human beings," and that the president "must be prepared to exercise the fullest powers of his office—all that are specified and some that are not." JFK's vision of American omnipotence led him to proclaim that the United States would "bear any burden, pay any price" to defend liberty around the globe, including in the swamps of South Vietnam.[37]

In an address to the United Nations on September 20, 1963, Kennedy went beyond the promises of his inflated 1960 campaign rhetoric or his inaugural address. Speaking to this international audience, Kennedy claimed that if mankind put aside their differences, there were no limits to what could be accomplished: "Never before has man had such capacity to control his own environment, to end thirst and hunger, to conquer poverty and disease, to banish illiteracy and massive human misery. We have the power to make this the best generation of mankind in the history of the world—or to make it the last."[38] The belief that mankind could banish all earthly ills has something of an ancient pedigree. But the track record of regimes that have attempted to alleviate these inequities in life offers little hope. Unfortunately, history is riddled with utopian visions which degenerated into totalitarianism. But it is not simply ahistorical to claim such a "capacity," for a clear-eyed understanding of human nature is also at odds with this sentiment, something the American founders understood. Americans have a "can do" quality about them, which has led to impressive economic and technological breakthroughs, but a due regard for the history of mankind requires one to acknowledge that human nature is fixed. And that nature is composed in part, perhaps in good part, of avarice, greed, and rapaciousness. This is not a conservative belief, rather it is a belief that is grounded in the lessons of history and philosophy. It is the essence of realism.

But this was not a lesson heeded by some members of Kennedy's Harvard brain trust, many of whom admired Woodrow Wilson and believed in his doctrine of perpetual progress. Candidate Kennedy hailed Wilson during his acceptance speech at the Democratic Convention in 1960, noting that Wilson's "New Freedom promised our nation a new political and economic framework," and later, just three weeks prior to the election, Kennedy reminded voters that he was "the standard bearer of a party which in this century has run men like Woodrow Wilson, and Franklin Roosevelt, and I run in their tradition."[39]

Kennedy made sure that Wilson's widow attended his inauguration on January 20, 1961, and invited her to the Oval Office that October as he signed legislation creating the Woodrow Wilson Memorial Commission.[40] Kennedy's conception of presidential power was as sweeping and assertive as Wilson's. JFK believed that the American president was the nation's visionary in chief, responsible for the fate of the free world, if not the entire planet. When he announced that he was running for the presidency in January 1960, Kennedy noted that

> the presidency is the most powerful office in the Free World. Through its leadership can come a more vital life for our people. In it are centered the hopes of the globe around us for freedom and a more secure life. For it is in the Executive Branch that the most crucial decisions of this century must be made in the next four years . . . [including] how to give direction to our traditional moral purpose, awakening every American to the dangers and opportunities that confront us.[41]

Kennedy repeated many of the same themes during a speech at the National Press Club less than two weeks later, adding that *the* central issue of the 1960 campaign was "not the farm problem or defense or India. It is the presidency itself." The history of the United States was in fact the history of the presidency: "the history of this nation—its brightest and its bleakest pages—has been written largely in terms of the different views our Presidents have had of the Presidency itself." Not since Woodrow Wilson's time had "any candidate spoken on the presidency itself," and Kennedy hoped that the proper scope of executive power would be the central focus of the election of 1960. Dwight Eisenhower's stodgy Rotary Club presidency was simply not suited for the challenges of the "revolutionary" 1960s—what was needed was a reinvigorated Wilsonian presidency to replace Ike's "detached, limited concept of the Presidency."

The presidency demanded, in Kennedy's view, "a man capable of acting as the commander in chief of the Great Alliance" who would not permit constitutional niceties to constrain his actions.. He must also fulfill Professor Woodrow Wilson's vision of a president serving as "educator in chief," by "reopen[ing] channels of communication between the world of thought and the seat of power." Additionally, the chief executive must be something of the nation's "preacher in chief," for the presidency "must be the center of moral leadership." Dwight Eisenhower's constricted view of presidential power was inappropriate for the central role "the Presidency was meant to have in American life." Foreshadowing the great issue that would dominant and divide the nation in the 1960s, Kennedy noted that the proper conception of presidential power including extinguishing a "brushfire [that] threatens some part of the globe—he alone can act, without waiting for the Congress." The founding fathers drafted a "Constitution [that] envisioned: a Chief Executive who is the vital center of action in our whole scheme of Government." Kennedy's beau ideal of a president was one who embraced the idea that "upon him alone converge all the needs and aspirations of all parts of the country, all departments of the Government, all nations of the world."[42]

Despite the opposition of most of his party's leaders, JFK was selected as the Democratic Party's nominee for president in July 1960. Kennedy's insurgent candidacy set the stage for a series of Democratic nominees, including George McGovern, Jimmy Carter, and Barack Obama, securing their party's nomination in defiance of party leaders. This same phenomenon began to occur in the Republican Party as well but took much longer to develop. In his acceptance speech, the junior senator from Massachusetts argued that his activist presidency would get the country moving again after the stagnant Eisenhower years. Kennedy saw himself as the heir to a series of presidents who understood the need for action and had succeeded lethargic caretakers.

After Buchanan this nation needed Lincoln; after Taft we needed Wilson; and after Hoover we needed Franklin Roosevelt. . . . Woodrow Wilson's New Freedom promised our nation a new political and economic framework. Franklin Roosevelt's New Deal promised security and succor to those in need.

It is time, in short, for a new generation of leadership. All over the world, particularly in the newer nations, young men are coming to power, men who are not bound by the traditions of the past, men who are not blinded by the old fears and hates and rivalries—young men who can cast off the old slogans and the old delusions.

Kennedy added that the march of history in the 1960s would bring with it "new breakthroughs in weapons of destruction, but also a race for mastery of the sky and the rain, the ocean and the tides, the far side of space, and the inside of men's minds." There were, in other words, no limits to man's ability to remake the world, and the United States must be in the forefront of this great transformation. The nation stood on "the edge of a New Frontier—the frontier of the 1960s—a frontier of unknown opportunities and perils—a frontier of unfulfilled hopes and threats." All was possible if men of courage and vigor, "pioneers on that New Frontier," responded to Kennedy's clarion call.[43]

The torpid Eisenhower years saw the United States slip behind the Soviet Union on several fronts. Kennedy claimed in his final debate with Richard Nixon that "the Communists have been moving with vigor—Laos, Africa, Cuba—all around the world today they're on the move. I think we have to revitalize our society. I think we have to demonstrate to the people of the world that we're determined in this free country of ours to be first—not first if, and not first but, and not first when—but first."[44] On the campaign trail, Kennedy noted that the nation's "enemies" had "rolled the Iron Curtain to 90 miles from our shores onto the once friendly island of Cuba."[45] Kennedy made Eisenhower's alleged complacency regarding the Soviets a key issue in his campaign against Vice President Richard Nixon in 1960. He called for the use of "fighters for freedom" to overthrow Castro, and jokingly told a campaign aide that he had no qualms about doing so, since "they never told us how they [the Republicans] would have saved China."[46]

Remarkably, President Kennedy's inaugural address surpassed the call to arms of his campaign rhetoric. The nation's youngest elected president committed the United States to paying "any price, bear[ing] any burden, meet[ing] any hardship, support[ing] any friend, oppos[ing] any foe to assure the survival and the success of liberty. This much we pledge—and more." He also called for an international effort to "explore the stars, conquer the deserts, eradicate disease, tap the ocean depths and encourage the arts and commerce," and appealed for "a struggle against the common enemies of man: tyranny, poverty, disease, and war itself."[47]

"A Fluid Presidency"

President Kennedy's management style went well beyond Woodrow Wilson's notion of centralizing power in the executive branch. For Kennedy, centralizing power meant centralizing it in the Oval Office itself. Kennedy was not only impatient with separation of powers, he viewed his own cabinet, and the federal bureaucracy writ large, as an impediment to progress as well. Determined to be his own secretary of state, Kennedy slighted his choice to head that department, Dean Rusk, whose selection was based in part on his deferential manner. Ted Sorensen would later write with glee that "no decisions of importance were made at Kennedy's Cabinet meetings and few subjects of importance, particularly in foreign affairs, were ever seriously discussed." Sorensen also boasted of the fact that "not one staff meeting was ever held, with or without the President," adding that Kennedy "paid little attention to organization charts and chains of command which diluted his authority." Kennedy, in fact, had no chief of staff, and saw himself playing that role. There would be no Sherman Adams in the Kennedy White House, since, in JFK's view, Adams typified Eisenhower's propensity for importing stultifying military practices into the more free-wheeling world of politics.[48]

Kennedy adopted what Arthur Schlesinger Jr. referred to as "a fluid presidency" and wanted to engage in every White House issue, leading to a remarkably undisciplined presidency. His national security advisor, McGeorge Bundy, tried to inject some semblance of organization and discipline, but to little avail. He told Kennedy, "We can't get you to sit still. . . . Calling three meetings in five days is foolish—and putting them off for six weeks at a time is just as bad." JFK's administration lurched from crisis to crisis, a situation the president seemed to thrive on. Bundy added to his rebuke of the president that, "right now it is so hard to get to you with anything not urgent and immediate that about half the papers and reports you personally ask for are never shown to you because by the time you are available you clearly have lost interest."[49]

From the first day of his presidency, Sorensen claimed, Kennedy "abandoned the notion of a collective, institutionalized presidency."[50] In other words, presidential government under Kennedy was the personification of micromanagement from the Oval Office. This was policymaking by the select few, by the band of brothers. This was a presidency that put a premium on action, or more accurately stylish action, and woe to those like Rusk or Chester Bowles who lacked that style and were noted for their unattractive propensity for deliberation. Again, Sorensen captured the mood of this action-oriented presidency by describing the lethargic response of one misguided administration official: "When he [JFK] returned one assistant's six-page, single-spaced memorandum with the request that the author set down its action consequences, he received back another long memorandum recommending: two presidential speeches, a policy paper and a 'systematic review of the situation'—and shortly thereafter that aide was moved to one of the departments."[51]

The fleeting Kennedy presidency, the first television presidency, was from the beginning to its tragic end a media event. Kennedy was made for television, and his bronzed appearance in four televised debates had helped him defeat a sweaty, shifty-eyed, and ghostly Richard Nixon.[52] As historian Alan Brinkley has noted, Kennedy was "a witty and articulate speaker, [who] seemed built for the age of television. To watch him on film today is to be struck by the power of his presence and the wit and elegance of his oratory."[53]

Kennedy was the first president to hold press conferences on live television, and his sharp intellect and mastery of detail impressed his fellow Americans. One reporter noted that "we were props in a show. We should have joined Actors Equity," while another remembered Kennedy looking "right over our heads, right into the camera. . . . This was a man who was extraordinarily professional." Indeed, the God of American politics, public opinion polls, gave the president a 91 percent approval rating for his press conference performances.[54]

Jack and Jackie served as the inspiration for Rob and Laura Petrie on *The Dick Van Dyke Show,* and Caroline and "John-John" were the subject of affecting photo essays in *Life* magazine (a media-savvy president would arrange for the photos to be taken while the First Lady was absent from the White House). This same media, drawn in good part from JFK's fellow World War II veterans, liked the new president, in part because he was interested in their work and his photogenic family was good for business. The American public was taken by the contrast between the chic Kennedys and the dowdy, coupon-clipping, bridge-playing Eisenhowers. The nation's oldest president (at the time) had been succeeded by one of the nation's youngest, at a point when youth was becoming all the rage. As Arthur Schlesinger Jr. described it, Kennedy's ascension to the presidency marked "the shift from the Old Frontier to the New Frontier."[55]

It is no accident that a presidency obsessed with action, with "getting the country moving again," should have one of its chief chroniclers celebrate the number of crises that confronted Kennedy in his brief presidency, a fact that Ted Sorensen repeatedly mentions in his hagiographic biography of the nation's thirty-fifth president. Presiding over the nation as an effective administrator doing the unglamorous work of governing does not make for a progressive hero.

The jolt of the Kennedy assassination for those Americans who were alive in 1963 was rivaled only by the events of December 7, 1941, or later by September 11, 2001. The poignant images of the thirty-four-year-old First Lady kissing the president's casket and his three-year-old son saluting the same were almost too much to bear. When the news broke from Dallas, the nation's three television networks suspended their normal broadcasting schedule for the first time in their short history to focus nonstop on the funeral of the president, followed shortly by the murder of his assassin.[56] After Kennedy's death, 65 percent of the American public claimed they voted for him, although he had only received 49.7 percent of the popular vote.[57]

Jacqueline Kennedy was determined to elevate her husband into a mythic figure and she set the stage for this by planting the Camelot myth in the mind of presidential chronicler Theodore White. Mrs. Kennedy recoiled at the idea that a nonentity like Lee Harvey Oswald had murdered her husband, noting that Jack "didn't even have the satisfaction of being killed for civil rights. . . . It had to be some silly little communist. It . . . robs his death of any meaning." The myth of Camelot has persisted into the twenty-first century through the works of Arthur Schlesinger Jr., along with Ted Sorensen, Robert Dallek, Larry Sabato, Sean Wilentz, and countless others.

For these chroniclers the Kennedy years were a brief, shining moment in which the world of ideas merged seamlessly, and gracefully, with the world of power. Schlesinger, the Kennedy family's favored biographer, wistfully observed that "the capital city, somnolent in the Eisenhower years, had suddenly come alive . . . [with] the release of energy which occurs when men with ideas have a chance to put them into practice."[58] Schlesinger's view was shared by his colleague Sorensen, the author of the worshipful biography

Kennedy. Both men saw JFK, and later Robert Kennedy, as martyrs for world peace and racial equality.

With John F. Kennedy unable to write a memoir, the torch was passed to Schlesinger and Sorensen, the latter of whom had played a very influential role in the administration, earning the label of JFK's "intellectual alter ego" and "a lobe of Kennedy's mind."[59] Schlesinger and Sorensen helped shape the Kennedy legacy by publishing the first insider accounts of that short-lived presidency. *A Thousand Days* and *Kennedy* were both released in 1965, with each author celebrating the Kennedy presidency as an exceptional moment in the nation's history. Schlesinger and Sorensen quickly emerged as the creative talent behind a carefully managed marketing strategy.[60]

At times, Schlesinger's and Sorensen's accounts of President Kennedy read like excerpts from a romance novel. The Kennedy brothers were "so filled with love of life and so conscious of the ironies of history" that they never would have countenanced killing Fidel Castro, Arthur Schlesinger Jr. claimed.[61] Schlesinger, in fact, noted that after the 1960s he was unable, politically speaking, to "fall hopelessly in love again. I don't suppose I will ever enjoy the careless rapture of my engagement with . . . JFK or RFK." Sorensen observed that he worked for JFK for eleven years and that he "loved him," so much so that his first marriage failed due to his all-consuming relationship with Kennedy.[62] Schlesinger, responding to historians who criticized Kennedy for being a "macho Cold Warrior," believed that Kennedy's critics were "paying [him] back" for being "too handsome, too popular, too rich, [and having] too beautiful a wife."[63]

Schlesinger and Sorensen were not alone in terms of falling in love with John F. Kennedy, for he was the embodiment of the progressive dream of supplanting party leaders and removing the obstacles to popular selection of presidential candidates. Kennedy, as mentioned, was not the choice of party leaders in 1960—that honor belonged to perennial candidate Adlai Stevenson, or Senate Majority Leader Lyndon Johnson, or the respected senator from Missouri, Stuart Symington. John F. Kennedy's presidential campaign was a family operation bankrolled by the family patriarch, Joseph P. Kennedy, and managed by his brother Robert. Outside endorsements were sought, but outsiders were always viewed with some degree of skepticism by family insiders.

Kennedy's powerful rhetoric, and his domination of the new media of television, allowed him to fulfill Woodrow Wilson's vision of a charismatic leader forming a life bond with his people and transforming the polity. Kennedy's hold on the American imagination is based in part on the acceptance of the Camelot myth, of the notion of his one thousand days in office as "one brief shining moment." Large segments of the American public continue to believe this, as do many scholars who should know better, and probably do.

A Presidency of Unlimited Expectations

The Kennedy legend celebrated by so many progressive politicians and scholars has distorted expectations of what the presidency can achieve, and in the long run eroded the prestige and effectiveness of the office. The notion of the presidency as the center of action and of presidential power resting on the personal qualities of the president, reached its apogee under John F. Kennedy. James MacGregor Burns, the author of *Presidential Government: The Crucible of Leadership* (1965), welcomed the rise of a presidency-centric government that would circumvent the archaic checks and balances that impeded government effectiveness and prevented coherent, visionary leadership. The founders' presidency was part of a system designed for "deadlock" and worthy of replacement.[64] Burns was a devoted admirer of Kennedy, having ghostwritten a fawning campaign biography of the future president in 1960. Burns hoped that JFK, and later Senator Edward Kennedy, could break this deadlock. "Our system was designed for deadlock and inaction,"[65] Burns bemoaned, suggesting a transition to something resembling a parliamentary system. Burns glowingly sang the praises of "presidential government," for it was "a superb planning institution. . . . Better than any other human instrumentality he [the president] can order the relations of his ends and means."[66]

Another scholar who influenced Kennedy, and was influenced by Kennedy, was Richard Neustadt, whose book *Presidential Power: The Politics of Leadership* (1960) was read by Kennedy and some members of his inner circle. Neustadt recommended that the president focus on chapters 3 and 7, but according to Arthur Schlesinger Jr., Kennedy read the entire book. Neustadt observed that *Presidential Power* was about "how to be on top in fact as well as name." Neustadt was somewhat dismissive of those who focused on constitutional questions related to presidential power, for "the probabilities of power do not derive from the literary theory of the Constitution." He acknowledged that some elements of presidential power were rooted in the "formal" powers granted by the Constitution, and thus these formal powers were an essential prerequisite to the exercise of the president's "personal influence."[67] But he added that his book was "not about the presidency as an organization, or as legal powers, or as precedents, or as procedures."[68] In perhaps the most damaging passage of all, Neustadt claimed that "a president's success in maximizing power for himself serves objectives far beyond his own. . . . what is good for the country is good for the president, and vice versa."[69] In fairness, it should be noted that Neustadt added in the 1990 edition of his book, thirty years after its original publication, that chief executives needed to think about presidential power "in its symbolic and constitutional dimensions."[70] But arguably, by then, the damage had been done.

Kennedy asked Neustadt to prepare transition memos for the new administration and asked him to join his White House staff, but Neustadt demurred. But *Presidential Power* was a publishing hit, eventually selling over one million copies, "arguably the greatest number in history for a book on a single political institution," as political scientist Charles O. Jones has noted. Jones added:

> Recognition of the book's contribution was not limited to Presidents and the Washington political elite. In 1961, *Presidential Power* won the American Political Science Association's Woodrow Wilson Foundation Award as the best book published in 1960 on government, politics, or international affairs. This is the most prestigious award given out by the APSA. The book clearly met the author's goals of having an impact in the public service sphere and, by his own declaration, of convincing his academic colleagues that he "was serious about their business."[71]

Neustadt also contributed to enshrining Kennedy's legacy in the American pantheon, playing, as Ted Sorensen would later note, "an indispensable part in guiding the Kennedy family and legatees in the establishment of the Kennedy Library, [and] the Kennedy School of Government at Harvard."[72]

By the mid-1960s the Constitutional approach to examining the American presidency was out of the mainstream of American political science. It was perhaps inevitable that as the role of the Constitution and its system of checks was displaced, a handbook would be written to guide scholars and citizens in choosing the correct presidential personality. James David Barber's *The Presidential Character: Predicting Performance in the White House* (1972) recommended adopting a psychological matrix as a replacement for the shattered constitutional and electoral restraints.[73] Barber designed a system to determine proper presidential character; his goal was to move the science of politics, or the study of the presidency, from "theory to prediction." According to Barber, presidential personality boiled down to four distinct categories: active-positive, active-negative, passive-positive, and passive-negative. The most desired qualities could be found in the active-positive category, for these men possessed high self-esteem, enjoyed political life, and were adaptive and flexible in confronting the issues of their time. Active-positive presidents included Franklin Roosevelt, Harry Truman, and John F. Kennedy. Barber's book was released just prior to the election of 1972, and Barber found candidate George McGovern to possess precisely the qualities needed for the Oval Office.[74]

Many of the aforementioned scholars who promoted a version of Wilsonianism on steroids had some sober second thoughts regarding presidential power in the wake of Vietnam and Watergate. But it took the ascension of Richard Nixon for this sobering up to occur. This transformation was most evident among scholar-activists such as Schlesinger, Burns, Neustadt, and Henry Steele Commager, who all believed, with minor differences of emphasis, in Burns's "presidential government." However, when Richard Nixon was elected in 1968, these men suddenly discovered the importance of limiting presidential power. What conservatives dreamed of doing during two decades of Democratic rule from FDR to Truman, limiting executive power both at home and abroad, now became a battle cry for progressive scholars and activists.

The fact that scholarly concerns over executive power emerged in modern times during the tenure of assertive Republican presidents undermines the argument of those favoring a restrained presidency. As with the rule of law, this principle, in order to be credible, should be consistently applied regardless of partisan affiliation or the "charismatic" personal qualities of the president.[75] Despite a period of retrenchment during the Nixon, Ford, and Reagan presidencies, the progressive love affair with strong presidents, as the Obama presidency revealed, remains as vital as it was during the days of Franklin Roosevelt or John F. Kennedy. Even at the height of his despair over Nixon's "imperial presidency," Arthur Schlesinger Jr. always hoping for a Kennedy restoration, warned that the United States could not afford "a generation of weak presidents in an age when the turbulence of race, poverty, inflation, crime and urban decay [is] straining the delicate bonds of national cohesion and demanding, quite as much as in the 1930s, a strong domestic Presidency to hold the country together."[76]

A century of progressive disregard for the Constitution, in which John F. Kennedy and his scholarly supporters played a key role, damaged our nation's polity, possibly beyond repair. While Woodrow Wilson, and Teddy Roosevelt to a lesser extent, laid the foundation for the modern presidency, it was John F. Kennedy's star quality, his charisma, conveyed through modern technology, that permanently embedded Kennedy's personalized presidency in the American psyche. While many of Kennedy's contemporaries took a more progressive stance on the issues, Hubert Humphrey, for instance on civil rights, or Adlai Stevenson on the Cold War, Kennedy captured the progressive imagination particularly after his tragic assassination in Dallas, when many Americans concluded that he was the victim of a conspiracy involving racist, right-wing extremists, or the "deep state," or a combination of both.[77]

John F. Kennedy's allure persists even though the proponents of a personalized presidency promised too much of the federal government. Unfortunately, John F. Kennedy's inspiring rhetoric, which his successors have attempted to mimic, usually in vain, produced an "expectations gap" of epic proportions. In the years following Kennedy's tragic assassination, his successors escalated this rhetoric to even more unhealthy levels.

Progressive Martyr

John F. Kennedy's greatest domestic achievement was his ringing endorsement of civil rights for African Americans. He reminded his fellow citizens in June 1963 that the time had come to dispense with one hundred years of Jim Crow, a reminder that was grounded in the noblest principles of the American political tradition: "We are confronted primarily with a moral issue. It is as old as the Scriptures and is as clear as the American Constitution. . . . This is one country. . . . it has become one country because all of us and all the people who came here had an equal chance to develop their talents."[78] Belated though this was, it was nonetheless a costly political move for a president who hoped to retain the support of Southern Democrats in the 1964 election—thus the trip to Dallas in November 1963.

Even more remarkable was the robust endorsement of a civil rights agenda, including the invocation of the language of the civil rights movement, by Kennedy's successor, Lyndon Johnson of Texas, who threw the weight of his entire presidency to secure the adoption of major civil rights initiatives. No other president comes close to Johnson's accomplishments in this regard. These initiatives changed the face of America and began the process of breaking the doctrine that "the majority was to govern" at the expense of minorities. For this, these two presidents, perhaps Lyndon Johnson especially, although Johnson's success was due in part to Kennedy's death, rightly secured their place in American history. And they did so at great electoral cost to themselves and their party.

While President Kennedy's willingness to defy majority sentiment in the South and offer unqualified rhetorical support for the goals of the civil rights movement was impressive, his abbreviated presidency left a destructive legacy in other areas. The Kennedy presidency continued the process of undermining the office with its inflated promises, its excessive focus on personality, on "charisma," and with its elevation of television to become the central player in American politics. Ironically, Kennedy understood that television had the potential to distort American politics. In 1959, a year before he ran for president, he acknowledged that "political success on television is not, unfortunately, limited only to those who deserve it." This new medium "lends itself to manipulation, exploitation and gimmicks. It can be abused by demagogues, by appeals to emotion and prejudice and ignorance."[79]

Kennedy's movie-star looks, his attractive family, and his manipulation of the media along with his tragic early death fostered a cult-like following devoted to celebrating and restoring "Camelot." And, it is important to note, as author Michael J. Hogan has documented, that the marketing of John F. Kennedy continued long after the murder in Dallas's Dealey Plaza.[80]

The Camelot legend took hold despite the preponderance of evidence that President Kennedy expanded American involvement in Vietnam, lied about his serious health issues, engaged in several risky extramarital affairs, including one with the girlfriend of the Chicago mob boss and another with a nineteen-year-old intern whom he bedded on her fourth day on the job, and presided over an administration that tried repeatedly to assassinate Fidel Castro.[81]

Regardless of this mixed record, Kennedy remains an admired figure among the American public and among presidential scholars. A Gallup poll of Americans taken in 2008 ranked JFK at the top of the list in terms of presidents you wished "you could bring back" to be president. JFK came in at 23 percent followed by Ronald Reagan with 22 percent, Bill Clinton at 13 percent, and Abraham Lincoln at 10 percent. Another Gallup poll, this one taken in February 2000, ranked Kennedy as "the greatest president ever."[82] A poll taken during the fiftieth anniversary of Kennedy's assassination found that JFK was "by a wide margin, the most esteemed president since 1953. . . . Even more remarkable, his appeal transcends ideology: Fifty-two percent of Republicans and 79 percent of Democrats . . . called him one of America's best leaders. By contrast, other strong finishers, such as Ronald Reagan and Bill Clinton, are deeply disliked by members of the opposite party."[83] The 2017 *C-Span* presidential leadership survey of historians and political scientists ranked President Kennedy eight overall, slightly behind Jefferson and ahead of luminaries such as Jackson, Wilson, and Eisenhower.[84]

For many progressive politicians and scholars, JFK continues to be *the* standard of excellence for an American president. As Rutgers's historian David Greenberg rightly noted in 2013, during countless commemorations and media reports, there were no similar displays of emotion fifty years after William McKinley's assassination, or fifty years after Warren G. Harding's premature passing. Historian and educator Diane Ravitch summed up the views of many members of her generation when she wrote that "I was part of the generation that was moved by his [JFK's] eloquence, his humor, his charm, his intellect. He encouraged us to dream of a new world. I felt shattered by his assassination. It was one of the darkest days the nation had known."

Another commentator summed up the feeling of many Americans, noting that "much more than John F. Kennedy died in November 1963; in many ways our nation died with him." This commentator revealed the extent to which Woodrow Wilson's conception of executive power has been embraced by many Americans: "one of the roles of the president is to help focus us as a society—to give us goals, to steer us in a direction, to show us what matters and must be done, and motivate us to do it."

Historian David Greenberg attributed Kennedy's hold on the American imagination to a similar sense that Kennedy epitomized all that was right in Woodrow Wilson's reconstituted presidency. Kennedy remained a revered figure because of

> the way he used the presidency, his commitment to exercising his power to address social needs, his belief that government could harness expert knowledge to solve problems. In 1960, the United States was gripped by a quest for "national purpose," a yearning to find a meaningful goal for America's energies. . . . They reflect a wistfulness for the sense of common purpose and faith in a collective project that a proudly liberal president helped the nation achieve.[85]

Historian Robert Dallek once asserted that Kennedy's "thousand days spoke to the country's better angels, inspired visions of a less divisive nation and world, and demonstrated that America was still the last best hope of mankind."[86] Larry Sabato outdid them all, comparing JFK to the first Christian martyr, Saint Stephen. Kennedy was no saint, Sabato conceded, "but he had shown and earned grace during the better part of three years in power." Three weeks after attending a mass at St. Stephen's Church in Middleburg, Virginia, President Kennedy was assassinated, "proceed[ing] to his own martyrdom."[87] Sabato's over-the-top paean to Kennedy notwithstanding, he was correct to assert that regarding the American presidency, we have lived in the Kennedy–half century, and will likely do so well into the next half century. The allure of "presidential government" is simply too strong for progressives to abandon even after witnessing the havoc wreaked by the presidency of Donald Trump.

8

The Road to Degradation

The parameters of the modern popular presidency were set by Woodrow Wilson, Franklin Roosevelt, and John F. Kennedy. From Kennedy's time to the present, any alterations made to the office were rooted in the foundation built by these three presidents. While late twentieth- and early twenty-first-century presidencies worked within these parameters, each added some small element to the existing presidential model. This was particularly true in the technological arena, as Presidents Obama and Trump used the internet to appeal directly to the American people. While some of these presidents contributed much in the policy realm that is worthy of praise, they also further popularized the presidency and paved the way for Donald J. Trump.

All the Way with LBJ

One of these enablers was John F. Kennedy's successor, Lyndon Baines Johnson, who was perpetually insecure about his lack of charisma and his rhetorical shortcomings. Despite these insecurities, Johnson was positively euphoric about the curative powers of the federal government. Remarkably, Johnson's hyperbole exceeded that of Kennedy's, as when he noted in December 1964 that "these are the most hopeful times in all the years since Christ was born in Bethlehem." According to Johnson, mankind had progressed to the point where "as never before—man has in his possession the capacities to end war and preserve peace, to eradicate poverty and share abundance, to overcome the diseases that have afflicted the human race and permit all mankind to enjoy their promise in life on this earth." Johnson claimed that humanity had reached a stage where it could "think of broader and brighter horizons than any who have lived before these times."[1]

Invoking the legacy of Woodrow Wilson, Johnson noted in his Great Society speech of May 1964, that his administration was determined to eradicate

> poverty and racial injustice, to which we are totally committed in our time. But that is just the beginning. The Great Society is a place where every child can find knowledge to enrich his mind and to enlarge his talents. It is a place where leisure is a welcome chance to build and reflect, not a feared cause of boredom and restlessness. It is a place where the city of man serves not only the needs of the body and the demands of commerce but the desire for beauty and the hunger for community.[2]

Some of Johnson's advisors believed that poverty in the United States would be eliminated by 1975 because of their War on Poverty. Johnson's belief in the transformative power of the American government extended beyond the nation's borders. He hoped to create something akin to the Tennessee Valley Authority in the Mekong Delta of South Vietnam to assist in defeating the North Vietnamese and their Viet Cong allies.[3]

Additionally, in keeping with his populist predecessors, Johnson saw no boundary between his person and the office he held. On one occasion when he was being directed to a specific helicopter by a military escort, Johnson allegedly responded, "Son, they are all my helicopters." Most politicians are well endowed in the ego department, but Lyndon Johnson's was in a category all its own. He boasted of an ancestor who died at the Alamo, which was not true, and offered embellished accounts of his World War II career.[4] Johnson's ego led him to present Pope Paul VI with a bust of himself, while the pope presented Johnson with a reproduction of a nativity scene. LBJ allegedly told West German Chancellor Ludwig Erhard that while Lincoln was born in a log cabin, "I was born in a manger."

Johnson routinely abused those around him, beckoning aides and cabinet officers to join him in the men's room where he would defecate in front of them, an act designed to demean them. He urinated once on the leg of a secret service agent while noting, "It's my prerogative." He loved to swim naked with his aides in the White House pool and point out the size of his penis, "Jumbo," as he affectionately called it, while denigrating the size of those in the pool with him.[5] Historian Robert Dallek noted that "when people mentioned Kennedy's many affairs, Johnson would bang the table and declare that he had more women by accident than Kennedy ever had on purpose."[6] A sense of dignity, a major concern for those who created the presidency, and humility, which characterized the presidency of Abraham Lincoln, was ruthlessly extinguished in the Johnson White House.

While Johnson, as mentioned, deserves the greatest accolades for his civil rights legacy, his unbridled confidence in the federal government, and in American power, led to the debacle in Vietnam. Johnson's lack of personal boundaries bled over into his policy prescriptions, which were detached from reality. He believed he could conduct a war from nine thousand miles away in the situation room of the White House, fine tuning the bombing campaign over North Vietnam and splitting the difference on the number of troops requested by the military and the number of troops he considered politically palatable. And his inability to separate himself from the office he held led to abuses, as it had with some of his predecessors. Johnson continued the practice begun by Franklin Roosevelt of using the FBI as his private detective agency. The bureau monitored the activities of Johnson's political opponents, including civil right activists, and it appears that Johnson had numerous sources monitoring his Republican opponent in 1964, Senator Barry Goldwater. Some prominent Republicans were aware of Johnson's abuses of power and vowed to use the machinery of the federal government in a similar manner when the opportunity presented itself. It presented itself on January 20, 1969.

"A New Nixon"

While something of an astute student when it came to foreign policy, Richard M. Nixon also knew how to play the demagogue at home. Nixon committed himself to binding the nation's wounds during his inaugural address, hoping to fulfill his campaign promise of moving the country "forward together."

> When we listen to "the better angels of our nature," we find that they celebrate the simple things, the basic things—such as goodness, decency, love, kindness. Greatness comes in simple trappings. The simple things are the ones most needed today if we are to surmount what divides us, and cement what unites us. To lower our voices would be a simple thing.

> In these difficult years, America has suffered from a fever of words; from inflated rhetoric that promises more than it can deliver; from angry rhetoric that fans discontents into hatreds; from bombastic rhetoric that postures instead of persuading. We cannot learn from one another until we stop shouting at one another—until we speak quietly enough so that our words can be heard as well as our voices.

Nixon's warning that the nation suffered from "inflated rhetoric that promises more than it can deliver" was an appropriate diagnosis of what ailed the modern presidency.[7] But unfortunately, Nixon went on to commit his administration to goals as unattainable as his progressive predecessors, including declaring war on drugs—a war that is still in progress, and still being lost, almost fifty years later. And perhaps more than any president since Andrew Johnson, Nixon demonstrated little regard for the rule of law, considered his opponents to be "enemies," and drew no distinction between himself and the office. He devoted a remarkable amount of energy plotting how to "screw" his enemies and slighted the role of head of state in favor of a highly partisan presidency. In fairness to Nixon, just minutes after completing his inaugural address appealing to his fellow citizens' "better angels," he was greeted with a fusillade of rocks and bottles thrown by antiwar protestors during his inaugural parade.[8]

Nixon was also the first president since Millard Fillmore who did not win control of either house of Congress at any point during his tenure in office. Many members of the House and Senate loathed him, as did members of the news media, some of whom had developed an unhealthy affection for John F. Kennedy. Nixon was seen by his opponents as a "hatchet man," a loner who despised East Coast elites whether they were at Harvard or the State Department or the *Washington Post.*

Nixon tried to soften his hatchet-man image after his back-to-back losses to Kennedy in 1960 and to California Governor Edmund Brown in a gubernatorial race in 1962. In January 1968 a "new Nixon" appeared on the popular television show *Rowan and Martin's Laugh-In*, exclaiming "Sock it to me." This was a bit of a chore for Nixon, as it took six takes for him to get it right. The practice of presidential candidates going on talk shows began when Kennedy and Nixon appeared on the *Tonight Show* with Jack Parr in 1960. These late-night sojourns were designed to make the candidate appear to be warm and caring, and sometimes showcase their musical talents, whether it was

Richard Nixon banging away on the piano on Parr's show or Bill Clinton playing a version of "Heartbreak Hotel" on Arsenio Hall's late-night show.[9]

Nixon's media team in 1968 not only wanted to project an image of a warm and approachable Nixon, but also a statesmanlike Nixon. This multifaceted "new Nixon" was a fabrication of ad men like Roger Ailes, who would go on to become the chairman of *Fox News.* Ailes was hired by Nixon after the two met on the *Mike Douglas Show* in 1967.[10] Nixon had dismissed the use of television as a "gimmick," much to Ailes's despair, although television had saved Nixon's political career when he was almost dumped by Dwight Eisenhower as his running mate in 1952 after the existence of a fund established by conservative California Republicans to defray Nixon's political expenses came to light.[11] In the end, Nixon salvaged his place on the ticket with an emotional televised appeal later dubbed the Checkers speech after the vice president's cocker spaniel, Checkers. Nixon vowed never to return the dog to the person who sent it, because his little girls "love the dog, and I just want to say this right now, that regardless of what they say about it, we're gonna keep it."[12]

But Nixon the lovable dog owner was a distant memory by 1968, having been replaced by the scowling Nixon who was frequently portrayed in *Washington Post* editorial cartoons crawling out of a sewer. As he ramped up for another run, Nixon knew he had to soften his image. Ailes and other members of Nixon's communications team succeeding in portraying him in a less combative and more mature manner, as is brilliantly recounted in *The Selling of the President 1968* by Joe McGinniss.[13] As Ken Hughes has noted, "The centerpiece of this self-recreation was a series of carefully managed television interview programs packaged by the Nixon campaign. These programs showed Nixon at his best, answering questions posed by ordinary Americans, and shielded him from questions by reporters, who sometimes brought out his worst."[14] Enough Americans accepted the idea that there was a "new Nixon" to give him a narrow electoral victory over Vice President Hubert Humphrey in 1968. But there was no "new" Nixon, only the same old Richard Nixon who was an introvert in an extrovert's business, as Henry Kissinger would later observe. Nixon was a loner who brooded over slights both real and imagined, slights going back decades.[15] This emotionally damaged man would drag his country, and the office of the presidency, into an abyss from which it has yet to completely return. As his successor Gerald Ford once observed, "this man had real demons."[16]

Despite the healing rhetoric of his campaign and his inaugural address, Nixon never attempted to heal the divisions, although it is quite likely these attempts would have failed. Nixon reached out to the "silent majority" for support for his policies and welcomed "hard hats" to the White House who had beaten up antiwar protestors in New York City on the steps of Federal Hall where George Washington had been inaugurated as the nation's first president. He appointed one of their members to a cabinet post, and the White House would later fund a hard-hat movement to counter antiwar street action.[17]

Vice President Spiro Agnew, playing the role that Nixon performed for Eisenhower, escalated the rhetorical war by claiming that a divided nation was a sign of health. "If in challenging we polarize the American people," Agnew exclaimed, "I say it is time for positive polarization." And he added, in defiance of all that the founders intended for the unifying role of the executive branch, "It is time to rip away the rhetoric and divide on authentic lines." Leaders of the antiwar movement were "vultures," "ideological eunuchs," and "parasites of passion."[18] Agnew also compared antiwar protestors to Nazis and the Ku Klux Klan, and urged Americans to "act accordingly."[19]

Vice President Agnew took credit for triggering "a holy war" and added, "I have no regrets."[20] Agnew would later observe with pride that "dividing the American people has been my main contribution to the national political scene. I not only plead guilty to this charge, but I am somewhat flattered by it." Nixon welcomed this as well, telling his aides "don't worry about divisiveness—having drawn the sword, don't take it out—stick it in hard." Nixon hoped for some ugly incident that would advance his cause, as he mentioned in 1970. "If anybody so much as brushes against Mrs. Agnew, tell her to fall down. If the vice president were slightly roughed up by those thugs, nothing better could happen for our cause."[21] Both sides, aided and abetted by Nixon and Agnew and the equally irresponsible members of the antiwar movement, who routinely compared Nixon to Hitler and accused him of practicing "genocide" in Southeast Asia, began to see each other as un-American.

Nixon may have had Abraham Lincoln and his "better angels" in mind when he paid a surprise predawn visit to antiwar protestors at the Lincoln Memorial on May 9, 1970.[22] But much like the country itself, the president and the protestors talked past one another. This type of outreach was unusual for Nixon, who was never particularly comfortable in public settings, especially in impromptu, unscripted events, and much preferred to remain ensconced in his hideaway office in the Old Executive Office building, scribbling on his yellow legal pads with the air conditioning on and the fireplace crackling away, even on the warmest summer day.

Richard Nixon spent much of his time in front of the fireplace concocting ways to manipulate public opinion in his favor, primarily through divide-and-conquer tactics, and generating a false image of himself, often in some Kennedyesque pose, such as the time he walked on the beach at San Clemente, California, in his black wingtip shoes, failing miserably at his attempt to look like Jack Kennedy.[23] Of all of the forty-five individuals who have served as the nation's president, Nixon was the least comfortable in his own skin.

Nixon's aides worked doggedly to manufacture positive public expressions of support, including White House–sponsored letter writing campaigns from alleged private citizens, backing Nixon and attacking his critics.[24] At one point in 1972, Nixon ordered his chief of staff, H. R. Haldeman, to produce a fake poll showing Senator George McGovern in a strong position to challenge Nixon. "The best way to assure that we could win was to pick our opponent. We were much happier with McGovern than other possible foes," Haldeman observed.[25] To complement efforts such as this, a White House "dirty tricks" unit was deployed to destroy the public reputations of Nixon's more formidable foes, including Senator Edmund Muskie of Maine and Edward Kennedy of Massachusetts. The Nixon White House elevated the manufacturing of public opinion to an art form.

Richard Nixon was the target of the first serious impeachment since Andrew Johnson, a man who shared Nixon's obsession with his enemies and a resentment of his "betters" and practiced the politics of divisiveness. Nixon was an intellectual genius compared to Johnson but shared his fellow disgraced president's dyspeptic outlook on life. Neither of these men possessed a "first-class temperament," and in fact neither man was emotionally suited to be president. Both men carried far too many scars and wallowed in slights from the distant past.

Richard Nixon sullied the American presidency, and while his defenders are right to note that Franklin Roosevelt and Lyndon Johnson used the FBI as their private detective agency, Nixon abused his power in new and more dangerous ways. "I gave them a sword and they stuck it in and they twisted it with relish. And I guess if I had been in their position, I'd have done the same thing," he recalled in 1977.[26] Nixon left the presidency and the nation weaker than he found it, and the "White House horrors" that were exposed led to numerous restrictions enacted to rein in the "imperial presidency."

The damage Richard Nixon and Lyndon Johnson did to the American presidency stemmed in good measure from their deep character flaws. Johnson and Nixon squandered the remaining vestiges of respect for the presidency, in part due to their disregard for the rule of law, but also because they lacked the character, the self-discipline, the humility, that distinguished the nation's greatest presidents. Perhaps most importantly, they lacked the virtue of magnanimity. Nixon put it best on his last day in the White House: "Always remember, others may hate you, but those who hate you don't win unless you hate them, and then you destroy yourself."[27]

The Constitutional Presidency of Gerald Ford

Gerald Ford deserves more credit than he receives for stabilizing the nation after the "long national nightmare" of the Nixon presidency came to an end. Ford exemplified many of the same qualities of the preprogressive presidents, demonstrating an affinity for the founders' presidency that makes him something of a modern rarity. Ford never won an election outside of his congressional district centered in Grand Rapids, Michigan, becoming the first and only president to assume the office under the provisions of the Twenty-Fifth Amendment.

Ford became president on August 9, 1974, in a nation soured on the presidency and cynical about politics in general. His pardon of Richard Nixon a month after assuming the presidency cost him dearly in the public opinion polls but was nevertheless a courageous act designed to end the nation's focus on the Watergate scandal. Many members of Congress, the media, and the public wanted to see Richard Nixon frog-marched into a federal penitentiary, which, while somewhat understandable, would have further divided the country and perhaps even made Nixon a figure of sympathy. As it was, Ford found it difficult enough to govern in an atmosphere of distrust and heightened partisan differences. Congress was lopsidedly controlled by the Democratic Party in both the House and Senate, and on paper at least had the ability to override any Ford vetoes after January 1975.

Ford's task was complicated by his unwillingness to adopt one of the main tenets of the progressive presidency, that the president must offer a "vision" for the country. This was due in part to the fact that Ford had not campaigned for president and had no transition in which to formulate one. But he was also reluctant to package his administration as if it were a new consumer gadget, and mislead his fellow citizens, as many of his predecessors had, that it was his job to lead them into the promised land. As he recalled in his memoir, "If 'vision' is to be defined as inspirational rhetoric describing how this or that new government program will better the human condition in the next sixty days, then I'll confess I didn't have it."[28]

Ford still pays a price for the lack of the "vision thing," as George H. W. Bush referred to it, even among sympathetic biographers such as historian Douglas Brinkley, who operate under the assumption that the progressive presidency is a settled feature, a permanent aspect of the American constitutional order. According to Brinkley, Ford "didn't grasp, until it was too late, that the art of persuasion was the true essence of the modern presidency." Ford behaved "more like a Grand Rapids Rotarian leader" than "Theodore Roosevelt in the Bully Pulpit."[29] By 1975, the nation was overdosing on visions, some, such as Woodrow Wilson's, Franklin Roosevelt's, and Lyndon Johnson's, were utopian fantasies. What the nation needed was what Ford offered, which was stability, integrity, and a recalibration of what government could reasonably expect to accomplish.

Ford's embrace of the constitutional presidency has been brilliantly elucidated by Alex Hindman, who notes that Ford faced a level of "hostility and political opposition that few, if any, American presidents have had to face." Ford did not have "an electoral mandate, rhetorical skill, or the benefit of a presidential campaign to hone his policy agenda."[30] Under the standards of the progressive presidency, embraced by scholars and presidents alike, Ford was at a remarkable disadvantage in terms of his power to persuade, which was the linchpin of the modern presidency, and possessed precious little "personal political capital," which was also seen as a source of power by those who denigrated the importance of the founders' presidency.

Despite his political shortcomings, Ford was able to defend the presidency from congressional encroachments due to the system created by the founders, and thereby preserve the constitutional presidency. As Hindman notes, "Gerald Ford occupied an office empowered with all of the constitutional authorities of the 1787 Constitution" even during a time, like Ford's, when "a president's personal popularity or the popularity of his office is at its lowest ebb." The office retains, assuming the incumbent is willing to accept the challenge, as Ford was, the power to endure "even the most hostile of public moods." The constitutional presidency, as we have seen, was designed to "remain extraordinarily resilient in the face of changing popular moods and public opinion."[31]

The main constitutional weapon Ford utilized to resist congressional encroachments on the presidency was the veto power. To use this tool as frequently as Ford did in his relatively brief 895 days places him in a unique category among American presidents. Ford exercised the veto 66 times, with 12 of his vetoes overridden, a 75 percent success rate, placing him in the top ten of American presidents in terms of numbers of vetoes.[32] Many of these vetoes were designed to check what Ford believed to be excessive spending, but others were cast in defense of the president's Article Two powers.

In 1975, Congress took to steps to expand its management of the nation's intelligence community and restrict presidential authority over clandestine operations. Many of these proposed reforms would have fundamentally altered the ability of the president to act with secrecy and speed. This had been the historical norm since George Washington had requested a secret service fund in his first annual message to Congress in 1790. Reasonable concessions were made by President Ford in light of reports of domestic intelligence operations of questionable legality, along with revelations of assassination plotting by Dwight Eisenhower and John F. Kennedy and other controversial Cold War–era operations. Ford, again relying on his constitutional mandate, not a popular mandate, fended off the most extreme proposals, including one which would have prohibited the use of any covert operations by the American government.[33] In the end, Ford, as Alex Hindman observes, defended the president's foreign intelligence powers "against adverse public opinion and the intrusion of the other branches."[34]

Ford also defended the foreign policy and war powers prerogatives of the presidency granted by the Constitution. Events of his brief presidency led him to conclude, rightly, that "foreign policy made by Congress can be short-sighted, fickle, and prone to domestic faction."[35] Ford's decisive action in ordering the rescue of the crew of the American merchant ship *Mayaguez,* seized by the Khmer Rouge off the coast of Cambodia, and his evacuation of American personnel and Vietnamese refugees when South Vietnam collapsed, appeared to violate the provisions of the War Powers Act. Assuming his constitutionally mandated powers as commander in chief, Ford acted in the absence of congressional leadership and a desire on the part of Congress to wash its hands of any responsibility for actions in Southeast Asia. On the one hand, Congress sought to micromanage foreign policy, but at the same time it did not wish to assume overall responsibility for risky actions. Ford responded in a Hamiltonian manner, serving as an "energetic" executive capable of acting with "decision, activity, secrecy, and dispatch." As Hindman notes, Ford made it clear he was "prepared to act with or without" the support of Congress and the American people.[36]

Unlike his two immediate predecessors, Gerald Ford was a magnanimous man. He did the best he could in hyperpartisan times to govern from the center and to act in a simple but dignified manner. Ford never won an election outside of Michigan's Fifth District and yet he understood that he was now responsible for governing the entire nation—he was now chief of state. Furthermore, Ford did not hold the kind of grudges that undid Richard Nixon; in fact, he rarely disparaged others. One of his speechwriters later recalled that only on two occasions did he hear Ford speak ill of others, and "the worst he would say about someone was, 'he's a bad man.'"[37] Ford's native honesty, humility, and simplicity stood in marked contrast to Nixon and Johnson, both tortured souls who deigned to afflict others with their "issues."

Perhaps most importantly, Gerald Ford proved that a chief executive can defend the office of the presidency and not be a demagogue, and that a strong president does not have to pander to public opinion. A president can be rhetorically challenged, lack Franklin Roosevelt's bond with the public, and still govern effectively. As Alex Hindman notes, Gerald Ford "remains overlooked by many scholars of the presidency" even though "his time in office serves as an archetype for how presidents can successfully marshal" the constitutional powers of their office.[38]

Jimmy Carter: "Feeling Your Pain"

Gerald Ford lost the presidency in a close race with former Georgia Governor Jimmy Carter, an insurgent candidate most Americans would have been unable to identify just months before he secured his party's nomination. Carter was not the choice of party leaders, but his campaign effectively tapped into the public's hope to eradicate the cynical politics of Richard Nixon. Ford's courageous pardon of Nixon was used against Ford to great effect as accusations were leveled of a corrupt bargain, a quid pro quo, where Nixon would step aside and give Ford the presidency in exchange for a pardon. In the cynical atmosphere of post-Watergate America, this conspiratorial version of events was widely accepted.

Carter ran as an incorruptible Sunday school teacher who pledged to abolish depravity in government, promising an administration that was "as good and honest, decent, truthful, and competent, and compassionate, and as filled with love, as are the American people."[39] Carter promised to be a president "who feels your pain, and who shares your dreams and who draws his strength and his wisdom from you."[40] Feeling the public's pain, as Carter vowed to do, would later become the mantra of the Clinton presidency, and captures the essence of the popular presidency.

Carter launched his campaign with a simple pledge, "I'm Jimmy Carter and I'm running for President. I will never lie to you," adding that he would drain the swamp created by the Nixon-Ford administration. Carter also capitalized on his "outsider" status, boasting that "I haven't been part of the Washington scene" to a nation sickened by years of Vietnam and Watergate. Those national disgraces "could have been avoided if our government had simply reflected the . . . high moral character of the American people."[41] Carter made this claim even though the people had given Lyndon Johnson and Richard Nixon two of the largest electoral landslides in history, and that substantial numbers of Americans supported the war in Vietnam, many to the bitter end.

Carter's religious beliefs animated his presidential campaigns as well as his policy choices as chief executive. He claimed in 1976 that "I can be a better president because of my faith."[42] As one observer commented, "far from being coy or retiring about his values, Carter placed them on the table for all to see. He planned to corner the market on morality and beat the Republicans senseless with it."[43] Lest some members of the public found him to be a bit "holier than thou," Carter arranged for an interview with *Playboy* magazine to confess that "I've committed adultery in my heart many times. . . . Christ says, 'Don't consider yourself better than someone else because one guy screws a whole bunch of women while the other guy is loyal to his wife.'"[44]

Carter portrayed himself as a common man, selling the presidential yacht *Sequoia*, wearing cardigan sweaters in the Oval Office, carrying his own luggage on to *Air Force One*, dispensing with "Hail to the Chief" during public events, hosting a nationally broadcast call-in show where the public could ask him questions (one questioner wanted to know if the president would considering flying on a space shuttle mission), staying in the homes of private citizens on trips around the country, and inviting large numbers of average Americans to state dinners at the White House.[45]

Carter was committed to openness and transparency, but to an extent that eroded the dignity of his office. His White House announced in 1979 that the president was suffering from a severe case of hemorrhoids, leading Egyptian President Anwar Sadat to ask the world to pray for the president's relief. Twice in his post-presidency, Carter chose to discuss his battle with hemorrhoids, and also recounted a case of Montezuma's revenge he suffered in Mexico, an affliction he referred to in a toast to the president of that nation.[46]

The Carter presidency was thoroughly Jacksonian in its commitment to dispensing with anything that sniffed of elitism. Perhaps no modern president praised the public as much as Carter, and perhaps no modern president was as disappointed when the public appeared to turn against him. Carter's famous 1979 malaise speech (it should be noted that he never used the word "malaise") was seen by many as Carter scolding the public for not seeing things the way he did. But on the other hand, the speech was an act of courage for a president who, until that time, had nothing but praise for the American public. Carter noted that the nation was suffering from a "crisis of confidence." The problems confronting the nation were spiritual, in part, resulting from a widespread cultural decay: "It is a crisis that strikes at the very heart and soul and spirit of our national will. We can see this crisis in the growing doubt about the meaning of our own lives and in the loss of a unity of purpose for our Nation. The erosion of our confidence in the future is threatening to destroy the social and the political fabric of America." Carter expressed confidence that the American public could "conquer the crisis of the spirit" that afflicted the nation.[47]

Tellingly, Carter's vice president, Walter Mondale, warned the president not to deliver this address, arguing "you can't castigate the American people or they will turn you off once and for all."[48] But Mondale was a firm believer in the promise of the progressive presidency and of the ability of government to deal with any problem. Mondale would later claim that it was the role of government to assist "the sad."[49]

Jimmy Carter deserved credit for trying to govern from the center, much to the despair of some members of his party, and for arguing that there were limits to what government could do. But his administration also revealed the shortcomings of the popular presidency—that public opinion is fickle, that you can live or die on the allegiance of the public in remarkably rapid fashion, and that in the end the public wants to look up to their president. Carter was a master of the intricacies of policy but belatedly discovered that the president must also serve as the nation's head of state.

A Conservative Camelot

Carter's 1980 opponent, former California Governor Ronald Reagan, appreciated the head-of-state role and played it to the hilt. In some ways Reagan's victory over Jimmy Carter represented the triumph of elements of the progressive presidency being adopted by the Republican Party, in that Reagan was something of an outsider or insurgent, a candidate embraced more in the hinterlands than in the nation's power centers, and a man who understood the power of television better than any of his rivals. Reagan was a well-known B-list movie star and host of television's *Death Valley Days,* and was a natural on radio, a medium he used to great effect as president with his weekly Saturday radio addresses.

Reagan's transition from Hollywood to politics began with a remarkably successful televised address on behalf of Barry Goldwater during the latter's 1964 presidential campaign. Popular reaction to "the speech," later known as A Time for Choosing, led a group of wealthy Californians to persuade Reagan to challenge Governor Pat Brown in 1966 for governor of the Golden State. Reagan's speech was one of the few highlights from an otherwise dismal Goldwater campaign. The Goldwater campaign was arguably one of the least media-savvy campaigns of modern times, although in some ways this was intentional, in that Goldwater and his supporters did not care what the media, "the liberal media," thought of them. Goldwater was later quoted as saying that he would not have voted for himself in 1964 if he believed everything that had been written or broadcast about him.[50]

The success of "the speech" was partly attributed to the low expectations set by the feckless Goldwater campaign. Desperate to find a silver lining, conservatives, and some members of the news media, latched onto "the speech" as the one Republican highlight of 1964. As television began to transform presidential campaigns into spectacles of superficiality, Ronald Reagan emerged as the ideal candidate for a media-saturated nation. Looking toward the future, the GOP needed a star with hints of Kennedy glamor, including good teeth and hair, which had become the gold standard of American politics. Reagan had the teeth and the hair, and he was comfortable, arguably even at home, in front of the camera. Reagan would later observe near the end of his presidency, "There have been times in this office when I've wondered how you could do this job if you hadn't been an actor."[51]

This is not to suggest that Reagan was somehow superficial. He was an avid reader of current events and a devoted subscriber to *National Review* and *Human Events* and other conservative publications. A former New Deal Democrat, Reagan had undergone a gradual but steady conversion to the GOP through the 1950s, in part due to the enormous tax burden he faced as a well-compensated Hollywood star, but also due to his disgust with Communist attempts to infiltrate the Screen Actors Guild in the late 1940s and early 1950s, when he served as the guild's president.

Reagan was the favorite of the conservative wing of the Republican Party and the darling of the survivors of the Goldwater debacle. Reagan learned an important lesson from Goldwater's campaign—that snarling conservatism frightens American voters and that a sunny disposition is the only effective method of delivering a conservative message to a nation devoted to progress and the pursuit of happiness. Reagan was a genuinely happy and genial person, and his sunny optimism served him well in his contest with the dour Jimmy Carter. Ironically, Reagan was fond of quoting the least conservative member of the founding generation, Thomas Paine, that "we have it in our power to begin the world over again," which was altogether fitting for the perpetual optimist from Dixon, Illinois.[52]

Reagan devoted a remarkable amount of time as president to his speeches and was proud of his editorial skills, a talent that some of his speech writers admired as well.[53] Reagan considered speeches to be central to successful governing, and his eloquent public addresses were matched only in modern times by John F. Kennedy. His speeches celebrating the exploits of the boys who took the cliffs at Pointe du Hoc on D-Day or commemorating the lives of those lost in the Challenger disaster, or his tribute to John F. Kennedy delivered in front of the assassinated president's widow and children, were examples of the types of speeches expected of a head of state.[54]

Reagan was also a remarkably magnanimous man, a man who operated utterly without guile, and who seldom attacked his opponents. The man did not have a vicious bone in his body, contrary to all strained comparisons to Donald Trump. Reagan's first-class temperament matched that of his hero,

Franklin Roosevelt. He rejected the politics of personal destruction and was repulsed by cynicism, believing that the narrative of America was a narrative of heroic deeds. While he was no fan of the federal government, Reagan never viewed his opponents as un-American or as less patriotic or public-spirited than himself. Reagan serves as a reminder in these hyperpartisan and divisive times that there is an alternative vision of American politics that does not view it as blood sport.[55]

Unfortunately, Reagan had a tin-ear when it came to matters of race. Reagan was not a racist, not the least in the same league as Andrew Johnson or Woodrow Wilson. But his gratuitous remarks regarding Dr. Martin Luther King, that King may have been a Communist, did little to improve race relations, and represented a rare breach of Reagan's reputation as a man of civility. He pledged early in his first term to continue meeting with the African American leaders, including the Congressional Black Caucus, but he stopped the practice after some leaders strongly criticized him in the media. The caucus was dominated by Democrats but breaking off discussions was an odd strategy for a president who stated on numerous occasions that he wished for a dialogue. True presidential leadership requires rising above the hurt the president says he felt from being called a racist and reaching out with conciliatory actions. Legislation creating a national holiday for Martin Luther King was just such an occasion, but Reagan besmirched the occasion by implying that King was a Communist when asked if he would sign the legislation.[56]

Reagan also demonstrated a capacity for obtuseness regarding racial issues when he opened his 1980 campaign in the county in Mississippi where three civil rights workers were murdered in 1964; a simple expression of sympathy or an acknowledgment of the event was not forthcoming. Instead, Reagan made a pitch for states' rights. His 1980 platform was notable for the absence of even the most generic language paying tribute to his party's historic role in civil rights for African Americans.[57] Sadly, the party of Lincoln, and of the Thirteenth, Fourteenth, and Fifteenth Amendments to the Constitution, appeared to have swapped roles with the party of states' rights and Jim Crow. One could reasonably disagree with policies such as affirmative action or the Great Society's welfare programs, but the subtle and not so subtle messages sent by the Republican Party's Southern strategy, which began with Barry Goldwater and accelerated under Richard Nixon, required an abandonment of principle and a betrayal of the party's founding fathers. This was yet another casualty of the presidency of popular consent, where winning a majority of votes in the South and in parts of the North demanded this betrayal. Reagan should have been above this.

There was also a superficial quality to some aspects of the Reagan presidency that were driven by a White House focused on "spin." One prominent member of the president's "troika" of top advisors, Michael Deaver, served as guardian of the Reagan image and arranged for photo opportunities that were as staged as anything that came out of the Kennedy White House. Nancy Reagan allegedly vetoed the selection of certain personnel due to their appearance, including longtime Reagan associate Lyn Nofziger and former Nixon administration official William Casey. They were denied these roles because they did not "look the part." Nancy Reagan also intervened on matters related to President Reagan's schedule based on her astrologer's advice, while Reagan himself had developed an odd relationship with the "psychic" Jeane Dixon.[58] The Reagan White House was in many ways Hollywood transported to the Potomac, with its attendant wackiness and obsession with generating positive media, something all presidents care about, but some far more than others, and unhealthily so.

There appeared to be a constant struggle for Reagan's soul throughout his eight years in office, as he was pulled in conflicting directions between Michael Deaver and Nancy Reagan's advice that he follow the shifting current of public opinion more closely, and those advisors like Edwin Meese and William Clark who fought to "let Reagan be Reagan" and adhere to his conservative principles. Reagan sometimes succeeded in blending those two currents in a coherent manner, at other times, less so, lending an air of disarray to his administration. But Reagan restored some faith in the office of the presidency, reversing a trend that began in the Carter years when many political scientists, journalists, and practitioners called for a radical overhaul of the office. One of those calling for a massive overhaul was Carter's White House counsel, who argued for the adoption of a parliamentary system in the United States.[59]

By the end of Reagan's eight years in office those calls were gone. It is the height of irony that Reagan, who came in to office arguing that government was not the solution, but was in fact the problem, restored to some degree the public's confidence in the federal government. There also seemed to be a marked improvement in national pride between 1981 and 1989, which is at least partly attributable to Reagan's deft use of the ceremonial and symbolic role of the presidency. Reagan proved, once again, that the chief of state can play a vital role in binding the nation together. Throughout the history of the American presidency, there has been a proverbial struggle between Jeffersonian simplicity and high-toned Hamiltonianism in terms of presidential "style," and Reagan clearly preferred the latter with his proclivity for presidential pageantry. In the end, Reagan convinced many skeptical conservatives to embrace elements of the popular presidency they had once opposed.

"The Vision Thing"

Ronald Reagan was the first president since Martin Van Buren succeeded Andrew Jackson in 1837 to see his vice president immediately follow him in office. George H. W. Bush, however, wasted no time in separating himself from Reagan in one of the frostier transitions in the nation's history between two camps from the same party. The ruthlessness of the transition would have pleased the Borgia family. Reagan's secretary of defense noted that Secretary of State George Shultz "was dealt better than I was. At least he got a call from the president-elect." Reagan's friend Senator Paul Laxalt recalled, "The Bush people . . . did not treat the Reagan people well." And he added, "they were just brutal. . . . it was get-even time."[60]

Bush pledged in his inaugural address to work for a "kinder" and "gentler" America, a none-too-subtle slap at Reagan. Bush walked away from Reagan's legacy as fast as he could, which cost him in his race for reelection in 1992. He initially ran on Reagan's semi-populist platform, pledging at the 1988 Republican National Convention, "Read my lips: No new taxes," an irresponsible pledge that he broke shortly thereafter.[61] But Bush failed at playing the populist because he was not a populist. He professed a love for pork rinds and country music, but this son of a wealthy United States senator and Yale graduate simply could not make himself into something he wasn't, although success in the popular presidency demanded that he do so.[62]

George H. W. Bush was by all accounts a genial man whose gestures of personal kindness were noted by friends and adversaries alike. But the politics of the popular presidency required ruthlessness, which Bush contracted out to Roger Ailes and Lee Atwater, with the latter serving as Bush's campaign manager. Atwater raised dirty campaigning to an art form, including the use of "push-polls," fake surveys of public opinion designed to manufacture the "correct" opinions. Atwater learned the tricks of the trade in campaigns in

South Carolina with candidates like Strom Thurmond where the race card was routinely played against Democratic opponents. Atwater destroyed one opponent by leaking the fact that the man had been treated for depression with electroconvulsive therapy as a teenager. Atwater told reporters that the opponent got "hooked up to jumper cables."

In 1988 Atwater's tactics succeeded in portraying Massachusetts Governor Michael Dukakis as a liberal, which he was, although Dukakis preferred to avoid that label and run as a somewhat nonideological, "competent" administrator. Atwater pledged to "strip the bark off the little bastard" and "make Willie Horton his running mate." Horton was a criminal who was furloughed from prison in Massachusetts and who proceeded to rape and torture a couple. Atwater's team played the mental illness card against Dukakis as well, allegedly circulating rumors that the candidate suffered from serious depression.[63] These "negative campaigning" tactics were not invented by Atwater and the Republicans; in fact many participants in the 1988 campaign were intimately familiar with Lyndon Johnson's devastating Daisy Girl television ad, which ran once, which was enough to suggest that Barry Goldwater supported incinerating little girls with nuclear weapons while they were picking daisies.

George H. W. Bush's campaign for president was one of the ugliest and most demagogic campaigns in contemporary American politics and serves as a significant blemish on an otherwise remarkable career. Bush did, however, draw a firm line between campaigning and governing, and conducted himself as president in a bipartisan and statesmanlike manner. The nation would benefit from a restoration of Bush's high wall of separation between campaigning and governing, putting an end to the permanent campaign "war rooms" operating out of the White House.

Bush brought an impressive background to the presidency: congressman, ambassador to the United Nations, Republican Party chairman, envoy to the People's Republic of China, director of the Central Intelligence Agency, and vice president of the United States. He seemed to know everyone on the planet and had close relationships with many world leaders. These relationships contributed to Bush's deft management of the collapse of the Soviet Union and the First Gulf War. Like many contemporary presidents, Bush preferred dealing with foreign policy over domestic matters, a preference that would come to haunt him in his bid for re-election in 1992.

He was also always haunted by the accusation that he lacked a "vision" for the nation even though this was never part of the president's job description from 1789 to 1912. The "vision thing," as Bush put it in his usual ineloquent way, was a contributing factor in his loss in 1992 to Governor Bill Clinton of Arkansas, whose campaign "vision" was "it's the economy, stupid."

The War Room

Governor Clinton ran an effective campaign in 1992 in a three-man field against Bush and Texas businessman H. Ross Perot, a billionaire populist. Clinton was a skilled politician who moved his party to the center and became the first Democrat in almost fifty years to win a second term. Clinton did well on television, possessed a Kennedy-like mastery of detail, and could be remarkably charming. One key event in the 1992 campaign that revealed the power of television occurred when President Bush was caught glancing at his watch during a debate with Clinton and Perot. The president, it seemed to some, was either anxious to conclude the debate or was simply bored with it all. Television, particularly in its around-the-clock cable incarnation, had elevated "gotcha" journalism to high art.[64]

Bill Clinton presided over the end of the Cold War and delivered surpluses in the federal budget from 1998 through 2001, with the assistance of a Republican-controlled Congress. The American economy also performed robustly throughout much of his two terms in office, but Clinton's presidency will always be scarred by the fact that he was only the second American president to be impeached (Andrew Johnson was the first; Richard Nixon resigned before his expected impeachment). Clinton was accused of lying under oath in a sexual harassment lawsuit brought by a former Arkansas state employee, Paula Jones. The alleged harassment had occurred while Clinton was governor of Arkansas. Many Republican activists considered Clinton to be an illegitimate president and supported efforts by Jones and others to undermine the president's standing in the courts and in the court of public opinion.

A unanimous Supreme Court in the case of *Clinton v. Jones* (1997) sided with Jones and ruled that the president was not immune from these types of lawsuits while serving as chief executive. It was a misguided decision, but its unanimity added to its weight, and the president was forced to provide testimony in the Jones lawsuit, which he did after being administered an oath by a federal judge. During this testimony the president was asked if he had engaged in an affair with a young White House intern, Monica Lewinsky. Paula Jones's attorneys were attempting to establish a pattern on Clinton's part of soliciting sex from underlings. Clinton denied having an affair with Lewinsky.[65]

This later proved to be untrue, and it provided an independent counsel, Kenneth Starr, an opening to expand his investigation beyond alleged financial improprieties by Bill and Hillary Clinton during their time in Arkansas. In August 1998 Clinton appeared by video link before Starr's grand jury and admitted to having relations with Lewinsky but denied having provided misleading testimony in his Jones deposition, claiming the questions were ill-framed and offering a somewhat jarring definition of what constituted sexual relations. Starr eventually released a report of the president's alleged misdeeds and forwarded it to the House of Representatives.

The report was filled with graphic descriptions of Clinton and Lewinsky's trysts. The lurid report redounded to Clinton's benefit, with a somewhat stunned First Lady and congressional Democrats rallying to the president's defense. A party line vote in the House of Representatives saw two articles of impeachment pass; one charging the president with lying to the Starr grand jury regarding the Lewinsky case, the other charging the president with obstructing justice and suborning perjury. The Senate trial concluded on February 12, 1999, with Clinton acquitted on both counts, 45–55 on the lying charge, 50–50 on obstructing justice, well short of the two-thirds majority necessary for conviction.[66]

Clinton would later be held in civil contempt by the judge who presided over the Jones lawsuit for lying under oath. Judge Susan Webber Wright noted that Clinton had provided "false, misleading, and evasive answers that were designed to obstruct the judicial process." She fined the president $90,000 and referred him to the Arkansas Supreme Court for disbarment. Meanwhile, Kenneth Starr's successor Robert Ray struck a deal with Clinton's lawyers on the president's last full day in office, where Clinton's license to practice law was suspended for five years and he agreed to pay a $25,000 fine. In this agreement, the president admitted that he "knowingly gave evasive and misleading answers" in the Jones case.[67]

The president's constitutional obligation to take care that the laws be faithfully executed had been violated by the president, initially in a sexual harassment case which grew out of the adoption of laws Clinton supported. While Jones was put up to filing a lawsuit by conservative activists behind the so-called Arkansas Project, nevertheless, the president did not handle this case in a manner becoming the presidency, or the rule of law.

Throughout this entire process, Clinton's White House engaged in a full-court public relations campaign to convince the public that there were no crimes involved, that the matter was simply one of consensual sex between adults. Additionally, Paula Jones, Kenneth Starr, Monica Lewinsky, the House impeachment managers, and reporters who investigated the matter were targeted both overtly and covertly for various character failings. Clinton's own appointee as director of the FBI was also subject to repeated White House criticism. Louis Freeh recalled in his memoir that one of Clinton's White House counsel's told him that the worst advice the president believed he had ever been given was to appoint Freeh as director. Freeh noted that he wore that "as a badge of honor." In his almost eight years as director, Freeh met with Clinton "at most three times." There was "always some new investigation brewing, some new calamity bubbling just below the headlines." Freeh added, "not only was he [Clinton] actively hostile toward me, he was hostile to the FBI generally."[68] This hostility would take a more overt form when one of Clinton's Oval Office successors chose to publicly air his grievances with the FBI.

The Clinton's celebrated "war room," which featured in a widely acclaimed 1993 documentary, was fully engaged in the campaign to undermine the Starr investigation. "There's going to be a war," said James Carville, Clinton's 1992 campaign strategist and unofficial White House advisor. A coordinated effort directed by the White House was "part of our continuing campaign to destroy Ken Starr," another official noted.[69] Clinton's defenders even resorted to raising the specter of Joe McCarthy, arguing that the president was a victim of "sexual McCarthyism."[70]

The First Lady was enlisted in this effort, claiming her husband was the target of a "vast right-wing conspiracy," which had an element of truth to it. But the effort required her, as former Clinton advisor George Stephanopoulos noted, "to do what she had always done before: swallow her doubts, stand by her man and savage his enemies."[71] "Savaging" women who accused Clinton of sexual improprieties was practiced not only by the Clintons but also by James Carville, who once observed about Paula Jones, "If you drag a hundred-dollar bill through a trailer park, you never know what you'll find."[72] Starr was also subject to withering attacks that turned public opinion against his investigation. Clinton survived "because he made Ken Starr the enemy," the president's pollster would later confess.[73]

Clinton would note in 2018, when asked if he should apologize to Monica Lewinsky, that "I dealt with it 20 years ago plus, and two-thirds of the

American people sided with me."[74] There is no more concise definition of the presidency of popular consent than this—the rule of law, as well as traditional standards of conduct, are irrelevant when popular opinion is on your side. The tactic of citing opinion polls and election results would be employed twenty years later by President Donald Trump in his conflict with Robert Mueller, the Justice Department appointee who led the investigation into possible collusion between the Trump campaign and Russian intelligence operatives.

As Clinton biographer John F. Harris observed, "We can now see the Clinton of the 1990s as a man far ahead of his times. Whose side are you on—mine or the people who want to destroy me—was the question that Clinton asked to successful effect in 1998. And it is the same question Donald Trump has made the basis of his presidency 20 years later."[75]

The Clinton White House raised presidential polling to new levels and used it to great effect to save Clinton's presidency. As political scientist George Edwards noted, "the Clinton administration is the ultimate example of the public presidency, one based on a perpetual campaign and fed by public opinion polls, focus groups, and public relations memos." Clinton's polling guru Dick Morris made a major contribution to saving Clinton's presidency by polling which phrases and which terms would allow him to prevail in the impeachment struggle, as Diane J. Heith has written. George Stephanopoulos noted that Morris "spoke to the part of Clinton that wanted to be told what to do." Stephanopoulos added, "at his moment of maximum peril, the president chose to follow the pattern of his past. He called Dick Morris. Dick took a poll. The poll said lie."

Essentially, polling by Morris and others indicated that Clinton could survive if he admitted to adultery but not obstruction of justice and perjury. If the public could be convinced that this was simply the case of adultery on the part of the president, "the public would resist impeachment and even resignation." After numerous fits and starts, Clinton adopted this approach, as Heith notes. She added, "The Clinton White House represents the epitome of a new style of governing that finds the continuous surveying of the public essential. . . . During Clinton's first term, public opinion was a tool to help Clinton achieve his goals via delicate coalition building. During his second term, public opinion was a tool to help Clinton remain in office."[76]

Alexander Hamilton, discussing impeachment in *Federalist* no. 65, assumed that "factions," "passions," and "animosities," would influence impeachment proceedings. But there was also an assumption on the part of the framers that somehow, through the impeachment process, the public interest would ultimately be served. It would require senators to put aside their "partialities" and examine whether a president engaged in "abuse[s] or violation[s] of some public trust."[77] President Clinton's triumph reveals the extent to which the founders' Constitution had been displaced not only by a presidency of popular consent, but an entire political order venerating popular opinion instead of the rule of law.

There are legitimate grounds to argue that Clinton's "evasive and misleading answers" under oath did not rise to the level of an impeachable offense. Sadly, due to the efforts of Clinton's perpetual "war room," this issue was never given the thoughtful deliberation it deserved. Emotion, partisan and otherwise, stoked by the White House, was the determining factor in saving the Clinton presidency. But Clinton's cynical campaign to save himself was yet another example of a president ignoring the line between his interests and that of the office he held. This practice has been a consistent and costly feature of the personalized presidency.

The editor in charge of the *Washington Post*'s scandal coverage, Susan Glasser, observed twenty years after the Clinton scandals broke, "I believe that Donald Trump has learned from and will take to heart the lessons of how Clinton survived politically the year 1998. It was political genius how he [Clinton] handled it by lying. Lying was proven to work in some way that has enabled further the cynical and divisive political culture of Washington."[78]

Historian William E. Leuchtenberg noted in 2015 that, "it did not seem possible that, with only twenty-four hours of his tenure remaining, Clinton could do anything further to tarnish his presidency, but he managed to pull it off." Clinton issued 177 pardons and commutations on January 20, 2001, including one to Marc Rich, a fugitive on the FBI's Ten Most Wanted List, and whose former wife, Denise Rich, made lucrative contributions to the Democratic National Committee, Hillary Clinton's campaign for the Senate in 2000, the Clinton's defense fund, the proposed Clinton presidential library, and spent thousands purchasing furniture for the Clinton's post-presidential home in New York. Additionally, Denise Rich paid ninety-six visits to the White House in the last two years of Clinton's presidency.[79] Clinton's pardon of a fugitive from justice was an act rarely undertaken by his predecessors.[80]

The president also pardoned his half-brother, Roger Clinton, and another pardon recipient turned out to have been represented by Hillary Clinton's brother, Hugh Rodham, who was paid $200,000 for his services, although Rodham returned the money after these payments were revealed. A federal investigation into the Rich pardon closed in 2005 without any charges being filed. This investigation was led for a time by James Comey, who, as FBI director, would later figure prominently in the investigation of the Trump campaign's possible links to Russia. In 2008, Comey wrote that he was "stunned" by the Rich pardon, although he chose not to pursue any charges due to insufficient evidence.[81] But internal FBI documents opened in 2016 noted that "it appears that the required pardon standards and procedures were not followed."[82]

A president, under the Constitution, has near carte blanche authority over federal pardons, and Clinton was within his authority to do what he did, but the process created over the decades by the Department of Justice to screen pardon and clemency applications was ignored in many of these cases, particularly in the Rich case. Clinton's last-minute-pardon spree reinforced an image of lawlessness, or at the very least revealed a kind of disregard for the prudence usually shown by presidents when exercising this extraordinary power. It was another Clinton legacy that would be cited by President Donald Trump's defenders twenty years later.

W.

The electoral imbroglio of 2000 between Texas Governor George W. Bush and Vice President Al Gore, in a time of relative peace and prosperity, was evidence of the deep partisan divisions left from the Clinton years. Bush lost the popular vote to Gore, although Bush ultimately became president after a Supreme Court decision put a halt to another recount in the state of Florida, thus putting Bush over the top in the electoral college. The cloud over Bush's presidency lifted, albeit briefly, in the aftermath of the attacks on September 11, 2001, when the nation experienced a moment of bipartisan unity, and Bush rose to the occasion with his powerful impromptu remarks in the rubble at ground zero and his remarks at Washington's National Cathedral.[83] These remarks served to point the nation to something higher, and to remind the citizenry of its shared heritage. During Major League Baseball's World Series in Yankee Stadium in 2001, Bush threw out the first pitch, which happened to be a strike, as the smoke still rose from the World

Trade Center a short distance away. This small gesture did much to boost the spirits of the beleaguered city of New York and of the nation at large, and proved once again that the president, when he chooses to act as head of state, can serve as a healing force in American life. When he chooses to "solidify the base" at the expense of the national interest, the entire country loses.

But the remainder of the Bush years were marked by intense partisan divisions, aggravated by his decision to invade Iraq and the failure to discover the large stockpiles of weapons of mass destruction the administration claimed were held by Saddam Hussein. George W. Bush recorded one of the highest job approval ratings in the history of the Gallup poll, 90 percent in September 2001, and one of the lowest, 25 percent in October 2008.[84]

Bush was confronted with an array of difficult decisions in the wake of the al-Qaeda attacks on the United States, which led to the greatest single-day loss of American life since the Battle of Antietam in 1862.[85] His exercise of executive power generated considerable opposition, at least after the danger from al-Qaeda seemed to subside. Both Bush and Vice President Dick Cheney pushed the nation's security entities to undertake extraordinary measures and did so in the tradition of many of their wartime predecessors, who had authorized the suspension of civil liberties, warrantless wiretapping, assassination, and innumerable domestic and foreign covert operations. Bush's approval of the use of torture on captured al-Qaeda members appeared to add a new chapter to the list of extraordinary presidential measures.

The legitimacy of Bush's actions in the War on Terror is beyond the scope of this book.[86] But ironically, in pressing the case for a broad interpretation of executive power, public trust in the presidency fell to its lowest level since the Watergate scandal, with 42 percent of the public claiming they had a "great deal" or a "fair amount" of trust, in contrast to 40 percent in 1974.[87]

This decline was due partly to the economic collapse of 2008 and the war in Iraq, but Bush also contributed to this decline by overpromising on what government could deliver. Bush embraced Woodrow Wilson's idea that self-government was a universal ideal, and that nations like Iraq and Afghanistan could be transformed into democracies. As a candidate in 2000, Bush promised a humble foreign policy and one that did not engage in nation building. However, events of September 2001 radicalized Bush and led him to abandon a more circumscribed foreign policy in favor of a Wilsonian foreign policy on steroids. While acknowledging that different "customs and traditions" existed around the globe, and that the success of this endeavor required the support of the citizenry of each nation, Bush announced that

> It is the policy of the United States to seek and support the growth of democratic movements and institutions in every nation and culture, with the ultimate goal of ending tyranny in our world. . . . The great objective of ending tyranny is the concentrated work of generations. The difficulty of the task is no excuse for avoiding it. America's influence is not unlimited, but fortunately for the oppressed, America's influence is considerable, and we will use it confidently in freedom's cause.[88]

Bush's commitment to worldwide democracy, and his ambiguous War on Terror, was as sweeping as any pledge made by his more progressive predecessors. "We will rid the world of the evildoers," Bush announced within a week of the September 11th attack, adding, "this administration . . . will do what it takes to rout terrorism out of the world."[89] The popular presidency habitually pledges more than it can deliver, and the presidency of George W. Bush was no exception.

There was another phenomenon that occurred during the Bush presidency that did not bode well for the future of the republic, and that was the embrace of bizarre conspiracy theories by the public. A survey taken in July 2006 found that 36 percent of Americans believed that the United States government assisted in the 9/11 attacks, or deliberately chose not to prevent the attacks. This was followed by a May 2007 survey which found that 35 percent of the nation's Democrats believed that Bush knew in advance of the 9/11 attacks.[90] Conspiracy theories have always been with us, but in the twenty-first century the Internet permitted conspiracy mongers to peddle their views in a sophisticated manner and disseminate them widely. This fact was not lost on Russian intelligence operatives, who would later exploit this opportunity to undermine public confidence in the American government and its electoral process.

The Transformational Presidency of Barack Obama

Barack Obama's election as the nation's first African American president was a genuinely historic moment in the history of the republic. It was especially notable that he won the office running as the nominee of a party that spent just shy of 150 years fighting to disenfranchise African Americans, or worse. Obama did not debase the presidency, as his successor did, but he did inflame passions by emphasizing the partisan presidency (he urged Hispanic American voters to adopt an attitude of "punish[ing] our enemies," although he later backtracked from the comment) at the expense of his role of head of state, and he continued the pattern of inflated presidential rhetoric that inevitably led to disappointment.[91]

Barack Obama was yet another candidate who was not the choice of party leaders. His rise to the presidency was meteoric, even by contemporary American standards. When he secured his party's nomination for president, he was only four years removed from his service in the Illinois State Senate and had only been in the United States Senate for two years before he began his race for president.[92] Obama appealed to the progressive belief that government could, and should, "fundamentally transform" American society, continuing in the tradition of Wilson and Roosevelt. Obama uttered one of the most extravagant claims ever made by a candidate when he clinched his party's nomination in 2008, noting that "this was the moment . . . when the rise of the oceans began to slow and our planet began to heal."[93] Candidate Obama vowed that he would preside over a "transformational presidency" that would "change the world."[94] During his 2008 race against Hillary Clinton, Obama remarked that the success of his movement "would make this time different than all the rest."[95] He was also fond of noting that he had a "limitless faith in the capacity of the American people."[96] In a speech to a group of evangelical Christians in South Carolina, Obama remarked "I am confident that we can create a kingdom right here on Earth."[97]

With rhetoric such as this, it was perhaps no surprise that Obama developed something of a cult-like following. The forty-fourth president possessed a healthy ego, as his authorship of two semi-autobiographical works prior to his election in 2008 indicated. His passionate supporters at rallies sometimes fainted while wearing shirts emblazoned with "The One" or "Jesus Was a Community Organizer."[98] A normally skeptical, secular media seemed at times to accept this version of an Obama from on high, including *Newsweek*, where one of its editors observed that "in a way, Obama's standing above the country, above—above the world. He's sort of God. He's going to bring all different sides together."[99] That same magazine's cover for its inaugural 2013 issue featured a photo of the president with the headline, "The

Second Coming," a line also used by the more scholarly journal *Foreign Policy* in its January 2013 edition.[100]

Additionally, Obama's use of social media continued the ongoing process of eroding what little dignity remained of the office. President Obama relied on social media to bond with voters, particularly younger voters, and while the man himself was quite dignified, there were actions he took that were beneath the dignity of the office. He appeared on the actor Zack Galifianakis's faux talk show *Between Two Ferns* on the website *Funny or Die.* (Galifianakis: "You said if you had a son, you would not let him play football. What makes you think he would want to play football? What if he was a nerd like you?") He granted interviews to social media "journalists," including one who was noted for filming herself lying in a bathtub filled with cereal that she ate. Another of the interviewers posted videos such as "How to Apologize without Being a Fartbag."[101] In another instance, the president filmed a video for *Buzzfeed* to promote the Affordable Care Act where he alternately posed in the mirror wearing sunglasses, made a series of funny faces, including sticking out his tongue, and walked around with a selfie stick striking various poses.[102]

Both the president and the First Lady danced with Ellen DeGeneres on her popular talk show, and the president appeared on the *Tonight Show* to "slow jam the news." In addition to *The Ellen Show* and the *Tonight Show,* Obama appeared on *The Daily Show, The Colbert Report, Real Time with Bill Maher, Full Frontal with Samantha Bee, Jimmy Kimmel Live!, The Late Show* with Stephen Colbert and David Letterman, *Anthony Bourdain: Parts Unknown, American Idol, MythBusters,* and *Running Wild with Bear Grylls.*

It is perhaps not surprising that a key figure in the Obama administration, Ben Rhodes, observed that he and other staff members watched the television show, *The West Wing,* to "mentally" prepare themselves to work in the White House. The Obama presidency witnessed a near complete blending of the presidency with the entertainment world, a development that the public appeared to welcome. As one of Obama's spokespersons observed, the public gets their news in a variety of ways, including "turning on *Entertainment Tonight* and seeing what the latest news is out there."[103]

Near the end of Barack Obama's presidency, more than 70 percent of the country claimed that the nation was more divided, or as divided, as it was in 2009. There were times when Obama demonstrated an absence of magnanimity, as when he rebuked the Supreme Court, some of whose members were seated in front of him, at his State of the Union address in January 2010. This unprecedented public rebuke made for dramatic television and would have pleased Andrew Jackson or Franklin Roosevelt, but it was beneath the dignity of the office and was further evidence of an erosion of respect for the principle of the separation of powers.

Race relations arguably worsened under President Obama due to a series of events involving police using excessive or deadly force against African Americans, which generated justifiable outrage around the nation.[104] Russian hackers also took advantage of the nation's openness to exploit America's racial divide, conducting a dry run for the 2016 presidential election. In one highly publicized incident, the case of Michael Brown in Ferguson, Missouri, investigators ultimately concluded that Brown had attempted to wrestle a gun from the police officer involved in the shooting. Some public figures rushed to judgment to conclude that the shooting was unwarranted before an investigation was completed. The president directly intervened in another incident involving the arrest of an African American professor in Cambridge, Massachusetts, where the president opined that the police had "acted stupidly," again, before all the facts were in. In both cases, the stories were more complicated than the initial reports indicated, and President Obama eventually admitted that he should have "calibrated those words differently."[105] Elected officials, particularly the president, are well advised to avoid rushing to judgment. But the popular presidency demands that presidents comment on the issues of the day, regardless of whether they have all the facts at hand. Deliberation is lost in the tyranny of the 24/7 news cycle, and in the constant din emanating from online.

The Obama presidency adeptly capitalized on the ability of the Internet to allow a president to reach the people in an unfiltered way. Part of their outreach effort included establishing a "We the People" webpage as part of the White House's website. After acquiring 150 signatures, a petition would be placed online, and if 100,000 signatures were posted within thirty days the administration was compelled to respond. The site was a culmination of the dreams of the architects of the popular presidency and led to petitions urging the prosecutions of forty-seven United States senators opposed to Obama's deal with the Islamic Republic of Iran, deporting specific individuals including an anchor for *Cable News Network*, establishing a legal system of judges on motorcycles "who serve as police, judge, jury, and executioner all bundled into one," and the building of a "death star" weapon derived from the movie *Star Wars.*[106]

It was a fitting coda to a two-hundred-year campaign designed to remove any filters between the president and the people and to elevate public opinion as the cornerstone of the American regime. Remarkably, the worst was yet to come, as a television reality-show star who promised to speak for the common man and who had mastered social media became the nation's forty-fifth president.

9

The Apotheosis of the Popular Presidency
Donald J. Trump

Assessing a president who recently left office is a precarious enterprise, but the risks are even greater when it comes to a president who is still in office. Partisan passions are heightened, information remains classified, media accounts are frequently incomplete, and the impact of his policies cannot be fully assessed until the passage of time. This has not prevented scholars with a partisan agenda from engaging in such a practice, as could be seen in the premature condemnations of Eisenhower's presidency by progressive scholars in the 1950s and 1960s. The Eisenhower example provides a cautionary note for those who are inclined to make hasty judgments about a presidency; in Ike's case it took decades before a balanced assessment of his presidency emerged.

Hamilton's Nightmare

With that disclaimer in mind, it does appear that the presidency of Donald J. Trump has hastened the office's descent into a media-saturated, cultish, hyperpartisan, public-opinion pandering enterprise. Trump is the logical culmination of a century of experimentation with the Wilsonian presidency. Alexander Hamilton began and ended the *Federalist Papers* by warning that demagogues represent the primary threat to republics. Having discarded this warning, along with Hamilton's principle that the people do not always reason right, proponents of the popular presidency gradually destroyed the institutional props as well as the norms and traditions designed to sustain, and restrain, the office. Trump is precisely the type of demagogue Hamilton and the other founders feared, and the pace at which Trump is continuing the process of destroying norms and traditions is truly breathtaking.

Trump is completing the task that was initially undertaken by Jefferson and Jackson, updated for the twentieth century by Wilson, and slightly repackaged by Franklin Roosevelt and Kennedy, and their successors. If presidents pursued progressive policies, scholars, the media, large segments of the public, and political practitioners were delighted with the popular presidency. It is only when "aberrations" like Nixon and now Trump emerged that sober second thoughts surface about the popular presidency. Having linked Nixon with Trump, it is important to note that Nixon brought real attributes to the office, including a grasp of world affairs that eludes Trump. And it is also important to recognize that Jefferson, Wilson, Roosevelt, and Kennedy would likely be horrified at the Trump presidency. The presidential predecessors who most closely resemble Donald Trump are Andrew Jackson and Andrew Johnson, the latter president closest of all. Johnson's vicious demagoguery, blind hatreds, and limited intellect disrupted the possibility for a more successful outcome of the post–Civil War era.

A complete account of the daily outrages emanating from the Trump White House would require a volume dwarfing Leo Tolstoy's *War and Peace*. What follows is thus a partial recitation of some of the president's statements and actions that have left much of the nation and the world in a state of shock.

Donald Trump was opposed by Republican Party leaders in part because he supported Democratic candidates for much of his life, although it would be a mistake to attribute any political principles to him at all. As with some of his more egregious populist peers, Trump dabbles in conspiracies theories, particularly those involving murder. He suggested that the father of one of his opponents in the Republican primaries of 2016 had assassinated President Kennedy and implied that Supreme Court Justice Antonin Scalia had been suffocated in his sleep.[1] He also suggested that a former member of Congress turned television host had murdered an intern who worked in the congressman's office.[2]

Trump was something of a spokesman for the "birther" movement that claimed that his presidential predecessor, Barack Obama, was born in Kenya, and he also argued that two of his primary opponents, Ted Cruz and Marco Rubio, were ineligible to run for president due to similar citizenship issues.[3] Echoing Noam Chomsky and Howard Zinn, Trump repeatedly raised the specter of a "criminal deep state" comprised of the nation's intelligence and law enforcement entities that covertly manipulate the American government.[4] Candidate Trump seemed to endorse the so-called 9/11 truther movement when he proclaimed that if he were elected, "you will find out who really knocked down the World Trade Center. Because they have papers in there that are very secret . . . But you will find out."[5] He also repeatedly suggested a link between vaccines and autism, a claim dismissed by nearly every reputable physician and researcher dealing with the disorder.[6]

One of the fundamental tenets of the progressive presidency is that the chief executive must marshal all the rhetorical skills at his disposal to move the nation. Trump has limited rhetorical skills but has mastered the art of weaponizing words. Trump uses these words to destroy opponents in the media and in the opposition party, as well as in law enforcement. He has also singled out corporations that irk him, including Amazon and Harley-Davidson, questioning their patriotism and threatening government retribution.[7] His words never inspire, but they effectively keep him in the limelight, all the while dividing Americans and fueling cynicism, encouraging citizens to belittle those who disagree with them, to reduce politics to the equivalent of an Internet food-fight. He has described people and places from the Third World as "shitholes" (or "shithouses" as some heard it) and repeatedly focuses on the threat presented by gang members from Central America who have illegally immigrated, or as he puts it, "infest[ed]" the United States. These gang members are "not people" but "animals."[8]

Trump did not begin the practice of weaponizing words, as any review of partisan newspapers dating back to the 1790s reveals. But by and large presidents prior to the twentieth century relied on surrogates to savage their opponents, although there were some exceptions to this norm. Pre-twentieth century, presidents generally confined personal attacks to private correspondence, a tradition which is sadly lost. Degraded by decades of both television talk shows and "shock" radio, which placed a premium on insults and ad hominem attacks, Trump is a representative man of his era. The former reality television star knows how to master the news cycle, a task made somewhat easier by his support from the entertainment wing of the conservative movement, including *Fox News*, Rush Limbaugh, Laura Ingraham, and Sean Hannity.

Trump has publicly defended the size of his penis and boosted in 2005 that his status as a star works "like a magnet. . . . I don't even wait. . . . When you're a star they let you do it. You can do anything. Grab them by the pussy. You can do anything."[9] On another occasion he noted "you know, it doesn't really matter what they write as long as you've got a young and beautiful piece of ass." All of the women on his reality television show "flirted with [him]—consciously or unconsciously. That's to be expected." Commenting on one of his 2016 Republican primary opponents, former Hewlett-Packard Chief Executive Officer Carly Fiorina, Trump observed, "look at that face! Would anyone vote for that? Can you imagine that, the face of our next president?" His narcissism knows no bounds, as when he observed that "part of the beauty of me is that I am very rich."[10]

He disparaged Senator John McCain's status as a prisoner of war during the Vietnam conflict by claiming "he's not a war hero. He was a war hero because he was captured. I like people who weren't captured."[11] Years earlier, Trump had boasted on talk radio that his own "Vietnam" consisted of avoiding sexually transmitted diseases, for which he should be given the Congressional Medal of Honor.[12] His irresistible attractiveness to women was matched by his remarkable Intelligence Quotient (IQ), which, as he put it to "losers and haters," was "one of the highest—and you all know it. Please don't feel so stupid or insecure, it's not your fault."[13] The president boasted of having a higher IQ than his secretary of state, who had been quoted as saying Trump was a "moron."[14]

On another occasion, the president referred to himself as "a very stable genius."[15] Despite his impressive intellect and his mastery of the English language, or as he put it, "I'm very highly educated, I know words, I have the best words," he was proud of his support from the "poorly educated," whom he loved and who loved him back.[16] He could, in fact, "stand in the middle of 5th Avenue and shoot somebody" without losing votes from his loyal base."[17] Trump has repeatedly claimed to know more than anyone else about taxes, trade, banking, building walls, infrastructure, jobs, debt, renewables, social media, the military, money, national defense, the visa system, and "the horror of nuclear."[18]

True to the Base

Donald Trump is everything critics of the popular presidency warned about—a demagogue who practices the "little arts of popularity," a man lacking the attributes of a magnanimous soul, a purveyor of conspiracy theories, and a president incapable of distinguishing between himself and the office he temporarily holds. On top of this, as former George W. Bush speechwriter Michael Gerson observes, Trump understands that "cynically exploiting fear is an art. And Trump is a Rembrandt of demagoguery."[19] The president panders to fears both real and imagined, boasts of himself as the answer to what ails the nation, and routinely overpromises. Trump pledged to build a "great wall" on the US southern border since "nobody build[s] walls better than me" and he would "make Mexico pay for that wall." He claimed that once he became president, among other things, "we're going to start saying 'Merry Christmas' again!"[20] Positive news is due to his exertions, negative news to those of his predecessors, although Trump did not invent this practice.

While many of Trump's policies are not that different from the policies his 2016 Republican primary challengers likely would have pursued, his insults and invectives, along with a complete disregard for his role as head of state, distinguish him from the rest of the field. Spewing insults had been part of Trump's celebrity repertoire, as when he took the occasion of the anniversary of the 9/11 attacks to post the following on Twitter: "I would like to extend my best wishes to all, even the haters and losers, on this special date, September 11th."[21] He also paid tribute again to the "haters and losers" on Thanksgiving 2013; Father's Day 2014; the Fourth of July 2014; Easter 2015; and Memorial Day 2015. While they are all jarring, Trump's wish for "a very happy Easter" to "haters and losers" indicates a complete lack of any religious sensibility.[22] The hope that Trump would abandon this type of invective upon becoming president turned out to be wishful thinking.

Trump's demagoguery exceeds that of any of his predecessors, again with the lone exception of Andrew Johnson, as he revealed in his endorsement of violence against hecklers and demonstrators. In one instance Trump encouraged a crowd to "knock the crap out of him [a heckler], would you? I promise you I will pay your legal fees." On another occasion, he noted, "the problem is no one wants to hurt each other anymore." Other similar comments about hecklers included "I'd like to punch him in the face," "I'll beat the crap out of [him]," and "maybe he should have been roughed up."[23] Like Andrew Johnson, Trump rejects the idea that he should behave in a dignified manner, arguing that "it's a lot easier to act presidential than to do what I do." At many of his rallies Trump mocks those who suggest that he should be more "presidential" by speaking in a monotone, which prompts considerable laughter: "And then you go, 'God bless you, and God bless the United States of America.'" He argues that his free-wheeling, slash-and-burn approach "is much more effective" at moving an audience.

Even an event such as the annual, highly nonpartisan Boy Scouts of America Jamboree was used by President Trump to praise himself and denigrate his opponents. Paeans to scouting and to the nation were overshadowed by attacks on an opponent defeated nine months earlier and by encomiums to his own accomplishments. At the jamboree, Trump threatened to fire his secretary of health and human services and told a meandering story about a man who "got bored with this life of yachts and sailing" and "lost all of his money." The down-on-his-luck ex-millionaire later ran into Trump at a cocktail party with "the hottest people in New York. . . . It was very sad."[24]

Another occasion where the president chose to forego the traditional role as head of state was at the Coast Guard Academy's 2017 commencement exercises, where Trump complained that he was treated "more unfairly" than any other American political figure.[25] The popular presidency encourages chief executives to "solidify the base" at the expense of his unifying role as head of state, and when this occurs, as it has increasingly over the past one hundred years, the nation loses. Trump is proud of his skill at energizing his base and dismissive of the importance of unifying the nation. When asked what he could do to bring the nation together, the first thing that came to mind was his "base": "our people are so incredible. You know, there's probably never been a base in the history of politics in this country like my base."[26]

True to form, Donald Trump's presidency is a nonstop celebration of the man himself. In June 2017, cabinet officers were asked in a meeting, in front of the media, to pay tribute to the president's leadership, producing a kind of groveling at the highest levels of the executive branch not seen since the days of Lyndon Johnson.[27] While the president's progressive forbears routinely overpromised on matters of policy, as has Trump, he has also inflated what is expected of the president even further by claiming that he draws the biggest crowds or delivers the greatest speeches, or accomplished more than any of his predecessors. After months of bullish growth in the stock market, Trump observed, "the reason our stock market is so successful is because of me. I've always been great with money." When pressed on the high number of unfilled posts in the Department of State, the president noted, "the one that matters is me. I'm the only one that matters."[28] Trump took credit for the fact that there were no fatalities on commercial airline flights in the United States in 2017, an accomplishment unrelated to his presidency.[29]

The first few days of Trump's presidency were devoted to embellishing the size of the crowd that attended the president's inauguration, with the White House claiming, inaccurately, "that was the largest audience to witness an inauguration, period."[30] Even mundane items such as the commander in chief's "challenge coin" has been modified to suit what appears to be Trump's massive but fragile ego. Trump was apparently personally involved in designing the coin, which serves as a presidential memento and is frequently exchanged on visits to military bases. The changes made in 2017 included replacing the presidential seal with an eagle bearing Trump's signature, the removal of the national motto "E Pluribus Unum" (Out of Many, One), with Trump's campaign slogan, Make America Great Again, which appears on both sides of the coin. Trump's name is mentioned three times on the coin and the silver and copper metals used in the past have been replaced by gold.[31]

On another occasion, the president boasted that he drew bigger crowds than the performer Elton John, and revealed a mixture of incoherence and narcissism without equal in the history of the presidency:

> I have broken more Elton John records, he seems to have a lot of records. And I, by the way, I don't have a musical instrument. I don't have a guitar or an organ. No organ. Elton has an organ. And lots of people helping. No we've broken a lot of records. We've broken virtually every record. Because you know, look, I only need this space. They need much more room. For basketball, for hockey and all of sports, they need a lot of room. We don't need it. We have people in that space. So we break all of these records.[32]

Trump's 2016 Democratic opponent, former Secretary of State Hilary Clinton, "crooked" Hillary Clinton according to Trump, ran an ineffective campaign and was carrying baggage, fair or not, from her husband's scandals, her use of private email servers as secretary of state, and from questions raised about the Clinton Foundation. Trump frequently spoke before cheering crowds chanting "lock her up," which became something of an unofficial campaign slogan. In November 2016 Trump lost the popular vote but became president due to his win in the electoral college, the fifth time this had occurred in American history. More than a year after his victory over Hillary Clinton, Trump was still calling for a criminal investigation of the former secretary of state, whom he referred to as "the worst (and biggest) loser of all time."[33]

The Rule of Law

Trump and his surrogates were the subject of an investigation into allegations of collusion with Russia during the 2016 campaign. On various occasions he labeled the inquiry as a "witch hunt," a "total hoax," and a "phony cloud" that "makes the country look very bad."[34] And he lambasted his own attorney general for recusing himself in this investigation and criticized the deputy attorney general and the special counsel, Robert Mueller, a Republican of long standing. He has also encouraged prosecutions of his political opponents, including the former chairwoman of the Democratic National Committee. These public calls, directed at the Department of Justice, are unparalleled in the history of the presidency.[35] Trump's actions make Richard Nixon appear to be a champion of the rule of law, particularly when he calls for jailing his 2016 opponent, or urges stiff sentences for those who have testified against him or for the prosecution of their relatives.[36]

The public relations campaign Trump directed against Robert Mueller was somewhat unique, and only equaled in modern times by a campaign conducted against Kenneth Starr during Bill Clinton's presidency. Clinton generally used surrogates to denigrate Starr's investigation, for the most part, while Trump chose to directly intervene, primarily through social media.

Trump's repeated use of Twitter as a vehicle to make pronouncements on policy, personnel, and a wide array of matters unrelated to the presidency has strained the judicial branch, which frequently must decide whether to abide by challenges in a variety of court cases to force the government to turn over information supporting the president's contentions. In many of these cases, the courts have ruled that the president's tweets are "speculation" and the government is not required to turn over the relevant information.[37] The judiciary itself has been the subject of Trump's attacks, and while there are persuasive arguments to be made that the judicial branch has overstepped its bounds in a number of areas, Trump's objections frequently revert to demeaning comments about individual judges. This sets him apart, although not entirely, from his populist forbears including Jefferson, Jackson, and Franklin Roosevelt. Those three made strident attacks against the federal judiciary, but not as fervently as Trump. Trump questioned the impartiality of one judge due to his "Mexican heritage," in a separate case criticized an "Obama judge" who ruled against his administration, and in another instance referred to a federal judge as a "so-called judge."[38]

Trump's approach to manipulating public opinion and his contempt for the rule of law was shaped by Roy Cohn, a former aide to Senator Joseph McCarthy and a longtime Manhattan attorney known for his "no holds barred" approach to defending his clients. Trump met Cohn in a Manhattan nightclub in 1973 and the two maintained a professional and personal relationship until Cohn's death in 1986. Trump stood by Cohn even after the latter was disbarred for unethical conduct shortly before he died.[39] A former assistant United States attorney for the Southern District of New York described Cohn as a master of "the art of the smear, the lie, and the counterattack. . . . As Cohn later wrote, 'people are bored; they want entertainment.'"[40]

Entertainment was the vehicle by which both Cohn and Trump enhanced their status in a media-saturated New York City perpetually in search of a new spectacle. Cohn was also an advocate for never apologizing, which is President Trump's position as well, no matter how egregiously wrong he is on a factual matter or how insulting he can be to a disabled reporter or to prisoners of war. Asked whether he believes in the importance of apologizing, the president responded, "I think apologizing's a great thing, but you have to be wrong. I will absolutely apologize, sometime in the hopefully distant future, if I'm ever wrong."[41]

Following his highly publicized summit in Singapore with North Korean Dictator Kim Jung Un in 2018, Trump expressed optimism regarding the prospects for successful negotiations. But when pressed on whether he might be wrong, he noted, "I mean I may stand before you in six months and say, 'Hey I was wrong.' I don't know that I'll ever admit that, but I'll find some kind of an excuse."[42] The results of the negotiations appeared to be a secondary concern for Trump; the success of the summit could be found in the fact that "they have 1,000 cameras at the Oscars and we had 6,000 cameras in Singapore. The buzz was fantastic."[43]

Trump frankly acknowledged his manipulation of the public and the media in his book *The Art of the Deal* (1987):

> The final key to the way I promote is bravado. I play to people's fantasies. People may not always think big themselves, but they can still get very excited by those who do. That's why a little hyperbole never hurts. People want to believe something is the biggest and the greatest and the most spectacular. I call it truthful hyperbole. It's an innocent form of exaggeration—and a very effective form of promotion.

It is precisely this combination of hyperbole, bravado, and viciousness that sets the Trump presidency apart from almost all of its predecessors. Trump has completed the transformation of the American presidency into the voice of the people, or at least the people who voted for him, and in return he tells these people what they want to hear in the most bombastic language ever used by an American president, save Andrew Johnson.

A Reality-Show Presidency

It is difficult not to conclude that the Trump administration is the nation's first reality-show presidency. According to the *New York Times*, this is precisely the presidency Trump wants: "Before taking office, Mr. Trump told top aides to think of each presidential day as an episode in a television show in which he vanquishes rivals."[44] Trump often praises his "performances" and their positive "reviews," and at one point in his presidency he greeted reporters in his "studio" in the White House.[45] In 2018 he alerted the media and the public that he was about to sign an agricultural bill by tweeting out a video of himself singing the theme song from the 1960s television show, *Green Acres.*[46] Trump described a meeting he held at the Department of Defense as "a meeting . . . with lots of generals. They were like a movie. Better looking than Tom Cruise, & stronger. And I had more generals than I've ever seen."[47]

As of this writing, the reality-show presidency proceeds apace, with Trump threatening publicly to fire various cabinet officers and advisors, dominating the news cycle with inflammatory tweets, and inviting other reality-show stars to advise him on public matters, including Kim Kardashian West, who made a highly publicized visit to the White House to plea for a pardon for an individual convicted for drug violations and also to lobby for prison reform.[48] Trump hired one of his reality show costars, Omarosa Manigault, whom he had fired three times from his show, *The Apprentice,* for a position in the White House Office of Public Liaison.[49] Trump's White House communications director, Anthony Scaramucci, who was removed from his post ten days into his job, segued into a role as a contestant on CBS Television's *Celebrity Big Brother.*[50] Trump is hardly the first public official to turn to celebrities for advice, as this odious practice became part of the ongoing degradation of the presidency that occurred over the past fifty years. The reduction of the presidency to a low-budget reality TV show is the natural consequence of what writer Kevin Williamson refers to as the "celebritization of our politics.'"[51]

Donald Trump has elevated the celebrity aspect, and so many other aspects of the popular presidency, to the point where the office would be completely unrecognizable to those who sought to build a dignified presidency. Boorish and crude behavior are the hallmarks of the Trump presidency, an aspect of the man that many of his supporters seem to admire, especially when he "owns the libs [liberals]."[52] Trump repeatedly "define[s] deviancy down," regarding appropriate presidential conduct, to borrow from Daniel Patrick Moynihan. He is the only chief executive inducted into the World Wrestling Entertainment (WWE) Hall of Fame, and actively participated in many of the WWE's broadcasts. These scripted wrestling events, with patriotic American's tackling cartoonish evil foreigners in front of shouting crowds, provides the perfect metaphor for the Trump presidency.[53]

Extremism in the Defense of Vice

Trump is shattering presidential norms almost daily, and according to his more intellectually inclined admirers, he is creating "new modes and orders," refounding the American regime, or more precisely, restoring control over the regime to the American people. The nation's "ruling elite" (a favorite tag line of Trump's more scholarly admirers) composed of members of prestigious universities, the media, and the administrative state (the federal bureaucracy), have all been put on their heels by the blunt-talking tycoon from Manhattan who speaks for "Joe the Plumber."

His admirers claim that Trump is "authentic," "tells it like it is," which for many members of the baby boomer generation is the gold standard of behavior. For decades "authenticity" was the battle cry of liberal baby boomers, of whom there were many, but it is now embraced by Trump supporters. Both groups consider "authenticity" and an aversion to compromise with those who corrupted the nation as the only true path to salvation. The end was near, time was running out, Americans were told by many on the left in the 1960s. Then, in 2016, the year of the "Flight 93" election, according to former Trump administration official Michael Anton, only Donald Trump stood between the American people and the apocalypse.[54] The time had come to strip away the niceties and the traditions, and deconstruct the conventions that allowed the "ruling elite" to create a society where the toiling taxpayer who arrived in the United States legally and went to church and paid his bills got a raw deal.

Unlike his Republican primary opponents in 2016, Donald Trump was seen by his supporters as someone who punched back, below the belt if necessary, in a manner mimicking his liberal opponents. Many of these academic supporters of Trump had condemned, for decades, the extremism they saw on the left, but they had now come full circle and endorsed the notion that the ends, e.g., judicial appointments, justified Trump's destructive means.

In the view of these same supporters, extremism in the defense of "true" Americanism was no vice, while moderation toward members of "the swamp" and their enablers was no virtue. Further soiling an already tainted presidency through crude and boorish conduct was a small price to pay for overturning the old order, for knocking the Ivy League–educated "ruling elite" off their pedestal and "making America great again."

Trump's victory has been described, rightly so, as akin to Andrew Jackson's election as president in 1828. Former Speaker of the House Newt Gingrich frequently compared Trump to Jackson, while former New York Mayor Rudolph Giuliani claimed that Trump's triumph was "like Andrew Jackson's victory. This is the people beating the establishment." Steve Bannon, one of the architects of Trump's upset victory, noted "like [Andrew] Jackson's populism, we're going to build an entirely new political movement."[55] Vice President Mike Pence noted "There hasn't been anything like this since Andrew Jackson." "The New Old Hickory," as journalist Linda J. Killian describes Trump, will likely have as much impact on the office of the presidency, if not more, than the man whose portrait he installed near his desk in the Oval Office.[56] Asked about that portrait, Trump noted "They say that his campaign and his whole thing was most like mine. That was interesting. . . . That's the great Andrew Jackson, who actually was a great general, and he was a great president—but a controversial president."[57]

Unfortunately, it may be impossible to arrest the damage done by Trump, and one shudders to think what may come next. The history of the American presidency indicates a steady, if somewhat halting procession toward decline. Unfortunately, the office may not have hit bottom yet. A reversal of these trends and a return to some semblance of health is possible, but it is equally likely that Trump has permanently redefined the office and will eventually be followed by someone equally demagogic or worse.

10

The Prospects for Renewal

The American founders repeatedly warned of the dangers presented by demagogues and the "little arts of popularity" they employ in their rise to power. Flattering the majority and ostracizing an unpopular minority is standard practice for demagogues, as is the absence of magnanimity and humility in their character. True statesmanship sometimes requires the courage to defy public opinion and to elevate the role of the president as head of state over partisan or parochial concerns, and a statesman also understands that the national interest is not always consonant with their own interest.

Statesmen also acknowledge the limits of the office and of government writ large, and understand, as President Calvin Coolidge put it, that "the words of a president have an enormous weight and ought not to be used indiscriminately. It would be exceedingly easy to set the country all by the ears and foment hatred and jealousies." This would, Coolidge added, "help nobody and harm everybody."[1] Coolidge is derided by most presidential historians, but his appreciation for rhetorical restraint was shared by Washington, Hamilton, Madison, and Lincoln. The nation seems to have forgotten these lessons, for they are nowhere to be seen in the presidency of Donald J. Trump, nor were they especially apparent in the administrations of many of his predecessors.

A review of the history of the American presidency reinforces the clichéd but sometimes contested notion that personal integrity determines whether the office will be elevated or diminished. George Washington had that integrity, the two Adamses had it, Lincoln had it, Taft had it, Trump does not. Character above all else, especially a sense of humility about one's own potential and the potential of the office they hold, is a vital characteristic for healthy republican statesmanship, along with an awareness that they are merely temporary inhabitants of the presidency and of life on earth.

Promiscuous Promises

The unraveling of the American presidency began when Thomas Jefferson took the first steps to transform the office into one legitimized by public consent, not the Constitution. The work of Jefferson's "Revolution of 1800" was completed by Andrew Jackson who democratized the office even further and whose assertive conduct as president would be celebrated by twentieth-century progressives. But while twentieth-century progressives embraced Jeffersonian and Jacksonian notions of the president as the voice of the people, there was an important difference between them and the progressives, in that the latter believed in an activist federal government, a view shared by neither Jefferson or Jackson. The progressives created a federal government that could be as big as it wanted to be, led by a president who was as big a man as he wanted to be.

Jefferson's great rival, the alleged father of "big government," Alexander Hamilton, would also never have endorsed the massive commitments the federal government made in the twentieth century. Hamilton acknowledged limits to what the presidency and the federal government could do—it should concentrate on administering the government, conducting foreign negotiations, overseeing military preparations, and if need be, directing a war. In contrast to the progressives, Hamilton believed that the federal government should undertake a limited number of tasks but do them well. Government could not be all things to all people, Hamilton would argue, and he would understand the dangers inherit in an inflated government agenda.

Inflated expectations, along with the demagoguery and pandering that fuels it, has eroded public confidence in the American government. To keep the public engaged and mobilized, a series of progressive presidents declared an endless array of ill-defined "wars"—on poverty, on cancer, on inflation, on terror, on drugs—the latter war now approaching the fiftieth anniversary of its commencement. These "wars" would confirm the founders' worst fears about the republic they created: that it might transition from a republic into a participatory democracy, which required constant "mobilization" of the public, precisely the goal of some twentieth-century progressives. The founders also understood that the more one democratized the office of the presidency, making it the mouthpiece of the majority, the more it would bc disrespected.

The constitutional presidency, the one advocated most cogently by Alexander Hamilton, provided both a floor and a ceiling that protects but also energizes the office; without this, the office is vulnerable either to abuse or to diminution, as we are witnessing. The American founders understood that "enlightened statesmen will not always be at the helm" and these norms, this "floor and ceiling," was an acknowledgment of this likelihood.[2] The popular presidency stripped these boundaries away, to the point where Wilson and others could boast without the slightest hesitation that the president was free to be as big a man as he wanted to be. Donald Trump is proving that the president can be as big a man as he wants to be, or as small as he wants to be. He is Woodrow Wilson's dream turned into a nightmare.

An office intended to be a unifying force in the life of the nation instead became a pulpit where petty men convinced of their righteousness spewed invectives at their opponents. The role of party spokesman and "policy formulator in chief" has led too many presidents, including Wilson, FDR, Truman, Nixon, and Trump, to question the loyalty of their opponents. This required them to reject George Washington's intentions for the office, thus weakening the office and damaging the nation. Washington understood the vital role the head of state played in a healthy political order, in binding the nation together, and to some extent a small number of modern presidents have grasped this as well, including Eisenhower, Kennedy, and Reagan. The ceremonial and symbolic role of the president needs to be restored as a step toward reinvigorating civility and pride in the American polity.

There is a role to play for presidential rhetoric in this restoration, as Abraham Lincoln understood, better than any president before or since. Lincoln demonstrated at Gettysburg in 1863 or in his second inaugural address that a president can appeal to "mystic chords of memory" and help bind the nation's wounds. Franklin Roosevelt's Day of Infamy speech, John F. Kennedy's speech at the Berlin Wall in 1963, Reagan's remarks at Pointe du Hoc on the fortieth anniversary of D-Day, even George W. Bush's off-the-cuff comments in the rubble at ground zero all served to point the nation to something higher, and to remind the citizenry of its shared heritage. The president does not need to be a visionary, but he is in a sense a keeper of the American tablets, the temporary possessor of an office that came to symbolize much of what was good in the first modern republic—an office that extends back to George Washington.

Back to the Future

A return to the founders' presidency would restore the office and mitigate, somewhat, the deep divide in the American polity. One step in that direction would be for the political parties to empower so-called superdelegates. This should be a priority for both parties to prevent a recurrence of the 2016 fiasco which saw the Republican Party become the victim of a hostile takeover, and the Democratic Party almost nominate a candidate who was not a Democrat.

Additionally, in an ideal world the Electoral College would be restored to its original purpose, which was to prevent a manifestly unfit character from becoming president. The president was to be selected by electors who would choose a person of character and judgment, a person who held the national rather than the parochial interest close to heart and would resist the prevailing fads and passions of the day. While the original intention of the Electoral College was quickly rendered moot by the rise of political parties, those parties sought to replicate the Electoral College by filtering out unstable and unqualified individuals, at least during the nineteenth century. Unfortunately, as noted, the parties no longer filter—John F. Kennedy, Barry Goldwater, Jimmy Carter, George McGovern, Bill Clinton, Barack Obama, and Donald Trump were not the choice of party leaders.

The chances of restoring the original Electoral College are nil, as almost all Americans have accepted the popular presidency. The notion of any intermediary body filtering the will of the people runs contrary to the mantra of all right thinkers, and woe to anyone who breaks from this narrative. Yet it must also be noted that a return to institutions like the Electoral College and other elements of the constitutional presidency would not only rejuvenate the presidency, it might also restore Congress to its rightful place in the system of separation of powers. Congress no longer checks the executive, but as many recent presidencies have revealed, the legislative branch marches to the beat set by the president, and when it does break ranks, it does so at the margins.

The current process of selecting the nation's presidents has contributed to the decline of the office. Former South Dakota Senator George McGovern, building on the proposals of Woodrow Wilson, numerous progressive scholars, and former Democratic Party Chairman Paul Butler, proposed in the wake of the disastrous 1968 Democratic National Convention to curtail the power of party leaders and strengthen that of the "rank and file." These reforms eventually triumphed in both parties. Oddly, the Republican Party resisted these reforms longer than the Democrats but ultimately succumbed to its worst manifestation. One result of this more democratic selection process is that the party activists have moved their parties away from the "vital center." Each party became more ideologically "pure," rendering the prospects for compromise and consensus more remote.

McGovernism opened each party to insurgent campaigns, including those of Bernie Sanders and Donald Trump. If party leaders, including large numbers of superdelegates composed of governors, members of Congress, and mayors, maintained control over presidential selection, there would have been no George McGovern and no Donald Trump. Of course, this would have also made it more difficult for Barack Obama or possibly John F. Kennedy to secure their party's nomination.

Many of the architects of the nation's two-party system, included one whom I have criticized in this book, Martin Van Buren, understood that the party process of selecting a presidential nominee, in the wake of the demise of the original Electoral College, had become an informal but vital element of America's constitutional regime.[3] Character, experience, and a minimal sense of the national interest was vital, not simply the ability to generate passion and "solidify the base."

For Alexander Hamilton, "generating passion" was precisely the quality you did not want in a president. Martin Van Buren was more accepting of the "little arts of popularity," but even he acknowledged the necessity of some type of filtering mechanism to weed out undesirable presidential contenders. The process was not foolproof, Andrew Johnson being a case in point, but it was something of a process, and one with a purpose. The old party system may have produced several mediocrities, but in the end, a Benjamin Harrison is preferable to a Donald Trump. (The lowly Harrison, it should be noted, once observed that "no political party can long pursue advantage at the expense of public honor or by rude and indecent methods without protest and fatal disaffection in its own body.")[4] Two twentieth-century professors,

Woodrow Wilson and George McGovern, devoted to abstract principle over prudence, destroyed these filters and opened the doors to allow patently unfit persons to secure a party's nomination.

Parties were strong enough in the past to resist the likes of a Henry Wallace, a Strom Thurmond, a Pat Buchanan, or a Ross Perot, all of whom were forced to peddle their views outside of the two parties. The ability of parties to weed out the unfit, the demagogues, was beneficial not only to the party but to the republic at large. Party filtering of presidential nominees lent stability to policymaking at home and abroad. This prevented constant upheavals in American foreign policy and unstable relations abroad. The founders understood, and we should as well, that constant upheaval is not healthy for a political order. Presidents, at the very least, should do no harm, and insurgent nominees intend to do harm. Stability has its place, a radical concept for an era that worships change. Any refugee from a regime that experiences violent swings in government control can attest to the erosion these swings have on the rule of law and the effect it has on undermining confidence in the future.

In response to the public's perennial affection for "change" and its current disaffection with the two parties, both Republicans and Democrats perpetually turn to outsiders who pledge to "drain the swamp in Washington." This appeal has been made, in some form or another, by Dwight Eisenhower, John F. Kennedy, Barry Goldwater, George McGovern, Jimmy Carter, Ronald Reagan, Bill Clinton, Barack Obama, and Donald Trump. Even longtime "insiders" contort themselves to come off as outsiders. This pandering to the desire for perpetual change ignores the fact that overall the American two-party system has served the nation well. This system, until very recently, encouraged moderation, compromise, and coalition building. Interest groups, the Internet, talk radio, and 24/7 cable news have all contributed to weakening the ability of the government to govern, as all sides are held hostage to their "base" and commit themselves to defeating the "enemy" rather than working with it.

Presidential scholars have also contributed to the democratization and degradation of the presidential selection process and the presidency itself. There is an unhealthy academic tendency to celebrate presidential change agents—at least those presidential change agents who pursue a progressive agenda. This field of study would benefit from an appreciation for those presidents of moderate temperament who actually govern, who abide by and enforce the rule of law, and who are averse to sweeping transformative visions. There is a place for a John Quincy Adams, a William Howard Taft, a Gerald Ford, a George H. W. Bush, none of whom believed it was their task to deliver the American people to the promised land. These presidents and their peers will never make it to the real or figurative Mount Rushmore, but perhaps it is time for a new Mount Rushmore, one where Thomas Jefferson and Teddy Roosevelt are removed and replaced with John Quincy Adams and William Howard Taft, assuming the latter will fit.

Those polls of presidential greatness that appear around Presidents Day almost yearly could also use some sober second thoughts as the "top ten list" is replete with progressive presidents, including one who served for two years and ten months out of the republic's 230-year life span. And academics need to reject the popular 1960s notion of "presidential government," which still has some adherents, as dangerous to constitutional government and detrimental to the presidency itself. The lesson of a century's worth of Wilsonian "presidential government" is clear: executive leadership will remain suspect and oddly fragile yet potentially dangerous without the moderating influence of constitutionalism. We simply should not expect, as political scientist Clinton Rossiter once endorsed, that the occupant of the Oval Office had to be "a combination of scoutmaster, Delphic oracle, hero of the silver screen, and father of the multitudes."[5]

Hyperdemocracy

The central thesis of this book is that shifting presidential power away from its constitutional foundation toward a presidency of popular consent contributed to the decline of the office and of the American polity. Unfortunately, most of the influences at work in 2019 are pushing the system even further in the direction of popularizing the presidency. Supporters of these trends are motivated by a belief that technological advances have progressed to a point where the voices of the citizenry can play a more assertive role in the political process, including in the executive branch. Due to technological advances, it is argued, the American people are better informed and better educated (so it is believed) than they were 220 years ago, and their views need to be reflected in the governing process. Democratized decisions lead to better policy, the argument goes; "crowd sharing" leads to more representative and smarter policy. This is also a far more egalitarian form of decision making than a select few members drawn from America's "ruling elite," an ill-defined group if there ever was one, but one repeatedly cited by supporters of Donald Trump on the right and Bernie Sanders on the left.[6]

The notion that increased citizen awareness of and participation in decision making will produce better, more just results, is not borne out by history. The founders understood, rightly so, that the public can err, sometimes tragically so. Statewide legislative majorities in the nineteenth and twentieth centuries routinely denied unpopular minority groups equal protection under the law. Franklin Roosevelt struggled for years, at times covertly, to nudge his reluctant citizens toward recognizing the threat presented by Adolf Hitler. The American public's support for the war in Vietnam was strong, if not stronger, than support for the war with the nation's elites. In March 2003, a Pew Research Center poll indicated that 72 percent of the American public supported President George W. Bush's decision to use force in Iraq.[7]

Couple these views with the public's lack of understanding of international affairs, and you have a problematic situation. For instance, a 2006 Roper poll found that only 37 percent of Americans between the ages of eighteen and twenty-four could find Iraq on a map. This was three years after the United States invaded that country. That same year, 88 percent of these Americans could not locate Afghanistan on a map, five years after that invasion.[8] In 2002, 11 percent of this same group could not find the United States on a map.[9] These gaps in rudimentary knowledge are compounded by the tendency of substantial portions of the public to believe in conspiracy theories, be it President Obama's Kenyan birth or George W. Bush's plot to attack the Twin Towers or the fake moon landing in 1969.

It is frequently assumed that more openness, more governmental responsiveness to public opinion will reverse this persistent downward trend in American confidence in their government, which is at near-record lows.[10] Yet a strong case can be made that our increasingly democratized, poll-driven politics fails to inspire, and in fact serves to demoralize the citizenry. (Public opinion polls, remarkably enough, dictated who could participate in the Republican Party's presidential primary debates in 2016. The Trump campaign, meanwhile, paid "a tech guy" to rig online polls in favor of their candidate that year.)[11]

"Hyperdemocracy" is the term coined by political scientist Hugh Heclo to describe the phenomenon of the displacement of the Constitution and of deliberative representation with a politics of "participatory openness" that has polarized the electorate and made thoughtful decision making problematic. Compromise and civility are lost in the din of "publicity, exposure, investigation, revelation" in our 24/7, media-saturated environment. Confounding the hopes of openness advocates, the rejection of deliberation and the courting of public opinion has contributed to the mistrust and alienation that characterizes the American political order in the twenty-first century.[12]

Another element of America's hyperdemocracy, according to Matthew Continetti, is the nation's "continuous cycle of revolt, where the only things that change are the names of the protesters on the march. The Tea Party, Occupy Wall Street, Deplorables, Black Lives Matter, the Women's March, alt-right, antifa-elections are a sideshow to the parade of networked crowds outraged at whichever elite temporarily finds itself in power." The endless cycle of "challenge and response, proposal and rejection, election and protest, Tweet and counter-Tweet . . . is the way of things in a networked and fractured and data-rich world."[13] Endless examples abound on Twitter of the phenomenon of "what aboutism," where partisans defend some new presidential outrage by noting a similar precedent committed by a president of the opposite party. A cycle of escalation ensues, with all participants dragged into an abyss of charge and countercharge, often culminating in an accusation disparaging the morals of someone's mother.

The Internet has changed American politics for the worse, allowing the former isolated village crank to network with fellow cranks around the globe. James Kirchick rightly notes that "we live in a country where the very archetype of the tinfoil-hat-wearing-crackpot, whose claim to fame is standing on a street corner shouting obscenities, can have the ear of the most powerful person in the world."[14] And the current most powerful person in the world has a propensity to retweet those street-corner cranks, or endorse their thinking in his own inimitable way.

The architects of the American Constitution believed that the permanent interests of the community were enhanced through a republican form of government rooted in representation and resistant to the whims of public opinion or street action. As a result, the office of the presidency was designed to rebuff public sentiment, if need be, or at the very least moderate these sentiments. While the founders rejected the notion of parroting the will of the public, a more transparent system where the Internet becomes a tool to force elected officials "to think twice," as Michigan Congressman Justin Amash recently put it, is now seen as a central tenet of the regime. This is contrary to

James Madison's claim in *Federalist* no. 10 that representation will "refine and enlarge" the public views. "I defend liberty & explain every vote @facebook .com," Amash boasted. This congressman is so focused on his Internet reputation that his own chief of staff once observed that "when the voting was every two minutes, there was a real danger he might miss a vote while he was updating his Facebook page."[15]

The founders were opposed to pandering to the public, and rejected the type of populist, demagogic appeals that inevitably emerge from a more transparent and democratized Congress or presidency. Representation was designed to act as a filter; members of Congress as well as the president were not intended to be automatons translating public passions into policy. Both presidents and legislators owe the public their "unbiased opinion," "mature judgment," and "enlightened conscience," which ought not to be "sacrificed . . . to any man," as Edmund Burke observed.[16]

Openly formulated policies are more subject to the whims of the day and tend to focus on near-term results, while bold presidential initiatives, planned in secret, can change the course of world history. Policies hatched in secret enhance the chances of a strategic breakthrough, such as Franklin Roosevelt's covert and overt assistance to Great Britain in the months leading to America's formal entry into World War II, or President Richard Nixon's opening to China in 1972, or Barack Obama's opening to Cuba in 2014–2015.[17]

It must also be noted that a return to the constitutional presidency will not weaken the executive in time of war but rather strengthen it. The president will be seen less as a partisan figure and more as a head of state and a legitimate commander in chief. George Washington and Abraham Lincoln were strong commanders in chief and yet obedient to the Constitution. As this book attempted to convey, the problem is not one of the "imperial presidency" but the populist presidency.

Presidential leadership which defied the conventional wisdom of the day contributed greatly to America's superpower status, whether it was George Washington's support for a national bank or the Jay Treaty; or John Quincy Adams's refusal to match Andrew Jackson's demagoguery and maintain the dignity of the presidency; or Abraham Lincoln's refusal to vilify his Civil War opponents and his transformation of the purpose of the war into a "new birth of freedom"; or William Howard Taft's resistance to the demagoguery of Teddy Roosevelt and Woodrow Wilson and his eloquent appeals for the preservation of constitutional government; or John F. Kennedy's and

Lyndon Johnson's politically costly support for civil rights; or Gerald Ford's courageous pardon of Richard Nixon. These actions were taken in defiance of majority opinion and stand as monuments to the positive influence the constitutional presidency can have on the body politic.

Again, as mentioned, the odds are against recovering the lost soul of the American presidency. The public, as with any political body, is reluctant to surrender power. But it is remotely possible that a civically starved body politic may someday yearn for a return to the founders' constitutionalism, and that an American president who acts as some of his or her dignified forbears did, can draw enough support to steady the ship of state.

A return to health would be further assisted if the American public rediscovered its past and civics was restored to its rightful place in the American educational system. Unfortunately, this seems especially unlikely at a time when traditions of any kind are under attack, and the Internet has convinced far too many citizens that they are self-taught experts on climate change or international trade or intercontinental ballistic missiles, or countless other complex issues.[18] Democracy encourages the deceit that all opinions are equal, and encourages a healthy, and at other times, unhealthy, reluctance to defer to those in positions of power. This is not to say that all would be well if the nation were to defer to government by the "best and the brightest." Elites have made their share of mistakes, undoubtedly, but unless one is willing to abandon the entire Western experiment, there is much to be said for knowledge and expertise, for a system that permits those of talent to rise and to challenge the conventional wisdom of the day. Americans have examples from the past of this type of "elite" leadership they can be proud of, and they can learn from them if they open their minds.

What will follow in Donald Trump's wake remains to be seen, but if history is any guide, he could eventually be followed by Trump squared. But this is not inevitable. The nation would do well to return to the constitutional presidency proposed and enacted by George Washington and Alexander Hamilton. They created an "energetic executive," but did not pander to public opinion, nor attempt to bear any burden, nor engage in the kind of destructive hubris found in the proclamation that "man can be as big as he wants" and that "no problem of human destiny is beyond human beings." Nor would they ever dream of proclaiming that the moment of one's nomination for president marked the time "when the rise of the oceans began to slow." And they did not stir the pot to "solidify the base."

Presidents make a difference. The way they conduct themselves affects the entire body politic. Presidents can choose to unite or divide, to appeal to what binds us or to wallow in partisan or ideological slights. It is within their grasp to reach for something higher. But presidents cannot do this alone. The effort to restore the presidency will require Americans to "think continentally," to move beyond the parochial, beyond the immediate, and reject the siren call of those who flatter them. It will be difficult to recover the lost soul of the American presidency, but we can take solace from the fact that the past offers an alternative to the debased presidency of the present.

NOTES

INTRODUCTION: THE LONG, DECLINING ROAD

1. Frank Freidel, ed., *The Presidents of the United States of America* (Washington, DC: White House Historical Association and National Geographic Society, 1964).

2. Jeremi Suri deals with similar themes in his book *The Impossible Presidency: The Rise and Fall of America's Highest Office* (2017), which focuses on the unrealistic expectations that formed around, and ultimately undermined, the American presidency. Suri holds that American presidents ignored Thomas Jefferson's admonition that "restrained, modest, and cautious leaders" were essential elements of a healthy republic. Jefferson's "heirs did not heed his words" regarding the limited role of the presidency, an office characterized by "self-denial," "introspect[ion]," and "ascetic[ism]" (x, xi). In fact, Jefferson paved the way for the modern presidency by replacing the constitutional presidency with one whose legitimacy rested on public opinion, the main vehicle by which the office expanded in a myriad of unhealthy directions. Jefferson broadened the office's portfolio by democratizing the presidency, seeing the office as the implementer of public opinion and the lone national leader suitably positioned to direct the affairs of his party and its faction in Congress.

Suri offers an insightful account of Andrew Jackson's effort to refound the presidency and remake American society. He notes that "for all its sins, Jacksonian leadership became modern American leadership" and rightly claims that Jackson "anticipated the rhetorical belligerence of later presidents" (55, 71). But Suri overstates the link between Jackson's precedents and Abraham Lincoln's presidency; for instance, when he argues that "Jackson's populist presidency made Lincoln's war presidency possible" (71). While it is true that Lincoln came from "Jackson's world, not Washington's" (75), Lincoln recoiled from Jacksonianism and embraced Washington's principles and practices with an almost religious fervor. Suri adds, "Like Jackson, Lincoln claimed to 'derive all his authority from the people,' not the Constitution. . . . Lincoln and Jackson both believed that the president needed to set a public agenda for the people and pursue it vigorously." Yet Lincoln rejected Jackson and Jacksonianism as the epitome of lawlessness and did not share Jackson's view that the president, as Suri puts it, should be "a powerful and passionate actor" (75). Lincoln also did not, as Suri claims, "use executive powers to promote the economic, political, and social changes that the voters demanded" (79).

Abraham Lincoln, a meticulous lawyer, was always careful to ground his actions in the Constitution and rejected Jackson's notion that "the majority is to govern." Lincoln understood that there were certain fundamental precepts undergirding the American regime that were not subject to majority rule. Slavery, for instance, was at odds with natural law and the principles of the Declaration of Independence—its demise was mandated by these principles, not because the "voters demanded [it]."

Suri rightly notes the important role played by Theodore Roosevelt in placing the presidency on an unsustainable path, but he slights the critical role played by Woodrow Wilson in providing the intellectual imprimatur for "presidential government"—the notion that the president should be as "big a man as he can." Wilson is only dealt with in two brief passages, despite his outsized role in transforming the presidency.

Suri concludes his book by noting that "a single executive is just no longer practical" and proposes an "institutionalized division of responsibilities between a president and perhaps a prime minister" who would be elected by the people "at different intervals" (293). I conclude that the constitutional presidency is salvageable, and that we have several historical precedents to show us how to properly conduct the office. A plural executive as proposed by Suri would be subject to all the difficulties outlined by Alexander Hamilton in *Federalist* no. 70, including a dilution of executive responsibility, a quality particularly essential in times of war. See Jeremi Suri, *The Impossible Presidency: The Rise and Fall of America's Highest Office* (New York: Basic Books, 2017).

CHAPTER 1. THE FOUNDERS' PRESIDENCY: WASHINGTON, HAMILTON, AND AN OFFICE OF SOBER EXPECTATIONS

1. George Washington to Alexander Hamilton, 28 August 1788, https://founders.archives.gov/documents/Washington/04-06-02-0432.

2. For a libertarian perspective on Hamilton see Thomas DiLorenzo's *Hamilton's Curse: How Jefferson's Arch Enemy Betrayed the American Revolution—and What It Means for Americans Today* (New York: Crown Forum, 2009). Many twentieth-century mainstream historians accepted the simplistic Jeffersonian caricature of Hamilton as a militarist who was hostile to the "spirit of 1776." See for instance the work of Dumas Malone, Adrienne Koch, Julian Boyd, and Henry Steele Commager. For one of the most caricatured accounts, see Howard Zinn's widely circulated *A People's History of the United States* (New York: Harper & Row, 1980).

3. The great beast "quote" appears to be a fabrication. For a complete account of all the myths surrounding Hamilton, many of which originated in the imagination of Jefferson and his lieutenants, see my *Alexander Hamilton and the Persistence of Myth* (Lawrence: University Press of Kansas, 2002).

4. Alexander Hamilton to George Washington, 11 November 1794, *The Papers of Alexander Hamilton*, ed. Harold C. Syrett (New York: Columbia University Press, 1972), vol. xvii, 366.

5. Stephen F. Knott and Tony Williams, *Washington and Hamilton: The Alliance That Forged America* (Naperville, IL: Sourcebooks, 2015), 246–247.

6. Stephen F. Knott, "The Four Faces of Alexander Hamilton: Jefferson's Hamilton, Hollywood's Hamilton, Miranda's Hamilton, and the Real Hamilton," *Amer-*

ican Political Thought: A Journal of Ideas, Institutions, and Culture vol. 7 (Fall 2018): 554–561; Alexander Hamilton, "A Letter from Phocion to the Considerate Citizens of New York," 1–27 January 1784, https://founders.archives.gov/documents/Hamilton/01-03-02-0314.

7. For an insightful account of this case, see Peter Charles Hoffer, *Rutgers v. Waddington: Alexander Hamilton, the End of the War for Independence, and the Origins of Judicial Review* (Lawrence: University Press of Kansas, 2016).

8. Knott, "The Four Faces of Alexander Hamilton," 554–561; Knott and Williams, *Washington and Hamilton*, 247–248.

9. Glenn A. Phelps, *George Washington & American Constitutionalism* (Lawrence: University Press of Kansas, 1993), 181.

10. Knott and Williams, *Washington and Hamilton*, 246–247; Knott, "The Four Faces of Alexander Hamilton," 557.

11. Jacob E. Cooke, ed., *Federalist*, no. 6 (Middletown, CT: Wesleyan University Press, 1961), 28.

12. Hamilton, "A Letter from Phocion"; Knott, "The Four Faces of Alexander Hamilton," 557.

13. George Washington to Catherine Sawbridge Macauley Graham, 9 January 1790. https://founders.archives.gov/documents/Washington/05-04-02-0363.

14. Quoted in Richard D. Brown and Richard L. Bushman, "The Politics of Civility: From George Washington to Donald Trump," *Yale Books Unbound*, 9 October 2017, http://blog.yalebooks.com/2017/10/09/the-politics-of-civility-from-george-washington-to-donald-trump/; Stephen F. Knott, "George Washington and American Power," *Providence: A Journal of Christianity and American Foreign Policy*, 19 February 2018, https://providencemag.com/2018/02/george-washington-american-power/.

15. George Washington to Henry Knox, 8 March 1787, https://founders.archives.gov/GEWN-04-05-02-0072.

16. General Orders, 10 July 1776, https://founders.archives.gov/documents/Washington/03-05-02-0185; Knott, "George Washington and American Power."

17. Thomas J. McInerney and Fred L. Israel, eds., *Presidential Documents: Words That Shaped a Nation from Washington to Obama* (New York: Routledge, 2013), 16; Knott, "George Washington and American Power."

18. Alexander Hamilton to Edward Carrington, 26 May 1792, https://founders.archives.gov/documents/Hamilton/01-11-02-0349.

19. Cooke, ed., *Federalist*, no. 1, 6; Knott, "The Four Faces of Alexander Hamilton," 557–558.

20. Cooke, ed., *Federalist*, no. 85, 594; Knott, "The Four Faces of Alexander Hamilton," 558.

21. Cooke, ed., *Federalist*, no. 71, 482, Knott, "The Four Faces of Alexander Hamilton," 558.

22. Alexander Hamilton, *The Defence No. 1*, 22 July 1795, https://founders.archives.gov/documents/Hamilton/01-18-02-0305-0002; Knott, "The Four Faces of Alexander Hamilton," 558.

23. Knott, "The Four Faces of Alexander Hamilton," 558; Hamilton, *The Defence No. 1.*

24. Knott and Williams, *Washington and Hamilton*, 208; Alexander Hamilton to George Washington, 5 May 1796, https://founders.archives.gov/documents/Washington/99-01-02-00489.

25. Cooke, ed., *Federalist*, no. 10, 62.

26. Cooke, ed., *Federalist*, no. 63, 425.

27. Knott, "The Four Faces of Alexander Hamilton," 559; Thomas S. Engeman, Edward J. Erler, and Thomas B. Hofeller, eds., *The Federalist Concordance* (Chicago: University of Chicago Press, 1988), 390–391.

28. Quoted in Noah Feldman, *The Three Lives of James Madison, Genius, Partisan, President* (New York: Random House, 2017), 653n54.

29. James Madison, "Speech in the Virginia Convention," 2 December 1829, http://rotunda.upress.virginia.edu/founders/default.xqy?keys=FOEA-print-02-02-02-1924.

30. Cooke, ed., *Federalist*, no. 63, 428.

31. Cooke, ed., *Federalist*, no. 10, 62.

32. Greg Weiner, *Madison's Metronome: The Constitution, Majority Rule, and the Tempo of American Politics* (Lawrence: University Press of Kansas, 2012); Peter Wehner, "The Man the Founders Feared," *New York Times*, March 20, 2016.

33. Cooke, ed., *Federalist*, no. 10, 62.

34. James Madison to Unknown, "Re Majority Governments," December 1834, http://rotunda.upress.virginia.edu/founders/default.xqy?keys=FOEA-print-02-02-02-3066.

35. Ralph Ketcham, *James Madison: A Biography* (Charlottesville: University Press of Virginia, 1990), 181.

36. Thomas Jefferson to James Madison, 3 August 1795, https://founders.archives.gov/documents/Jefferson/01-28-02-0335; Knott, "The Four Faces of Alexander Hamilton," 559.

37. Alexander Hamilton, Enclosure [Objections and Answers Respecting the Administration], [18 August 1792], https://founders.archives.gov/documents/Hamilton/01-12-02-0184-0002.

38. Knott, "The Four Faces of Alexander Hamilton," 559–560.

39. This quote, ironically, was a favorite of President Ronald Reagan, arguably one of the nation's most conservative presidents. The quote can be found in the appendix to the third edition of *Common Sense.*

40. Quoted in Malcolm L. Cross, "Washington, Hamilton, and the Establishment of the Dignified and Efficient Presidency," in *George Washington and the Origins of the American Presidency*, eds. Mark J. Rozell, William D. Pederson, and Frank J. Williams (Westport, CT: Praeger, 2000), 102.

41. Cooke, ed., *Federalist*, no. 68, 458–459.

42. Cooke, ed., *Federalist*, no. 59, 403.

43. Cooke, ed., *Federalist*, no. 68, 458–459; James Ceaser, "Presidential Selection," in *The Presidency in the Constitutional Order*, eds. Joseph M. Bessette and Jeffrey Tulis (Baton Rouge: Louisiana State University Press, 1981), 250.

44. George Washington to Thomas Jefferson, 6 July 1796, https://founders.archives.gov/documents/Jefferson/01-29-02-0107.

45. Alexander Hamilton to George Washington, 8 April 1783, https://founders.archives.gov/documents/Hamilton/01-03-02-0204.

46. George Washington to the Marquis de Lafayette, *The Writings of George Washington, from the Original Manuscript Sources*, ed. John C. Fitzpatrick (Washington, DC: US Government Printing Office, 1938), vol. 26, 298.

47. Cooke, ed., *Federalist*, no. 1, 3.

48. Stephen F. Knott, "National Security and Foreign Policy," in *Debating Reform: Conflicting Perspectives on How to Fix the American Political System*, eds. Richard J. Ellis and Michael Nelson (Thousand Oaks, CA: Sage Publications, Inc., 2017), 390; John R. Vile, *Founding Documents of America: Documents Decoded* (Santa Barbara: ABC-Clio, 2015), 179.

49. Knott, "National Security and Foreign Policy," 390.

50. Quoted in Michael P. Federici, *The Political Philosophy of Alexander Hamilton* (Baltimore: Johns Hopkins University Press, 2012), 219.

51. Alexander Hamilton, "New York Ratifying Convention, First Speech of 21 June 1788," Francis Child's Version, https://founders.archives.gov/documents/Hamilton/01-05-02-0012-0011.

52. Knott and Williams, *Washington and Hamilton*, 195.

53. Quoted in Federici, *The Political Philosophy of Alexander Hamilton*, 166.

54. Knott, "The Four Faces of Alexander Hamilton," 560–561; Knott and Williams, *Washington and Hamilton*, 193–196.

55. Quoted in Byron W. Daynes, "George Washington: Reluctant Occupant, Uncertain Model for the Presidency," in *George Washington and the Origins of the American Presidency*, eds. Rozell, Pederson, and Williams, 25.

56. Daynes, "George Washington: Reluctant Occupant, Uncertain Model for the Presidency," 199–200; Max M. Edling, *A Revolution in Favor of Government: Origins of the U.S. Constitution and the Making of the American State* (Oxford: Oxford University Press, 2003), 135–136; John Ferling, "Hamilton and Jefferson: The Rivalry That Forged a Nation," *Time*, 20 January 2016, 48.

57. Jeffrey K. Tulis, *The Rhetorical Presidency* (Princeton, NJ: Princeton University Press, 2016), 47–48.

58. Sandra Moats, *Celebrating the Republic: Presidential Ceremony and Popular Sovereignty, from Washington to Monroe* (DeKalb: Northern Illinois University Press, 2010), 36–37.

59. Thomas Engeman and Raymond Tatalovich, "George Washington: The First Modern President? A Reply to Nichols," in *George Washington and the Origins of the American Presidency*, 71.

60. Alexander Hamilton to George Washington, 5 May 1789, https://founders.archives.gov/documents/Hamilton/01-05-02-0128; see also Knott and Williams, *Washington and Hamilton*, 180.

61. Quoted in Moats, *Celebrating the Republic*, 12–13, 29–30.

62. Moats, *Celebrating the Republic*, 40, 42.

63. David McCullough, *1776* (New York: Simon & Schuster, 2005), 247.

64. Moats, *Celebrating the Republic*, 34.

65. Forrest McDonald, "Today's Indispensable Man," in *Patriot Sage: George Washington and the American Political Tradition*, eds. Gary L. Gregg II and Matthew Spalding (Wilmington, DE: ISI Books, 1999), 37.

66. Richard Brookhiser, *Founding Father: Rediscovering George Washington* (New York: Free Press, 1996), 44.

67. John P. Kaminski, *George Washington: The Man of the Age* (Madison: Parallel Press, 2004), 33.

68. Thomas S. Langston, "George Washington as the First Head of State," in *The Powers of the Presidency* (Los Angeles: CQ Press, 2013), 49; John Adams to Benjamin Rush, 21 June 1811, https://founders.archives.gov/documents/Adams/99-02-02-5649.

69. T. H. Breen, *George Washington's Journey: The President Forges a New Nation* (New York: Simon & Schuster, 2016), 72–73, 124, 128.

70. Knott and Williams, *Washington and Hamilton*, 188–189; Langston, "George Washington as the First Head of State," 49.

71. Henry Wiencek, *An Imperfect God: George Washington, His Slaves, and the Creation of America* (New York: Farrar, Straus & Giroux, 2003), 191.

72. Erica Armstrong Dunbar, *Never Caught: The Washingtons' Relentless Pursuit of Their Runaway Slave, Ona Judge* (New York: Atria, 2017).

73. Knott and Williams, *Washington and Hamilton*, 254–255; McDonald, "Today's Indispensable Man," 29.

74. Wiencek, *An Imperfect God*, 362.

75. George Washington, "Circular to the States," 8 June 1783, http://press-pubs.uchicago.edu/founders/documents/v1ch7s5.html.

76. Knott and Williams, *Washington and Hamilton*, 184; Knott, *Alexander Hamilton and the Persistence of Myth*, 217.

77. Glenn A. Phelps, "George Washington and the Founding of the Presidency," *Presidential Studies Quarterly* vol. 17, no. 2 (Spring 1987): 351.

78. "George Washington's Last Will and Testament," 9 July 1799, https://founders.archives.gov/documents/Washington/06-04-02-0404-0001.

79. Moats, *Celebrating the Republic*, 39–40.

80. George Washington's Mount Vernon, "Washington's Southern Tour: An Interview with Warren Bingham," http://www.mountvernon.org/george-washington/the-first-president/george-washingtons-1791-southern-tour/.

81. Malcolm L. Cross, "Washington, Hamilton, and the Establishment of the Dignified and Efficient Presidency," 194.

82. Tulis, *The Rhetorical Presidency*, 47–48; Knott, "George Washington and American Power."

83. Quoted in Dorothy Twohig, "The Controversy over Slavery," in *George Washington Reconsidered*, ed. Don Higginbotham (Charlottesville: University Press of Virginia, 2001), 116.

84. Knott and Williams, *Washington and Hamilton*, 234–236; Alexander Hamilton to James Bayard, [16–21] April 1802, https://founders.archives.gov/documents/Hamilton/01-25-02-0321.

85. Knott, "George Washington and American Power."

86. George Washington, "Letter to the Hebrew Congregation at Newport," 21 August 1790, http://teachingamericanhistory.org/library/document/letter-to-the-hebrew-congregation-at-newport/; Jeffry H. Morrison, *The Political Philosophy of George Washington* (Baltimore: Johns Hopkins University Press, 2008), 154.

87. Knott, "George Washington and American Power."

CHAPTER 2. THE PRESIDENCY OF POPULAR CONSENT: THOMAS JEFFERSON AND THE "REVOLUTION OF 1800"

1. Quoted in Aaron N. Coleman, *The American Revolution, State Sovereignty, and the American Constitutional Settlement, 1765–1800* (Lanham, MD: Lexington Books, 2016), 235.

2. Joyce Appleby, *Thomas Jefferson* (New York: Times Books, 2003), 135, 146, 149.

3. Jeremy D. Bailey, *Thomas Jefferson and Executive Power* (Cambridge, UK: Cambridge University Press, 2007), 6.

4. Bailey, *Thomas Jefferson and Executive Power*, 6.

5. Bailey, *Thomas Jefferson and Executive Power*, 25.

6. Bailey, *Thomas Jefferson and Executive Power*, 9; Thomas Jefferson to James Madison, 20 December 1787, https://founders.archives.gov/documents/Jefferson/01-12-02-0454.

7. Bailey, *Thomas Jefferson and Executive Power*, 10.

8. Thomas Jefferson to Samuel Kercheval, 12 July 1816, http://www.let.rug.nl/usa/presidents/thomas-jefferson/letters-of-thomas-jefferson/jefl246.php.

9. Quoted in Forrest McDonald, *The American Presidency: An Intellectual History* (Lawrence: University Press of Kansas, 1994), 252.

10. Bailey, *Thomas Jefferson and Executive Power*, 11.

11. Thomas Jefferson to Albert Gallatin, 18 September 1801, https://founders.archives.gov/documents/Jefferson/01-35-02-0245.

12. Bailey, *Thomas Jefferson and Executive Power*, 212–213.

13. Bailey, *Thomas Jefferson and Executive Power*, 212–213, 217.

14. Bailey, *Thomas Jefferson and Executive Power*, 218–220.

15. Stephen F. Knott and Tony Williams, *Washington and Hamilton: The Alliance That Forged America* (Naperville, IL: Sourcebooks, 2015), 234–234.

16. Thomas Jefferson to Joseph C. Cabell, 2 February 1816, http://press-pubs.uchicago.edu/founders/documents/v1ch4s34.html.

17. Jefferson to Kercheval, 12 July 1816.

18. Jefferson to Kercheval, 12 July 1816.

19. Bailey, *Thomas Jefferson and Executive Power*, 15.

20. Jefferson to Kercheval, 12 July 1816.

21. Jefferson to Kercheval, 12 July 1816.

22. Quoted in Gordon Wood, "The Company of Giants," *New Republic*, 17 March 2011, https://newrepublic.com/article/85343/madison-jefferson-wood-american-con situtio n.

23. Dumas Malone, *Jefferson and the Ordeal of Liberty* (Boston: Little, Brown & Co., 1962), 418.

24. Linda K. Kerber, *Federalists in Dissent: Imagery and Ideology in Jeffersonian America* (Ithaca, NY: Cornell University Press, 1970), 22.

25. Jefferson to Kercheva1, 12 July 1816.

26. Gordon S. Wood, *Empire of Liberty: A History of the Early Republic, 1789–1815* (New York: Oxford University Press, 2009), 151.

27. Paul Finkelman, "The Problem of Slavery," in *Federalists Reconsidered*, eds. Doron Ben-Atar and Barbara B. Oberg (Charlottesville: University Press of Virginia, 1998), 148.

28. Quoted in Robert K. Landers, "Prophet of Abolition," *Wall Street Journal*, 28 March 2016.

29. Finkelman, "The Problem of Slavery," 145.

30. Donald R. Hickey, ed., *The War of 1812: Writings from America's Second War of Independence* (New York: Library of America, 2013), 657.

31. Van Gosse, "Fight for Black Voting Rights Precedes the Constitution," *Boston Globe*, 15 March 2015, https://www.bostonglobe.com/ideas/2015/03/12/fight-for-black-voting-rights-precedes-constitution/VM0V8vsrIFHXxPb1Qv9kAJ/story.html.

32. Jason Duncan, Review of *Jim Crow New York: A Documentary History of Race and Citizenship, 1777–1877*, H-Law, September 2007, http://www.h-net.org/reviews/showrev.php?id=13569; Alan J. Singer, *New York's Grand Emancipation Jubilee: Essays on Slavery, Resistance, Abolition, Teaching and Historical Memory* (Albany: State University of New York, 2018), 17.

33. Wood, *Empire of Liberty*, 302.

34. Lex Renda, "Between Freedom and Bondage: Race, Party, and Voting Rights in the Antebellum North," *Journal of Interdisciplinary History* vol. 41, no. 1 (Summer 2010): 154–156.

35. Don E. Fehrenbacher, *The Dred Scott Case: Its Significance in American Law and Politics* (New York: Oxford University Press, 2001), 110.

36. Thomas Jefferson to Albert Gallatin, 20 December 1820, https://founders.archives.gov/documents/Jefferson/98-01-02-1705.

37. Allen C. Guelzo, "Learning to Love the Federalists," *Claremont Review of Books*, 15 December 2003, http://www.claremont.org/crb/article/learning-to-love-the-federalists/.

38. Matthew Mason, "Federalists, Abolitionists, and the Problem of Influence," *American Nineteenth-Century History* vol. 10, no. 1 (March 2009): 1–27.

39. David Herbert Donald, *Lincoln Reconsidered: Essays on the Civil War Era* (New York: Vintage Books, 1989), 27.

40. Finkelman, "The Problem of Slavery," 138.

41. Bailey, *Thomas Jefferson and Executive Power*, 225–226.

42. Sidney Milkis and Michael Nelson, *The American Presidency: Origins and Development, 1776–2011* (Washington, DC: CQ Press, 2011), 110–111.

43. Milkis and Nelson, *The American Presidency: Origins and Development*, 148.

44. Bailey, *Thomas Jefferson and Executive Power*, 155; Forrest McDonald, *The Presidency of Thomas Jefferson* (Lawrence: University Press of Kansas, 1976), 37.

45. Alexis de Tocqueville, *Democracy in America* (New York: Library of America, 2004), 295.

46. Cooke, ed., *Federalist*, no. 10, 60–61.

47. Bailey, *Thomas Jefferson and Executive Power*, 63.

48. Thomas Jefferson to Thomas Ritchie, 25 December 1820, https://founders.archives.gov/documents/Jefferson/98-01-02-1702.

49. Robert K. Faulkner, "John Marshall," in *American Political Thought: The Philosophic Dimension of American Statesmanship*, eds. Morton J. Frisch and Richard G. Stevens (New Brunswick, NJ: Transaction Publishers, 2011), 165.

50. Thomas Jefferson to Thomas Ritchie, 25 December 1820.

51. Thomas Jefferson to Spencer Roane, 6 September 1819, in *The Writings of Thomas Jefferson*, ed. Paul Leicester Ford (New York: G. P. Putnam's Sons, 1899), vol. 12, 135–137.

52. Thomas Jefferson to William Charles Jarvis, 28 September 1820, https://founders.archives.gov/documents/Jefferson/98-01-02-1540.

53. Thomas Jefferson to Edward Livingston, 25 March 1825, http://rotunda.upress.virginia.edu/founders/default.xqy?keys=FOEA-print-04-02-02-5077.

54. James F. Simon, *What Kind of Nation: Thomas Jefferson, John Marshall, and the Epic Struggle to Create a United States* (New York: Simon & Schuster, 2002), 118.

55. McDonald, *The American Presidency*, 251.

56. Appleby, *Thomas Jefferson*, 11.

57. Wood, *Empire of Liberty*, 288.

58. McDonald, *The American Presidency*, 252.

59. Wood, *Empire of Liberty*, 288.

60. "Jefferson's Clothing," Thomas Jefferson's Monticello, https://www.monticello.org/site/research-and-collections/jeffersons-clothing.

61. Thomas Jefferson to Thaddeus Kosciusko, 2 April 1802, http://www.let.rug.nl/usa/presidents/thomas-jefferson/letters-of-thomas-jefferson/jefl145.php.

62. Stephen F. Knott, *Alexander Hamilton and the Persistence of Myth* (Lawrence: University Press of Kansas, 2002), 11–12.

63. Joseph Ellis, *American Sphinx: The Character of Thomas Jefferson* (New York: Alfred A. Knopf, 1997), 99.

64. Thomas Jefferson to William Short, 3 January 1793, https://founders.archives.gov/documents/Jefferson/01-25-02-0016.

65. Extract from William Short to John H. Cocke, 12 August 1826, Thomas Jefferson's Monticello, http://tjrs.monticello.org/letter/444.

66. Thomas Jefferson to James Madison, 1 October 1792, https://founders.archives.gov/documents/Madison/01-14-02-0339.

67. Cited in "Restore the First Bank of the United States," 13 April 2018, https://www.facebook.com/restorethefirstbank/.

68. Forrest McDonald, *The Presidency of Thomas Jefferson*, 151–152; and Wood, *Empire of Liberty*, 656–657.

69. Donald R. Hickey, ed., *The War of 1812: Writings from America's Second War of Independence* (New York: Library of America, 2013), 44.

70. Stephen F. Knott, "Republican Ideology and Its Failure in the War of 1812," *Law and Liberty*, http://www.libertylawsite.org/book-review/republican-ideology-and-its-failure-in-the-war-of-1812/.

71. R. R. Bernstein, *Thomas Jefferson* (New York: Oxford University Press, 2003), 182.

72. Knott, *Alexander Hamilton and the Persistence of Myth*, 240n5.

73. H. A. Washington, ed., *The Writings of Thomas Jefferson*, vol. 9 (Cambridge, UK: Cambridge University Press, 2011), 96.

74. Mark G. Spencer, "Alexander Hamilton," in *Conspiracy Theories in American History: An Encyclopedia*, ed. Peter Knight (Santa Barbara: ABC-Clio, 2003), vol. 1, 297.

75. Knott, *Alexander Hamilton and the Persistence of Myth*, 11.

76. Thomas Jefferson to Philip Mazzei, 24 April 1796, https://founders.archives.gov/documents/Jefferson/01-29-02-0054-0002.

77. Thomas Jefferson to George Washington, 9 September 1792, https://founders.archives.gov/documents/Jefferson/01-24-02-0330.

78. Knott, *Alexander Hamilton and the Persistence of Myth*, 10.

79. Thomas Jefferson to James Madison, 8 September 1793, https://founders.archives.gov/documents/Madison/01-15-02-0067.

80. Knott and Williams, *Washington and Hamilton*, 232; Knott, *Alexander Hamilton and the Persistence of Myth*, 11.

81. See Knott, *Alexander Hamilton and the Persistence of Myth* for a detailed account of the tendency of progressive historians and political figures to endorse a sinister view of Hamilton.

82. Cooke, ed., *Federalist*, no. 51, 349.

CHAPTER 3. ANDREW JACKSON: "THE MAJORITY IS TO GOVERN"

1. Stephen F. Knott, *Alexander Hamilton and the Persistence of Myth* (Lawrence: University Press of Kansas, 2002), 28.

2. Stephen F. Knott and Tony Williams, *Washington and Hamilton: The Alliance That Forged America* (Naperville, IL: Sourcebooks, 2015), 205.

3. Lynn Hudson Parsons, *The Birth of Modern Politics: Andrew Jackson, John Quincy Adams, and the Election of 1828* (New York: Oxford University Press, 2009), 15.

4. Fred Greenstein, *Inventing the Job of President: Leadership Style from George Washington to Andrew Jackson* (Princeton, NJ: Princeton University Press, 2009), 99.

5. Mary W. M. Hargreaves, *The Presidency of John Quincy Adams* (Lawrence: University Press of Kansas, 1985), 221.

6. Robert V. Remini, *Andrew Jackson and the Bank War: A Study in the Growth of Presidential Power* (New York: W. W. Norton, 1967), 49, 61–64.

7. Jon Meachem, *American Lion: Andrew Jackson in the White House* (New York: Random House, 2009), xxii.

8. Robert V. Remini, *Andrew Jackson and the Course of American Democracy, 1833–1845* (New York: Harper & Row, 1984), 51.

9. David T. Z. Mindich, *Just the Facts: How "Objectivity" Came to Define American Journalism* (New York: New York University Press, 1998), 33.

10. Jeffrey L. Pasley, "Andrew Jackson," in *Conspiracy Theories in American History: An Encyclopedia*, ed. Peter Knight (Santa Barbara: ABC-Clio, 2003), vol. 1, 362.

11. Robert V. Remini, *Andrew Jackson and the Course of American Empire, 1767–1821* (New York: Harper & Row, 1977), 145; and Robert V. Remini, *Andrew Jackson and the Course of American Freedom, 1822–1832* (New York: Harper & Row, 1981), 32.

12. Jack K. Williams, *Dueling in the Old South: Vignettes of Social History* (College Station: Texas A&M University Press, 1980), 18.

13. Daniel Walker Howe, "The Ages of Jackson," *Claremont Review of Books* vol. 10, no. 2 (Spring 2009).

14. Howe, "The Ages of Jackson."

15. Mark A. Graber, "Andrew Jackson," in *The Presidents and the Constitution: A Living History*, ed. Ken Gormley (New York: New York University Press, 2016), 111.

16. Remini, *Andrew Jackson and the Course of American Empire*, 310–312.

17. Graber, "Andrew Jackson," 112.

18. Andrew Jackson, First Annual Message to Congress, 8 December 1829, http://www.presidency.ucsb.edu/ws/index.php?pid=29471.

19. Kimberly C. Shankman, "Henry Clay and the Statesmanship of Compromise," in *History of American Political Thought*, eds. Jeff Sikkenga and Bryan-Paul Frost (Lanham, MD: Lexington Books, 2003), 307; Andrew Jackson, "Message to the Senate Protesting Censure Resolution," 15 April 1834, http://www.presidency.ucsb.edu/ws/?pid=67039.

20. Remini, *Andrew Jackson and the Course of American Democracy*, 518.

21. Robert V. Remini, *John Quincy Adams* (New York: Times Books, 2002), 74.

22. Pasley, "Andrew Jackson," 358.

23. Donald B. Cole, *The Presidency of Andrew Jackson* (Lawrence: University Press of Kansas, 1993), 31.

24. Remini, *John Quincy Adams*, 118–119.

25. Daniel Walker Howe, *What Hath God Wrought: The Transformation of America, 1815–1848* (New York: Oxford University Press, 2007), 283.

26. Howe, "The Ages of Jackson."

27. Howe, *What Hath God Wrought*, 488.

28. Greenstein, *Inventing the Job of President*, 85.

29. Forrest McDonald, *The American Presidency: An Intellectual History* (Lawrence: University Press of Kansas, 1994), 318; Remini, *Andrew Jackson and the Course of American Democracy, 1833–1845*, 73.

30. Ted Widmer, *Martin Van Buren* (New York: Times Books, 2005), 85–86.

31. Quoted in Howe, "The Ages of Jackson."

32. Cole, *The Presidency of Andrew Jackson*, 3–4.

33. Sidney Milkis and Michael Nelson, *The American Presidency: Origins and Development, 1776–2011* (Washington, DC: CQ Press, 2011), 134–135.

34. Milkis and Nelson, *The American Presidency*, 75–77; Stanley Elkins and Eric McKitrick, *The Age of Federalism: The Early American Republic, 1788–1800* (New York: Oxford University Press, 1995), 53–54.

35. Cole, *The Presidency of Andrew Jackson*, 45–46.

36. Cole, *The Presidency of Andrew Jackson*, 143.

37. Remini, *Andrew Jackson and the Course of American Democracy*, 63.

38. Greenstein, *Inventing the Job of President*, 94.

39. Bruce W. Dearstyne, "Can Books By a Fired High Official Like James Comey Damage a President?," *History News Network*, 20 April 2018, https://historynewsnetwork.org/article/168830.

40. Widmer, *Martin Van Buren*, 105–106.

41. Cole, *The Presidency of Andrew Jackson*, 226–227.

42. Mark R. Cheatham, "Andrew Jackson, Slavery, and Historians," *History Compass* vol. 9, no. 4 (2011): 326–338.

43. Howe, *What Hath God Wrought*, 500–501.

44. Sean Wilentz, *Andrew Jackson* (New York: Times Books, 2005), 124–125.

45. Wilentz, *Andrew Jackson*, 67.

46. Cole, *The Presidency of Andrew Jackson*, 114–117.

47. Robert V. Remini, *Andrew Jackson* (New York: Palgrave MacMillan, 2008), 42–43, 86.

48. Thomas R. Hietala, *Manifest Design: American Exceptionalism and Empire* (Ithaca, NY: Cornell University Press, 1985), 7n6.

49. Andrew Jackson, "First Annual Message," 8 December 1829, http://www.presidency.ucsb.edu/ws/index.php?pid=29471.

50. Cole, *The Presidency of Andrew Jackson*, 114.

51. Cole, *The Presidency of Andrew Jackson*, 111.

52. "Speech of Mr. Frelinghuysen, of New Jersey, Delivered in the Senate of the United States, 6 April 1830, on the Bill for an Exchange of Lands with the Indians Residing in Any of the States or Territories, and for Their Removal West of the Mississippi," https://catalog.hathitrust.org/Record/007645568.

53. Wilentz, *Andrew Jackson*, 160.

54. Michael Allen, "The Federalists and the West, 1783–1803," *Western Pennsylvania Historical Magazine* no. 61 (October 1978): 320.

55. Paul Finkelman, *Slavery and the Founders: Race and Liberty in the Age of Jefferson* (Armonk, NY: M. E. Sharpem, 2014), 165, 183.

56. Paul Finkelman, *Supreme Injustice: Slavery in the Nation's Highest Court* (Cambridge, MA: Harvard University Press, 2018).

57. Howe, *What Hath God Wrought*, 442.

58. Howe, "The Ages of Jackson."

59. Michael Lind, *What Lincoln Believed: The Values and Convictions of American's Greatest President* (New York: Random House, 2004), 11.

60. Joyce Appleby, *Thomas Jefferson* (New York: Times Books, 2003), 150.

61. Howe, *What Hath God Wrought*, 498.

62. Patricia Roberts Miller, *Fanatical Schemes: Proslavery Rhetoric and the Tragedy of Consensus* (Tuscaloosa: University of Alabama Press, 2009), 89.

63. Martin Van Buren, "Inaugural Address," 4 March 1837, http://www.presidency.ucsb.edu/ws/index.php?pid=25812.

64. Widmer, *Martin Van Buren*, 113.

65. Graber, "Andrew Jackson," 112.

66. John Quincy Adams, "First Annual Message to Congress," 6 December 1825, http://www.presidency.ucsb.edu/ws/index.php?pid=29467; Charles Francis Adams, ed., *Memoirs of John Quincy Adams, Comprising Portions of His Diary from 1795 to 1848* (Philadelphia: J. B. Lippincott & Co., 1876), vol. 10, 492.

67. James Traub, *John Quincy Adams: Militant Spirit* (New York: Basic Books, 2016), 492.

68. Howe, *What Hath God Wrought*, 514.

69. William Lee Miller, *Arguing about Slavery: John Quincy Adams and the Great Battle in the United States Congress* (New York: Vintage Books, 1998), 189.

70. Fred Kaplan, *John Quincy Adams: American Visionary* (New York: Harper Collins, 2014), 569–570; Charles N. Edel, *Nation Builder: John Quincy Adams and the Grand Strategy of the Republic* (Cambridge, MA: Harvard University Press, 2014), 250; Robert K. Landers, "Prophet of Abolition," *Wall Street Journal*, 28 March 2016.

71. Diana Schaub, "J. Q. Adams, Diarist," *Online Library of Law and Liberty*, 22 January 2018, http://www.libertylawsite.org/book-review/j-q-adams-diarist/#comment-1631178; Landers, "Prophet of Abolition."

72. James W. Ceaser, *Presidential Selection: Theory and Development* (Princeton, NJ: Princeton University Press, 1979), 166; Andrew Delbanco, "A Great American Hater," *New York Review of Books*, vol. lxvi, no. 1, 17 January 2019.

73. Hargreaves, *The Presidency of John Quincy Adams*, 48.

74. Hargreaves, *The Presidency of John Quincy Adams*, 66.

75. Hargreaves, *The Presidency of John Quincy Adams*, 300, 302.

76. Hargreaves, *The Presidency of John Quincy Adams*, 300.

77. Edel, *Nation Builder: John Quincy Adams and the Grand Strategy of the Republic*, 240.

78. Edel, *Nation Builder: John Quincy Adams and the Grand Strategy of the* Republic, 301.

79. Andrew R. L. Cayton, review of "John Quincy Adams: A Public Life, A Private Life, by Paul C. Nagel," *Los Angeles Times*, 5 October 1997.

80. Cole, *The Presidency of Andrew Jackson*, 17; Wilentz, *Andrew Jackson*, 51.

81. Milkis and Nelson, *The American Presidency: Origins and Development*, 134.

CHAPTER 4. ABRAHAM LINCOLN AND THE "MOBOCRATIC SPIRIT"

1. David Herbert Donald, *Lincoln* (New York: Simon & Schuster, 1985), 42, 109.

2. Douglas L. Wilson, *Honor's Voice: The Transformation of Abraham Lincoln* (New York: Alfred A. Knopf, 1998), 296–297.

3. Jon Meacham, *American Lion: Andrew Jackson in the White House* (New York: Random House, 2009), 247.

4. Donald, *Lincoln*, 63; Michael Burlingame, "Abraham Lincoln: Life before the Presidency," University of Virginia, Miller Center of Public Affairs, https://millercenter.org/president/lincoln/life-before-the-presidency.

5. Luke A. Harlow, *Religion, Race, and the Making of Confederate Kentucky, 1830–1880* (Cambridge, UK: Cambridge University Press, 2016), 46–47; Daniel Walker Howe, *What Hath God Wrought: The Transformation of America, 1815–1848* (New York: Oxford University Press, 2007), 433; Carl E. Prince, "'The Great Riot Year': Jacksonian Democracy and Patterns of Violence in 1834," *Journal of the Early Republic* vol. 5, no. 1 (Spring 1985), 1–19; Jeff Seuss, "1836 Cincinnati Riots Couldn't Stop Anti-Slavery Newspaper," 11 May 2017, https://www.cincinnati.com/story/news/2017/05/11/1836-cincinnati-riots-couldnt-stop-anti-slavery-newspaper/101497562/.

6. Sean Wilentz, *Andrew Jackson* (New York: Times Books, 2005), 128–129.

7. Quoted in Ted Widmer, *Martin Van Buren* (New York: Times Books, 2005), 115.

8. Joseph R. Fornieri, *The Language of Liberty: The Political Speeches and Writings of Abraham Lincoln* (Washington, DC: Regnery Publishing, Inc., 2009), 26.

9. Abraham Lincoln, "The Perpetuation of Our Political Institutions, Address before the Young Men's Lyceum of Springfield, IL," 27 January 1838, Abraham Lincoln Online, http://www.abrahamlincolnonline.org/lincoln/speeches/lyceum.htm.

10. Donald, *Lincoln*, 80–83; Abraham Lincoln, "The Perpetuation of Our Political Institutions, Address before the Young Men's Lyceum of Springfield, IL."

11. James Russell Lowell, *Abraham Lincoln, 1864–1865*, http://www.bartleby.com/28/16.html.

12. Fornieri, *The Language of Liberty*, 748–750.

13. Douglas L. Wilson, "William H. Herndon and His Lincoln Informants," *Journal of the Abraham Lincoln Association* vol. 14, issue 1 (Winter 1993): 15–34.

14. Stephen F. Knott, *Alexander Hamilton and the Persistence of Myth* (Lawrence: University Press of Kansas, 2002), 53–56.

15. Donald, *Lincoln*, 207–208; Abraham Lincoln, "House Divided Speech," 16 June 1858, Abraham Lincoln Online, http://www.abrahamlincolnonline.org/lincoln/speeches/house.htm.

16. Matthew Karp's *This Vast Southern Empire: Slaveholders at the Helm of American Foreign Policy* (Cambridge, MA: Harvard University Press, 2016) makes a strong case for the existence of a "slave power" in terms of directing American foreign and defense policy in the decades prior to the Civil War. Additionally, some members of this bloc sought to nationalize slavery and export the institution abroad.

17. Donald, *Lincoln*, 208; Paul Finkelman, *An Imperfect Union: Slavery, Federalism, and Comity* (Chapel Hill: University of North Carolina Press, 1981), 325–326.

18. Paul Finkelman, "*Scott v. Sandford:* The Court's Most Dreadful Case and How It Changed History," *Chicago-Kent Law Review* vol. 82 (December 2006): 46–47.

19. Glenn M. Linden, ed., *Voices from the Gathering Storm: The Coming of the American Civil War* (Wilmington, DE: Scholarly Resources, 2001), 151–152.

20. Phillip Shaw Paludan, *The Presidency of Abraham Lincoln* (Lawrence: University Press of Kansas, 1994), 55.

21. Paludan, *The Presidency of Abraham Lincoln*; Abraham Lincoln, "First Inaugural Address," 4 March 1861, http://avalon.law.yale.edu/19th_century/lincoln1.asp.

22. Paludan, *The Presidency of Abraham Lincoln*, 54.

23. Paludan, *The Presidency of Abraham Lincoln*, 55.

24. Robert W. Johannsen, *Stephen A. Douglas* (New York: Oxford University Press, 1973), 9, 23.

25. Johannsen, *Stephen A. Douglas*, 25.

26. Johannsen, *Stephen A. Douglas*, 27–28.

27. Johannsen, *Stephen A. Douglas*, 129–130.

28. Johannsen, *Stephen A. Douglas*, 139, 381.

29. Johannsen, *Stephen A. Douglas*, 570; Richard N. Current, "Stephen A. Douglas," *New York Times*, 22 April 1973, http://www.nytimes.com/1973/04/22/archives/stephen-a-douglas-by-robert-w-johannsen-illustrated-993-pp-new-york.html.

30. Peter Marshall and David Manuel, *Sounding Forth the Trumpet: 1837–1860* (Grand Rapids, MI: Revell Publishing, 2009), 513–514.

31. Johannsen, *Stephen A. Douglas*, 660.

32. Current, "Stephen A. Douglas."

33. Nicole Etcheson, "'A Living, Creeping Lie': Abraham Lincoln on Popular Sovereignty," *Journal of the Abraham Lincoln Association* vol. 29, issue 2 (Summer 2008): 1–26; Allen C. Guelzo, *Lincoln: A Very Short Introduction* (Oxford: Oxford University Press, 2009), 66–67.

34. Etcheson, "'A Living, Creeping Lie': Abraham Lincoln on Popular Sovereignty."

35. Jeffrey K. Tulis, *The Rhetorical Presidency* (Princeton, NJ: Princeton University Press, 2016), 5, 25, 79–81.

36. David Zarefsky, "'Public Sentiment Is Everything,' Lincoln's View of Political Persuasion," *Journal of the Abraham Lincoln Association* vol. 15, no. 2 (Summer 1994): 23–40; Abraham Lincoln, "Speech at a Republican Banquet," Chicago, IL, 10 December 1856, in *The Collected Works of Abraham Lincoln*, ed. Roy P. Basler (New Brunswick, NJ: Rutgers University Press, 1953), vol. 2, 386.

37. George S. Boutwell, "Hon. George S. Boutwell, Ex-Secretary of the Treasury," in *The Reminiscences of Abraham Lincoln, by Distinguished Men of His Time*, ed. Allen Thorndike Rice (New York: North American Publishing, 1886), 136.

38. Harry V. Jaffa, *Crisis of the House Divided: An Interpretation of the Issues in the Lincoln Douglas Debates* (Chicago: University of Chicago Press, 2009), 386.

39. Allen Nevins and Irving Stone, eds., *Lincoln: A Contemporary Portrait* (New York: Doubleday, 1962), 3.

40. Steven Kautz, "Abraham Lincoln: The Moderation of a Democratic Statesman," in *History of American Political Thought*, eds. Bryan-Paul Frost and Jeffrey Sikkenga (Lanham, MD: Lexington Books, 2003), 396–398.

41. Abraham Lincoln, Letter to Joshua Speed, 24 August 1855, http://www.abrahamlincolnonline.org/lincoln/speeches/speed.htm.

42. Abraham Lincoln, Letter to Joshua Speed, 24 August 1855, 400.

43. Paludan, *The Presidency of Abraham Lincoln*, 179.

44. "Coalition Government and National Unity," *CQ Researcher*, 17 October 1939, http://library.cqpress.com/cqresearcher/document.php?id=cqresrre1939101700; Donald, *Lincoln*, 263–264.

45. James M. McPherson, "'Team of Rivals': Friends of Abe," *New York Times*, 6 November 2005, http://www.nytimes.com/2005/11/06/books/review/team-of-rivals-friends-of-abe.html.

46. James M. McPherson, "'Team of Rivals': Friends of Abe."

47. Abraham Lincoln, "First Inaugural Address," 4 March 1861, http://www.presidency.ucsb.edu/ws/index.php?pid=25818.

48. Phillip Shaw Paludan, "Lincoln and the Greeley Letter: An Exposition," in *Lincoln Reshapes the Presidency*, ed. Charles M. Hubbard (Macon, GA: Mercer University Press, 2003), 89; "Abraham Lincoln and Public Opinion," Abraham Lincoln's Classroom, Lehrman Institute, www.abrahamlincolnsclassroom.org.

49. Abraham Lincoln, "Temperance Address," Springfield, IL, 22 February 1842, *The Collected Works of Abraham Lincoln*, vol. 2, 272–279.

50. Don E. Fehrenbacher and Virginia Fehrenbacher, eds., *Recollected Words of Abraham Lincoln* (Stanford: Stanford University Press, 1996), 232; "Abraham Lincoln and Public Opinion," Abraham Lincoln's Classroom.

51. William E. Gienapp, "Abraham Lincoln and Presidential Leadership," in *"We Cannot Escape History": Lincoln and the Last Best Hope of Earth*, ed. James M. McPherson (Urbana: University of Illinois Press, 1995), 68–69.

52. Richard D. Brown and Richard L. Bushman, "The Politics of Civility: From George Washington to Donald Trump," *Yale Books Unbound.*

53. Donald, *Lincoln*, 416–418, 529.

54. Quoted in "Abraham Lincoln and Public Opinion," Abraham Lincoln's Classroom; "The Dignity of Leadership from Washington to Lincoln," History-Essays, Lehrman Institute, 2012, http://lehrmaninstitute.org/history/the-dignity-of-leadership-from-washington-to-lincoln.html.

55. Michael Burlingame, ed., *Lincoln Observed: Civil War Dispatches of Noah Brooks* (Baltimore: Johns Hopkins University Press, 1998), 216; "The Dignity of Leadership from Washington to Lincoln," History-Essays, Lehrman Institute.

56. Joshua Speed quoted in *Recollected Words of Abraham Lincoln*, eds. Don E. Fehrenbacher and Virginia Fehrenbacher, 413; "The Dignity of Leadership from Washington to Lincoln," History-Essays, Lehrman Institute.

57. Harold Holzer, ed., *Lincoln as I knew Him: Gossip, Tributes, and Revelations from His Best Friends & Worst Enemies* (Chapel Hill: Algonquin Books of Chapel Hill, 2009), 179; "The Dignity of Leadership from Washington to Lincoln," History-Essays, Lehrman Institute.

58. James Oakes, *The Radical and the Republican: Frederick Douglass, Abraham Lincoln, and the Triumph of Antislavery Politics* (New York: W. W. Norton & Co., 2007), 93; "Abraham Lincoln and Public Opinion," Abraham Lincoln's Classroom.

59. The best scholarship on the issue of emergency executive power can be found in Benjamin Kleinerman, *The Discretionary President: The Promise and Peril of Executive Power* (Lawrence: University Press of Kansas, 2009) and Jeremy Bailey, *Thomas Jefferson and Executive Power* (Cambridge, UK: Cambridge University Press, 2007).

60. Abraham Lincoln, "Inaugural Address," 4 March 1861, http://www.presidency.ucsb.edu/ws/index.php?pid=25818; Abraham Lincoln, "Special Session Message," 4 July 1861, http://www.presidency.ucsb.edu/ws/?pid=69802.

61. Basler, *The Collected Works of Abraham Lincoln*, vol. 7, 282–283.

62. Joseph R. Fornieri, *Abraham Lincoln: Philosopher Statesman* (Carbondale: Southern Illinois University, 2014), 123.

63. Allen C. Guelzo, *Lincoln: A Very Short Introduction* (New York: Oxford University Press, 2009), 128; Allen C. Guelzo, *Abraham Lincoln: Redeemer President* (Grand Rapids, MI: William B. Eerdmans Publishing, 1999), 207.

64. Fornieri, *Abraham Lincoln: Philosopher Statesman*, 125.

65. William Lee Miller, *President Lincoln: The Duty of a Statesman* (New York: Random House, 2008), 5.

66. Quoted in Hans L. Trefousse, *Andrew Johnson: A Biography* (New York: W. W. Norton & Co., 1989), 53.

67. Annette Gordon-Reed, *Andrew Johnson* (New York: Times Books, 2011), 84–85; Albert Castel, *The Presidency of Andrew Johnson* (Lawrence: University Press of Kansas, 1979), 9–10.

68. Trefousse, *Andrew Johnson*, 53.

69. Gordon-Reed, *Andrew Johnson*, 36.

70. Gordon-Reed, *Andrew Johnson*, 57.

71. Gordon-Reed, *Andrew Johnson*, 59, 89.

72. Gordon-Reed, *Andrew Johnson*, 38–39; Andrew Johnson, National Historic Site, Tennessee, Slaves of Andrew Johnson, https://www.nps.gov/anjo/learn/historyculture/slaves.htm.

73. Quoted in Eric. C. Sands, *American Public Philosophy and the Mystery of Lincolnism* (Columbia: University of Missouri Press, 2009), 66.

74. Eric Foner, *A Short History of Reconstruction* (New York: Harper Perennial, 2014), 20.

75. Foner, *A Short History of Reconstruction*, 166.

76. Gordon-Reed, *Andrew Johnson*, 125–126.

77. Trefousse, *Andrew Johnson*, 244.

78. Tulis, *The Rhetorical Presidency*, 89–90; Hans L. Trefousse, *Thaddeus Stevens: Nineteenth-Century Egalitarian* (Chapel Hill: University of North Carolina Press, 1997), 197.

79. Ronald C. White, "Ulysses S. Grant Nominated for President 150 Years Ago," *Ronald C. White*, http://www.ronaldcwhite.com/2018/05/ulysses-s-grant-nominated-for-president-150-years-ago/.

80. Mary Stockwell, "Ulysses Grant's Failed Attempt to Grant Native Americans Citizenship," *Smithsonian*, 9 January 2019, https://www.smithsonianmag.com/history/ulysses-grants-failed-attempt-to-grant-native-americans-citizenship-180971198.

81. Charles W. Calhoun, *The Presidency of Ulysses S. Grant* (Lawrence: University Press of Kansas, 2017), 265–275, 405.

82. Andrew Johnson, "Third Annual Message to Congress," 3 December 1867, http://www.presidency.ucsb.edu/ws/?pid=29508.

CHAPTER 5. WOODROW WILSON: "TO BE AS BIG A MAN AS HE CAN"

1. David Schoenbaum, "A Question Asked since 1888: Why Can't Great Men Be President?" *Wilson Quarterly*, 12 January 2016, https://wilsonquarterly.com/quarterly/the-post-obama-world/a-question-asked-since-1888-why-cant-great-men-be-president/.

2. John Milton Cooper, *Woodrow Wilson: A Biography* (New York: Alfred A. Knopf, 2009), 58, 63. Bryce later became one of the foremost proponents of the League of Nations.

3. Woodrow Wilson, "The New Freedom: A Call for the Emancipation of the Generous Energies of a People," 1913, chapter 1, http://teachingamericanhistory.org/library/document/the-new-freedom/.

4. Joshua Zeitz, "Historians Have Long Thought Populism Was a Good Thing. Are They Wrong?," *Politico*, 14 January 2018, https://www.politico.com/magazine/story/2018/01/14/trump-populism-history-216320.

5. Quoted in Cooper, *Woodrow Wilson*, 97.

6. Woodrow Wilson, *Constitutional Government, Chapter 3: The President of the United States, 1908*, http://teachingamericanhistory.org/library/document/constitutional-government-chapter-iii-the-president-of-the-united-states/.

7. Sidney Milkis and Michael Nelson, *The American Presidency: Origins and Development, 1776–2011* (Washington, DC: CQ Press, 2011), 212.

8. Woodrow Wilson, *Constitutional Government in the United States* (New York: Columbia University Press, 1911), 169.

9. Woodrow Wilson, *Constitutional Government, Chapter 3*.

10. James Ceaser, "Presidential Selection," in *The Presidency in the Constitutional Order*, eds., Joseph M. Bessette and Jeffrey Tulis (Baton Rouge: Louisiana State University Press, 1981), 263. This essay should be required reading for any serious student of the American presidency.

11. William E. Leuchtenberg, *The American President: From Teddy Roosevelt to Bill Clinton* (New York: Oxford University Press, 2015), 70.

12. Milkis and Nelson, *The American Presidency: Origins and Development*, 226–227, 246.

13. Ceaser, "Presidential Selection," 262–263.

14. Ceaser, "Presidential Selection," 266–267.

15. Jeffrey Rosen, *William Howard Taft* (New York: Times Books, 2018), 15.

16. Michael J. Korzi, "Our Chief Magistrate and His Powers: A Reconsideration of William Howard Taft's 'Whig' Theory of Presidential Leadership," *Presidential Studies Quarterly* vol. 33, issue 2 (June 2003): 305.

17. Korzi, "Our Chief Magistrate and His Powers," 8–9.

18. Korzi, "Our Chief Magistrate and His Powers," 131.

19. Korzi, "Our Chief Magistrate and His Powers," 9.

20. Korzi, "Our Chief Magistrate and His Powers," 305.

21. Rosen, *William Howard Taft*, 5, 101.

22. Lewis L. Gould, *The William Howard Taft Presidency* (Lawrence: University Press of Kansas, 2009), 45.

23. Milkis and Nelson, *The American Presidency: Origins and Development*, 225.

24. Gould, *The William Howard Taft Presidency*, 45, 47.

25. Rosen, *William Howard Taft*, 131.

26. Rosen, *William Howard Taft*, 71.

27. Rosen, *William Howard Taft*, 86.

28. Woodrow Wilson, *Constitutional Government in the United States*, 78.

29. Forrest McDonald, *The American Presidency: An Intellectual History* (Lawrence: University Press of Kansas, 1994), 359.

30. Leuchtenberg, *The American President: From Teddy Roosevelt to Bill Clinton*, 70.

31. McDonald, *The American Presidency*, 359–360.

32. Arthur S. Link, ed., *The Papers of Woodrow Wilson* (Princeton, NJ: Princeton University Press, 1987), vol. 56, 17 March–4 April 1919, 517n1.

33. Jeffrey K. Tulis, *The Rhetorical Presidency* (Princeton, NJ: Princeton University Press, 2016), 151.

34. Quoted in Peter Knight, ed., *Conspiracy Theories in American History: An Encyclopedia* (Santa Barbara: ABC-Clio, 2003), vol. 2, 1.

35. Walter A. McDougall, *Promised Land, Crusader State: The American Encounter with the World since 1776* (Boston: Houghton Mifflin, 1997), 136; Lloyd E. Ambrosius, *Woodrow Wilson and American Internationalism* (New York: Cambridge University Press, 2017), 104.

36. McDonald, *The American Presidency*, 359–360.

37. Tulis, *The Rhetorical Presidency*, 159.

38. Tulis, *The Rhetorical Presidency*, 151.

39. Jacob E. Cooke, ed., *Federalist*, no. 68 (Middletown, CT: Wesleyan University Press, 1961).

40. Jacob Heilbrunn, "Reassessing Woodrow Wilson, Crusader President," *American Conservative*, 29 May 2018, http://www.theamericanconservative.com/articles/reassessing-woodrow-wilson-crusader-president/.

41. *Congressional Record: Proceedings and Debates of the 86th Congress*, Congressional Record—Senate (Washington, DC: US Government Printing Office), vol. 86, part 7, 31 May 1940, 7268.

42. Stephen F. Knott, *Rush to Judgment: George W. Bush, the War on Terror, and His Critics* (Lawrence: University Press of Kansas, 2012), 35–36.

43. Link, *The Papers of Woodrow Wilson, 1885–1888*, vol. 5, 561.

44. Quoted in Christopher Capozolla, "The United States Empire," in *Empires at War: 1911–1923*, eds. Robert Gerwath and Erez Manela (New York: Oxford University Press, 2014), 251.

45. Knott, *Rush to Judgment*, 36–37.

46. H. L. Mencken, *A Mencken Chrestomathy: His Own Selection of His Choicest Writings* (New York: Vintage Books, 1982), 248.

47. Cooper, *Woodrow Wilson*, 18.

48. Woodrow Wilson, *A History of the American People [Volume 5]: Reunion and Nationalization* (New York: Cosimo Inc., 2008), 58–64; Sheldon M. Stern, "The Puzzling Apologies for Woodrow Wilson's Racism in A. Scott Berg's Recent Biography," *History News Network*, 7 February 2016, https://historynewsnetwork.org/article/161837.

49. Woodrow Wilson, "The Reconstruction of the Southern States," *Atlantic Monthly*, January 1901, https://www.theatlantic.com/magazine/archive/1901/01/the-reconstruction-of-the-southern-states/520035/.

50. Ambrosius, *Woodrow Wilson and American Internationalism*, 67–70, 79–83; Gary Gerstle, "Race and Nation in the Thought and Politics of Woodrow Wilson," in *Reconsidering Woodrow Wilson: Progressivism, Internationalism, War, and Peace*, ed. John Milton Cooper Jr. (Washington, DC: Woodrow Wilson International Center for Scholars, 2008), 121.

51. Stern, "The Puzzling Apologies for Woodrow Wilson's Racism."

52. Stern, "The Puzzling Apologies for Woodrow Wilson's Racism."

53. Stern, "The Puzzling Apologies for Woodrow Wilson's Racism."

54. Deborah Yaffe, "Wilson Revisited: What the Presidential Portrait Left Out," Princeton Alumni Weekly, 3 February 2016, https://paw.princeton.edu/article/wilson-revisited.

55. Kendrick A. Clements, *The Presidency of Woodrow Wilson* (Lawrence: University Press of Kansas, 1992), 45; Dylan Matthews, "Woodrow Wilson Was Extremely Racist—Even by the Standards of His Time," *Vox*, 20 November 2015, https://www.vox.com/policy-and-politics/2015/11/20/9766896/woodrow-wilson-racist.

56. Arthur S. Link, ed., *The Papers of Woodrow Wilson: 1914* (Princeton, NJ: Princeton University Press, 1979), vol. 31, 361.

57. Yaffe, "Wilson Revisited."

58. Eric S. Yellin, "What Woodrow Wilson Did to Make 'Good Government' Mean

White Government," *History News Network*, 12 December 2015, https://historynewsnetwork.org/article/161456#sdendnote12sym.

59. *Addresses of President Wilson, January 27–February 3, 1916* (Washington, DC: US Government Printing Office, 1916), 64th Congress, 1st Session, House of Representatives, Document No. 803, 13.

60. Clements, *The Presidency of Woodrow Wilson*, 160.

61. Clements, *The Presidency of Woodrow Wilson*, 160.

62. David Krugler, "America's Forgotten Mass Lynching: When 237 People Were Murdered in Arkansas," *Daily Beast*, 16 February 2015, https://www.thedailybeast.com/americas-forgotten-mass-lynching-when-237-people-were-murdered-in-arkansas.

63. Clements, *The Presidency of Woodrow Wilson*, 46.

64. George Herring, *From Colony to Superpower: U.S. Foreign Relations since 1776* (New York: Oxford University Press, 2008), 386.

65. Max Boot, *Savage Wars of Peace: Small Wars and American Power* (New York: Basic Books, 2002), 149.

66. Michael Heale, *The United States in the Long Twentieth Century: Politics and Society since 1900* (London: Bloomsbury, 2015), 50.

67. Ambrosius, *Woodrow Wilson and American Internationalism*, 49; Christopher Burkett, "Remaking the World: Progressivism and American Foreign Policy," Heritage Foundation, 24 September 2013, https://www.heritage.org/political-process/report/remaking-the-world-progressivism-and-american-foreign-policy.

68. Aaron Delwiche, "Of Fraud and Force Fast Woven: Domestic Propaganda During the First World War," FirstWorldWar.Com, http://www.firstworldwar.com/features/propaganda.htm.

69. Clements, *The Presidency of Woodrow Wilson*, 152.

70. Edward L. Bernays, *Propaganda* (Brooklyn: IG Publishing, 2005), 127.

71. Bernays, *Propaganda*, 12.

72. Delwiche, "Of Fraud and Force Fast Woven."

73. Clements, *The Presidency of Woodrow Wilson*, 152–153.

74. Leon Fink, *Progressive Intellectuals and the Dilemmas of Democratic Commitment* (Cambridge, MA: Harvard University Press, 1977), 34.

75. John Maxwell Hamilton, "Happy 100th Birthday Information Warfare," *Washington Post*, 1 August 2014, https://www.washingtonpost.com/opinions/happy-100th-birthday-information-warfare/2014/08/01/3786e262-1732-11e4-85b6-c1451e622637_story.html?utm_term=.2121c419778a.

76. Delwiche, "Of Fraud and Force Fast Woven."

77. McDonald, *The American Presidency*, 438.

78. Clements, *The Presidency of Woodrow Wilson*, 152.

79. *Addresses of President Wilson, January 27–February 3, 1916*, 13.

80. The quotes from David Kennedy and Ira Katznelson can be found at "Woodrow Wilson, Special Features, Wilson's Legacy," www.pbs.org/wgbh/amex/wilson/sfeature/sf_legacy.html.

81. Stephen F. Knott, "Did Woodrow Wilson Destroy the American Presidency?,"

National Interest, 27 May 2014, http://nationalinterest.org/feature/did-woodrow-wilson-destroy-the-american-presidency-10531.

82. Milkis and Nelson, *The American Presidency: Origins and Development*, 245.

CHAPTER 6. FDR AND HARRY TRUMAN: "GIVE 'EM HELL"

1. Stephen F. Knott, *Alexander Hamilton and the Persistence of Myth* (Lawrence: University Press of Kansas, 2002), 99–100.

2. Knott, *Alexander Hamilton and the Persistence of Myth*, 99–101.

3. Knott, *Alexander Hamilton and the Persistence of Myth*, 118–119.

4. Knott, *Alexander Hamilton and the Persistence of Myth*, 120.

5. Knott, *Alexander Hamilton and the Persistence of Myth*, 101.

6. Robert Scigliano, *The Supreme Court and the Presidency* (New York: Free Press, 1971), 23; Franklin D. Roosevelt, "Fireside Chat," 9 March 1937, http://www.presidency.ucsb.edu/ws/index.php?pid=15381.

7. Franklin D. Roosevelt, "Address at the Democratic Party Victory Dinner," 4 March 1937, http://www.presidency.ucsb.edu/ws/index.php?pid=15378.

8. Roosevelt, "Fireside Chat," 9 March 1937.

9. Roosevelt, "Fireside Chat," 9 March 1937.

10. Knott, *Alexander Hamilton and the Persistence of Myth*, 118–119.

11. Knott, *Alexander Hamilton and the Persistence of Myth*, 121.

12. Knott, *Alexander Hamilton and the Persistence of Myth*, 116–118.

13. Knott, *Alexander Hamilton and the Persistence of Myth*, 120.

14. Franklin D. Roosevelt, "Address at the Jackson Day Dinner," 8 January 1938, http://www.presidency.ucsb.edu/ws/index.php?pid=15627.

15. Franklin D. Roosevelt, "Address at the Jackson Day Dinner," 8 January 1936, http://www.presidency.ucsb.edu/ws/index.php?pid=15256.

16. Roosevelt, "Address at the Jackson Day Dinner," 8 January 1936.

17. Roosevelt, "Address at the Jackson Day Dinner," 8 January 1936.

18. Franklin D. Roosevelt, "Address at the Jackson Day Dinner," 8 January 1938.

19. Franklin D. Roosevelt, "Address at Madison Square Garden," New York City, 31 October 1936, http://www.presidency.ucsb.edu/ws/?pid=15219.

20. Franklin D. Roosevelt, "Inaugural Address," 20 January 1937, http://www.presidency.ucsb.edu/ws/?pid=15349.

21. Franklin D. Roosevelt, "State of the Union Radio Address to the Nation," 11 January 1944, http://www.presidency.ucsb.edu/ws/index.php?pid=599.

22. Geoffrey C. Ward, *A First-Class Temperament: The Emergence of Franklin Roosevelt* (New York: Harper & Row, 1989).

23. Stephen F. Knott, *Rush to Judgment: George W. Bush, the War on Terror, and His Critics* (Lawrence: University Press of Kansas, 2012), 39–40.

24. Allen Weinstein, "Sure, the Tapes Were for History," *Washington Post*, 7 February 1982, https://www.washingtonpost.com/archive/opinions/1982/02/07/sure-the-tapes-were-for-history/b661a72d-912b-4507-b483-c912cbb82579/?utm_term=.a26d2f9dd47c.

25. Knott, *Rush to Judgment*, 42–43.

26. Rafael Medoff, "Why Didn't FDR Help European Jews? Hints in His Decision to Intern Japanese-Americans," *Tablet*, 14 February 2014, http://www.tabletmag.com/jewish-news-and-politics/162780/roosevelt-japanese-internment.

27. Greg Robinson, "FDR's Decision to Sign Executive Order 9066: Lessons from History," 4 March 2017, http://fdrfoundation.org/tag/greg-robinson/.

28. Knott, *Rush to Judgment*, 42–43.

29. Marina Koren, "A White House Tribute at Last," *Atlantic*, 29 September 2016, https://www.theatlantic.com/news/archive/2016/09/white-house-olympics-berlin/502325/; David Clay Large, *Nazi Games: The Olympics of 1936* (New York: W. W. Norton & Company, 2007), 233.

30. David Greenberg, "FDR's Nate Silver," *Politico Magazine*, 16 January 2016, https://www.politico.com/magazine/story/2016/01/emil-hurja-pollster-fdr-213537; Jill Lepore, *These Truths: A History of the United States* (New York: W.W. Norton & Company, 2018), 457-458.

31. Daniel Greene and Frank Newport, "American Public Opinion and the Holocaust," *Gallup*, 23 April 2018, http://news.gallup.com/opinion/polling-matters/232949/american-public-opinion-holocaust.aspx.

32. Greene and Newport, "American Public Opinion and the Holocaust."

33. Greene and Newport, "American Public Opinion and the Holocaust."

34. Medoff, "Why Didn't FDR Help European Jews?"

35. William E. Leuchtenberg, "Franklin D. Roosevelt: Foreign Affairs," University of Virginia, Miller Center of Public Affairs, https://millercenter.org/president/fdroosevelt/foreign-affairs.

36. Franklin D. Roosevelt, "Campaign Address at Boston, Massachusetts," 30 October 1940, http://www.presidency.ucsb.edu/ws/?pid=15887.

37. Medoff, "Why Didn't FDR Help European Jews?"

38. George McJimsey, *The Presidency of Franklin Delano Roosevelt* (Lawrence: University Press of Kansas, 2000), 262.

39. "Breckenridge Long," Holocaust Encyclopedia, United States Holocaust Memorial Museum, https://www.ushmm.org/wlc/en/article.php?ModuleId=10008298; McJimsey, *The Presidency of Franklin Delano Roosevelt*, 262–264.

40. Franklin D. Roosevelt, "Radio Address from Albany, New York: 'The Forgotten Man' Speech," 7 April 1932, http://www.presidency.ucsb.edu/ws/?pid=88408.

41. Sidney Milkis and Michael Nelson, *The American Presidency: Origins and Development, 1776–2011* (Washington, DC: CQ Press, 2011), 292.

42. "You Have a Marvelous Radio Voice, Distinct and Clear": The Public Responds to FDR's First Fireside Chat, *History Matters*, http://historymatters.gmu.edu/d/8126.

43. Patrick Novotny, *The Press in American Politics: 1787–2012* (Santa Barbara: Praeger, 2014), 115.

44. Ronald Isetti, "The Moneychangers of the Temple: FDR, American Civil Religion, and the New Deal," *Presidential Studies Quarterly* vol. 26, issue 3 (Summer 1996): 678.

45. Isetti, "The Moneychangers of the Temple," 678.

46. Abraham Lincoln, "Inaugural Address," 4 March 1865, http://www.presidency.ucsb.edu/ws/index.php?pid=25819.

47. Roosevelt, "Address at Madison Square Garden," 31 October 1936.

48. Franklin D. Roosevelt, "Acceptance Speech for the Renomination for the Presidency," 27 June 1936, http://www.presidency.ucsb.edu/ws/?pid=15314.

49. Roosevelt, "Inaugural Address," 20 January 1937.

50. Thomas W. Devine, *Henry Wallace's 1948 Presidential Campaign and the Future of Postwar Liberalism* (Chapel Hill: University of North Carolina Press, 2013), 129; J. Samuel Walker, "The New Deal and the Guru," *American Heritage* vol. 40, issue 2 (March 1989), https://www.americanheritage.com/content/new-deal-and-guru.

51. Donald R. McCoy, *The Presidency of Harry S. Truman* (Lawrence: University Press of Kansas, 1984), 106–108; Harry S. Truman, "Address before the National Association for the Advancement of Colored People," 29 June 1947, http://www.presidency.ucsb.edu/ws/index.php?pid=12686.

52. McCoy, *The Presidency of Harry Truman*, 107–108.

53. McCoy, *The Presidency of Harry Truman*, 157–158.

54. Stephen F. Knott, "As Election Day Nears, Trump Borrows from Harry Truman's Playbook," *Washington Post*, 5 November 2018, https://www.washingtonpost.com/outlook/2018/11/05/election-day-nears-trump-borrows-harry-trumans-playbook/?utm_term=.0e6112fca6b2.

55. John Dickerson, "How Truman Reinvented Campaigning," *Daily Beast*, 24 September 2016, https://www.thedailybeast.com/how-truman-reinvented-campaigning; Knott, "As Election Day Nears."

56. Zachary Karabell, *The Last Campaign: How Harry Truman Won the 1948 Election* (New York: Alfred A. Knopf, 2001), 247–248; Philip White, *Whistle Stop: How 31,000 Miles of Train Travel, 352 Speeches, and a Little Midwest Gumption Saved the Presidency of Harry Truman* (Lebanon, NH: University Press of New England, 2014), 156, 161; *The Public Papers of the Presidents of the United States, Harry S. Truman, 1948* (Washington, DC: US Government Printing Office, 1963), vol. 4, 505–506; Knott, "As Election Day Nears."

57. Karabell, *The Last Campaign*, 247–248; White, *Whistle Stop*, 156; Knott, "As Election Day Nears."

58. Karabell, *The Last Campaign*, 247; Knott, "As Election Day Nears."

59. Karabell, *The Last Campaign*, 250; Knott, "As Election Day Nears."

60. Roger Stone, "Trump Stole a Page from Give 'Em Hell Harry," *Real Clear Politics*, 15 February 2017, https://www.realclearpolitics.com/articles/2017/02/15/trump_stole_a_page_from_give_em_hell_harry_133085.html; Knott, "As Election Day Nears."

CHAPTER 7. IKE AND JACK: A STUDY IN CONTRASTING PRESIDENCIES

1. C-Span, Presidential Historians Survey, 2017, https://www.c-span.org/presidentsurvey2017/?page=overall.

2. Jean Edward Smith, *Eisenhower in War and Peace* (New York: Random House, 2012), 256–257.

3. Quoted in "The Eisenhower Model," *Washington Post*, 15 February 1981, https://www.washingtonpost.com/archive/opinions/1981/02/15/the-eisenhower-model/c944d668-20d6-4b3a-9e74-dba34c3b06e5/?utm_term=.c150aa879da1.

4. Smith, *Eisenhower in War and Peace*, 44, 566.

5. Fred Greenstein, *The Hidden-Hand Presidency: Eisenhower as Leader* (Baltimore: Johns Hopkins University Press, 1994), 80–81.

6. Chester J. Pach and Elmo Richardson, *The Presidency of Dwight D. Eisenhower* (Lawrence: University Press of Kansas, 1991), 42.

7. Stephen F. Knott, "John F. Kennedy: Prince of American Progressivism," *Blue Review*, 31 March 2017, https://thebluereview.org/john-f-kennedy/.

8. Quoted in Richard Neustadt, *Presidential Power and the Modern Presidents: The Politics of Leadership from Roosevelt to Reagan* (New York: Free Press, 1990), 10.

9. Peter W. Rodman, *Presidential Command: Power, Leadership, and the Making of Foreign Policy from Richard Nixon to George W. Bush* (New York: Alfred A. Knopf, 2009), 26.

10. Pach and Richardson, *The Presidency of Dwight D. Eisenhower*, 42.

11. Pach and Richardson, *The Presidency of Dwight D. Eisenhower*.

12. "The Eisenhower Model," *Washington Post*, 15 February 1981.

13. Greenstein, *The Hidden-Hand Presidency*, 58.

14. Greenstein, *The Hidden-Hand Presidency*, 5, 240.

15. Greenstein, *The Hidden-Hand Presidency*, 240.

16. Dwight D. Eisenhower, *Public Papers of the Presidents of the United States: Dwight D. Eisenhower: 1954* (Washington, DC: National Archives and Records Service, 1960), 88.

17. Dwight D. Eisenhower, "What Is Leadership," *Reader's Digest*, June 1965, 53–54.

18. Eisenhower, "What Is Leadership," 239.

19. Eisenhower, "What Is Leadership," 73–74.

20. Eisenhower, "What Is Leadership," 235.

21. Eisenhower, "What Is Leadership," 240–241.

22. Quoted in James David Barber, *The Presidential Character: Predicting Performance in the White House* (Abingdon, UK: Routledge, 2009), 179–181, 183.

23. Jeffrey K. Tulis, *The Rhetorical Presidency* (Princeton, NJ: Princeton University Press, 2016), 96n2.

24. Greenstein, *The Hidden-Hand Presidency*, 5–6.

25. Pach and Richardson, *The Presidency of Dwight D. Eisenhower*, 41.

26. Greenstein, *The Hidden-Hand Presidency*, 67.

27. Quoted in Jeffrey Frank, *Ike and Dick: Portrait of a Strange Political Marriage* (New York: Simon & Schuster, 2013), 74.

28. Smith, *Eisenhower in War and Peace*, 594.

29. Smith, *Eisenhower in War and Peace*, 591.

30. Jonathan Mahler and Matt Flegenheimer, "What Donald Trump Learned from Joseph McCarthy's Right-Hand Man," *New York Times*, 20 June 2016, https://www.nytimes.com/2016/06/21/us/politics/donald-trump-roy-cohn.html.

31. Pach and Richardson, *The Presidency of Dwight D. Eisenhower*, 150–154.

32. Pach and Richardson, *The Presidency of Dwight D. Eisenhower*, 148.

33. John F. Kennedy, "Report to the American People on Civil Rights," 11 June 1963, John F. Kennedy Library, https://www.jfklibrary.org/Asset-Viewer/LH8F_0Mzvoe6R01yEm74Ng.aspx. Kennedy, it should be noted, was also accused of unnecessarily delaying federal civil rights enforcement and of deferring to powerful Southern members of Congress from his own party who repeatedly blocked his civil rights legislation.

34. Smith, *Eisenhower in War and Peace*, 728–729.

35. Pach and Richardson, *The Presidency of Dwight D. Eisenhower*, 148–149.

36. Scott Slorach, Judith Embley, Peter Goodchild, and Catherine Shephard, *Legal Systems and Skills* (Oxford: Oxford University Press, 2013), 23; Carlo D'Este, *Eisenhower: A Soldier's Life* (New York: Henry Holt & Company, 2002), 679.

37. Stephen F. Knott, "What Might Have Been," *Review of Politics* vol. 76, no. 4 (Fall 2014): 661–670; Knott, "John F. Kennedy: Prince of American Progressivism."

38. John F. Kennedy, "Address before the 18th Assembly of the United Nations," 20 September 1963, http://www.presidency.ucsb.edu/ws/?pid=9416.

39. Address of Senator John F. Kennedy Accepting the Democratic Party Nomination for the Presidency of the United States—Memorial Coliseum, Los Angeles, 15 July 1960, http://www.presidency.ucsb.edu/ws/?pid=25966; John F. Kennedy Speeches, Remarks of Senator John F. Kennedy, Fulton and Nostrand, Brooklyn, New York, 20 October 1960, https://www.jfklibrary.org/Research/Research-Aids/JFK-Speeches/New-York-NY-Fulton-and-Nostrand_19601020.aspx.

40. President John F. Kennedy Signs Bill to Establish the Woodrow Wilson Memorial Commission, https://www.jfklibrary.org/Asset-Viewer/Archives/JFKWHP-AR6818-C.aspx; "Remembering Kennedy's Inauguration," 20 January 2011, http://edithbollingwilson.org/2011/01/remembering-kennedys-inauguration/.

41. "John F. Kennedy's Announcement as Candidate for President," 2 January 1960, https://www.jfklibrary.org/Research/Research-Aids/Ready-Reference/JFK-Fast-Facts/Announcement-of-Candidacy.aspx.

42. John F. Kennedy, "The Presidency in 1960," National Press Club, Washington, DC, 14 January 1960. http://www.presidency.ucsb.edu/ws/?pid=25795.

43. Address of Senator John F. Kennedy Accepting the Democratic Party Nomination for the Presidency of the United States.

44. The Commission on Presidential Debates, "The Fourth Kennedy-Nixon Presidential Debate, 21 October 1960 Debate Transcript," www.debates.org/index.php?page=october-21-1960-debate-transcript.

45. Excerpts of Remarks by Senator John F. Kennedy, Johnstown, PA, 15 October 1960, http://www.presidency.ucsb.edu/ws/index.php?pid=74041.

46. Quoted in Michael R. Beschloss, "Foreign Policy's Big Moment," *New York Times*, 11 April 1999.

47. John F. Kennedy, "Inaugural Address," 20 January 1961, http://www.presidency.ucsb.edu/ws/index.php?pid=8032&.

48. Knott, "John F. Kennedy: Prince of American Progressivism."

49. Alan Brinkley, *John F. Kennedy* (New York: Times Books, 2012), 59–61.

50. Theodore C. Sorensen, *Kennedy* (New York: Bantam Books, 1966), 294, 315–317.

51. Sorensen, *Kennedy*, 290–291; Knott, "John F. Kennedy: Prince of American Progressivism."

52. Knott, "What Might Have Been"; Knott, "John F. Kennedy: Prince of American Progressivism."

53. Alan Brinkley, "The Legacy of John F. Kennedy," *Atlantic*, Fall 2013, https://www.theatlantic.com/magazine/archive/2013/08/the-legacy-of-john-f-kennedy/309499/; Knott, "What Might Have Been."

54. James N. Giglio, *The Presidency of John F. Kennedy* (Lawrence: University Press of Kansas, 1991), 260.

55. Knott, "What Might Have Been"; Sean Wilentz, "The Vital Centrist," *New Republic*, 13 February 2008.

56. Knott, "What Might Have Been"; Wilentz, "The Vital Centrist."

57. Knott, "John F. Kennedy: Prince of American Progressivism"; Brinkley, "The Legacy of John F. Kennedy."

58. Knott, "What Might Have Been."

59. Knott, "What Might Have Been"; Robert Dallek, *An Unfinished Life: John F. Kennedy, 1917–1963* (Boston: Little, Brown, 2003), 76.

60. Knott, "What Might Have Been"; Knott, "John F. Kennedy: Prince of American Progressivism."

61. Arthur M. Schlesinger Jr., *Robert Kennedy and His Times* (Boston: Houghton Mifflin, 1978), 498.

62. Knott, "What Might Have Been"; Knott, "John F. Kennedy: Prince of American Progressivism."

63. Arthur M. Schlesinger Jr., *Journals: 1952–2000* (New York: Penguin Press, 2007), 558.

64. See James MacGregor Burns, *Presidential Government: The Crucible of Leadership* (Boston: Houghton Mifflin, 1973), especially 339, and James MacGregor Burns, *The Deadlock of Democracy: Four Party Politics in America* (Edgewood Cliffs, NJ: Prentice Hall, 1963).

65. Quoted in Sarah A. Binder, *Causes and Consequences of Legislative Gridlock* (Washington, DC: Brookings Institution, 2003), 5.

66. James MacGregor Burns, *John Kennedy: A Political Profile* (New York: Harcourt & Brace, 1960); James MacGregor Burns, *Edward Kennedy and the Camelot Legacy* (New York: W. W. Norton, 1976).

67. Joseph M. Bessette and Jeffrey Tulis, "The Constitution, Politics, and the Presidency," in *The Presidency in the Constitutional Order*, eds. Joseph M. Bessette and Jeffrey Tulis (Baton Rouge: Louisiana State University Press, 1981), 4.

68. Richard Neustadt, *Presidential Power: The Politics of Leadership* (New York: John Wiley & Sons, 1960), preface; 111.

69. Michael Nelson, "James David Barber and the Psychological Presidency," *Virginia Quarterly Review*, Autumn 1980, http://www.vqronline.org/essay/james-david-barber-and-psychological-presidency.

70. Quoted in Matthew J. Dickinson and Elizabeth A. Neustadt, eds., *Guardian of the Presidency: The Legacy of Richard E. Neustadt* (Washington, DC: Brookings Institution Press, 2007), 75.

71. Charles O. Jones, "Richard E. Neustadt: Public Servant as Scholar," *American Review of Political Science* vol. 6 (2003): 1–22.; "Presidential Power with Matthew Dickinson," https://sites.middlebury.edu/presidentialpower/2010/02/15/in-honor-of-presidents-day-2/.

72. Theodore C. Sorensen, "Richard E. Neustadt, Presidential Expert," in *Guardian of the Presidency*, eds. Dickinson and Neustadt, 77.

73. James David Barber, *The Presidential Character: Predicting Performance in the White House* (Englewood, NJ: Prentice Hall, 1972).

74. Bruce Mazlish, "The Presidential Character," *New York Times*, 8 October 1972; Raymond Tatlovich, Steven E. Schier, and Thomas S. Engeman, *The Presidency and Political Science: Paradigms of Presidential Power from the Founding to the Present* (London: Routledge, 2014), 146.

75. The preceding four paragraphs originally appeared in a slightly altered form in my *Rush to Judgment: George W. Bush, the War on Terror, and His Critics* (Lawrence: University Press of Kansas, 2012), 54–56.

76. Garry Wills, "A Pattern of Rising Power," *New York Times*, 18 November 1973.

77. See James Piereson, *Camelot and the Cultural Revolution: How the Assassination of John F. Kennedy Shattered American Liberalism* (New York: Encounter Books, 2007). Piereson deftly recounts the crafting of various myths that portray Kennedy as having been martyred for the cause of civil rights or world peace; Knott, "John F. Kennedy: Prince of American Progressivism."

78. Larry J. Sabato, *The Kennedy Half-Century: The Presidency, Assassination, and Lasting Legacy of John F. Kennedy* (New York: Bloomsbury 2013), 114; Knott, "What Might Have Been"; Knott, "John F. Kennedy: Prince of American Progressivism."

79. Alexis C. Madrigal, "John F. Kennedy on Television's Political Impact," *Atlantic*, 16 November 2010, https://www.theatlantic.com/technology/archive/2010/11/john-f-kennedy-on-televisions-political-impact/66644/.

80. Michael J. Horgan, *The Afterlife of John Fitzgerald Kennedy: A Biography* (Cambridge, UK: Cambridge University Press, 2017).

81. Knott, "John F. Kennedy: Prince of American Progressivism."

82. Lydia Saad, "JFK and Ronald Reagan Win Gallup Presidents Day Poll, Clinton Ranks Highest among Living Ex-Presidents," *Gallup Poll*, 18 February 2008; Lydia Saad, "C-Span 2009 Historians Presidential Leadership Survey," C-Span.org, February 2009; Mark Gillespie, "JFK Ranked as Greatest U.S. President," *Gallup News Service*, 21 February 2000; Knott, "What Might Have Been"; Knott, "John F. Kennedy: Prince of American Progressivism."

83. David Greenberg, "'The Kennedy Half-Century,'" by Larry J. Sabato," *Washington Post*, 25 October 2013; "The Kennedy Half-Century National Polling Results," 15 October 2013, http://www.thekennedyhalfcentury.com/pdf/Kennedy-Half-Century

-National-Polling-Results.pdf; Knott, "What Might Have Been"; Knott, "John F. Kennedy: Prince of American Progressivism."

84. "C-Span, Presidential Historians Survey 2017," *C-Span.org*, February 2017, https://www.c-span.org/presidentsurvey2017/?page=overall; Knott, "What Might Have Been"; Knott, "John F. Kennedy: Prince of American Progressivism."

85. David Greenberg, "JFK Was an Unapologetic Liberal," *New Republic*, 11 November 2013, https://newrepublic.com/article/115522/jfk-was-unapologetic-liberal; Diane Ravitch, "The Day President Kennedy Died," *Huffington Post*, 22 November 2013, http://www.huffingtonpost.com/diane-ravitch/the-day-president-kennedy-died_b_4327378.html; Peter Cummings, "Why the JFK Assassination Matters 50 Years Later," *Huffington Post*, 22 November 2013, http://www.huffingtonpost.com/peter-cummings/why-the-assassination-of-_b_4310463.html; Knott, "What Might Have Been"; Knott, "John F. Kennedy: Prince of American Progressivism."

86. Dallek, *An Unfinished Life*, 440, 467, 711.

87. Knott, "What Might Have Been"; Knott, "John F. Kennedy: Prince of American Progressivism."

CHAPTER 8. THE ROAD TO DEGRADATION

1. Lyndon B. Johnson, "Remarks at the Lighting of the Nation's Christmas Tree," 18 December 1964, http://www.presidency.ucsb.edu/ws/?pid=26766.

2. Lyndon B. Johnson, "Remarks at the University of Michigan," 22 May 1964, http://www.presidency.ucsb.edu/ws/?pid=26262%20.

3. Adam Wernick, "The Carrot and the Stick: LBJ Addresses the Nation on the Conflict in Vietnam, LBJ's War," *Public Radio International*, 22 September 2017, https://www.pri.org/stories/2017-09-22/carrot-and-stick-lbj-addresses-nation-conflict-vietnam.

4. William E. Leuchtenberg, *The White House Looks South: Franklin D. Roosevelt, Harry S. Truman, Lyndon B. Johnson* (Baton Rouge: Louisiana State University Press, 2005), 242; Peter Roff, "Commentary: A Late Look at LBJ's Medal," *United Press International*, 9 July 2001, https://www.upi.com/Archives/2001/07/09/Commentary-A-late-look-at-LBJs-medal/5828994651200/.

5. James T. Patterson, *The Eve of Destruction: How 1965 Transformed America* (New York: Basic Books, 2012), 46.

6. Robert Dallek, "Three New Revelations about LBJ," *Atlantic*, April 1998, https://www.theatlantic.com/magazine/archive/1998/04/three-new-revelations-about-lbj/377094/.

7. Richard Nixon, "Inaugural Address," 20 January 1969, http://www.presidency.ucsb.edu/ws/?pid=1941.

8. Rick Perlstein, *Nixonland: The Rise of a President and the Fracturing of America* (New York: Charles Scribner's Sons, 2009), 358–359.

9. Jack Martinez, "A History of Politicians on Late Night," *Newsweek*, 13 September 2015, http://www.newsweek.com/late-night-politicians-presidential-candidates-371394; Bill Higgins, "Hollywood Flashback: The Time Nixon Made an Appearance

on 'Laugh-In,'" *Hollywood Reporter*, 22 September 2016, https://www.hollywoodreporter.com/news/hollywood-flashback-time-nixon-made-930891.

10. Michael S. Rosenwald, "'Television Is Not a Gimmick: How Roger Ailes Made Richard Nixon Likable," *Washington Post*, 18 May 2017, https://www.washingtonpost.com/news/retropolis/wp/2017/05/18/television-is-not-a-gimmick-how-roger-ailes-made-richard-nixon-likable/?utm_term=.b7ecd63186aa.

11. Rosenwald, "Television Is Not a Gimmick."

12. Richard Nixon, "Address of Senator Nixon to the American People: The 'Checkers Speech,'" 23 September 1952, http://www.presidency.ucsb.edu/ws/index.php?pid=24485.

13. Joe McGinniss, *The Selling of the President 1968* (New York: Trident Press, 1969).

14. Ken Hughes, "Richard Nixon: Campaigns and Elections," UVA, Miller Center, https://millercenter.org/president/nixon/campaigns-and-elections.

15. Niall Ferguson, *Kissinger: 1923–1968, The Idealist* (New York: Penguin Books, 2015), 441.

16. John A. Farrell, "The Year Nixon Fell Apart," 26 March 2017, *Politico*, https://www.politico.com/magazine/story/2017/03/john-farrell-nixon-book-excerpt-214954.

17. Perlstein, *Nixonland*, 499; Ross Douthat, "E Pluribus Nixon," *Atlantic*, May 2008, https://www.theatlantic.com/magazine/archive/2008/05/e-pluribus-nixon/306765/; Farrell, "The Year Nixon Fell Apart."

18. Perlstein, *Nixonland*, 432.

19. Melvin Small, *The Presidency of Richard Nixon* (Lawrence: University Press of Kansas, 1999), 82.

20. Perlstein, *Nixonland*, 432.

21. Farrell, "The Year Nixon Fell Apart."

22. Farrell, "The Year Nixon Fell Apart."

23. Katelyn Fossett, "Richard Nixon, Awkward American Icon," *Politico*, 21 April 2014, https://www.politico.com/magazine/gallery/2014/04/richard-nixon-awkward-american-icon-000036?slide=0.

24. "Colson, Nixon's 'Hatchet Man,' Dead at 80," *United Press International*, 21 April 2012, https://www.upi.com/Colson-Nixons-hatchet-man-dead-at-80/23811335044902/.

25. Tim Weiner, *One Man against the World: The Tragedy of Richard Nixon* (New York: Henry Holt & Co., 2015), 183.

26. Stanley L. Kutler, *The Wars of Watergate: The Last Crisis of Richard Nixon* (New York: W. W. Norton & Co., 1990), 620.

27. Richard M. Nixon, *RN: The Memoirs of Richard Nixon* (New York: Grossett & Dunlap, 1978), 1089.

28. John Robert Greene, *The Presidency of Gerald R. Ford* (Lawrence: University Press of Kansas, 1995), 190.

29. Douglas Brinkley, *Gerald R. Ford* (New York: Times Books, 2007), 147.

30. Alex E. Hindman, *Gerald Ford and the Separation of Powers: Preserving the Constitutional Presidency in the Post-Watergate Period* (Lanham, MD: Lexington Books, 2017), 1.

31. Hindman, *Gerald Ford and the Separation of Powers*, 1, 33–34.

32. John Wooley and Gerhard Peters, "Presidential Vetoes, Washington—Obama," American Presidency Project, http://www.presidency.ucsb.edu/data/vetoes.php.

33. Stephen F. Knott, *Secret and Sanctioned: Covert Operations and the American Presidency* (New York: Oxford University Press, 1996), chapter 3 and 164–167, 171.

34. Hindman, *Gerald Ford and the Separation of Powers*, 177.

35. Hindman, *Gerald Ford and the Separation of Powers*, 107.

36. Hindman, *Gerald Ford and the Separation of Powers*, 122.

37. Brinkley, *Gerald R Ford*, 75, 148.

38. Hindman, *Gerald Ford and the Separation of Powers*, 237.

39. *Public Papers of the Presidents of the United States, Jimmy Carter, 1977, Book One, January 20, 1977–June 24, 1977* (Washington, DC: US Government Printing Office), 397.

40. Jimmy Carter, "Address to the Nation on Energy and National Goals: 'The Malaise Speech,'" 15 July 1979, http://www.presidency.ucsb.edu/ws/?pid=32596.

41. Greene, *The Presidency of Gerald R. Ford*, 175–176; Brinkley, *Gerald R. Ford*, 142.

42. Daniel Eric Schabot, "Jimmy Carter's Post-Presidential Rhetoric: Faith-Based Rhetoric and Human Rights Foreign Policy," (2012), http://aquila.usm.edu/dissertations/854.

43. Greene, *The Presidency of Gerald R. Ford*, 176.

44. Jimmy Carter, *Conversations with Carter*, ed. Don Richardson (Boulder: Lynne Reinner, 1998), 58.

45. Sidney Milkis and Michael Nelson, *The American Presidency: Origins and Development, 1776–2011* (Washington, DC: CQ Press, 2011), 366–367; Jimmy Carter, "'Ask President Carter'—Remarks During a Telephone Call-in Program on the CBS Radio Network," 5 March 1977, http://www.presidency.ucsb.edu/ws/index.php?pid=7119; Robert A. Wilson, *Character above All: Ten Presidents from FDR to George Bush* (New York: Simon & Schuster, 1996), 182–183.

46. Jimmy Carter, *Christmas in Plains: Memories* (New York: Simon & Schuster, 2001), 119; Jimmy Carter, *White House Diary* (New York: Farrar, Straus & Giroux, 2010), 292, 312; "Medicine: Carter's Injury," *Time*, 8 January 1979, http://content.time.com/time/magazine/article/0,9171,919965,00.html.

47. Jimmy Carter, "Address to the Nation on Energy and National Goals: 'The Malaise Speech,'" 15 July 1979.

48. Kevin Mattson, *"What the Heck Are You Up to Mr. President": Jimmy Carter, America's Malaise, and the Speech That Should Have Changed the Country* (New York: Bloomsbury, 2009), 6.

49. The Mondale quote can be found at George F. Will, "An Election to Call Voters' Bluff," *Washington Post*, 29 August 2012.

50. Bart Barnes, "Barry Goldwater, GOP Hero, Dies," *Washington Post*, 30 May 1998, 1.

51. Lou Cannon, *President Reagan: The Role of a Lifetime* (New York, Public Affairs, 2000), 32.

52. Stephen F. Knott and Jeffrey L. Chidester, *The Reagan Years* (New York: Facts on File, 2005), 391.

53. Knott and Chidester, *The Reagan Years*, 88.

54. Stephen F. Knott and Jeffrey L. Chidester, *At Reagan's Side: Insiders' Recollections from Sacramento to the White House* (Lanham, MD: Rowman & Littlefield, 2009), 7–8.

55. Knott and Chidester, *At Reagan's Side*, 8.

56. Knott and Chidester, *At Reagan's Side*, 4.

57. Knott and Chidester, *At Reagan's Side*, 4.

58. Knott and Chidester, *At Reagan's Side*, 5.

59. Knott and Chidester, *The Reagan Years*, 41, 99–101.

60. Knott and Chidester, *At Reagan's Side*, 211–212.

61. George H. W. Bush, "Address Accepting the Republican Nomination at the Republican National Convention in New Orleans," 18 August 1988, http://www.presidency.ucsb.edu/ws/index.php?pid=25955.

62. Kevin Bohn, "41 Things about Bush 41," *CNN Politics*, 29 March 2016, https://www.cnn.com/2014/06/12/politics/george-hw-bush-41-things/index.html.

63. Julian Zelizer, "Dirty Campaigning? He Perfected it," *CNN: Race for the White House*, 25 March 2016, https://www.cnn.com/2016/03/17/opinions/zelizer-lee-atwater-trump/index.html; Rowland Evans and Robert Novak, "Atwater without Apologies," *Washington Post*, 5 April 1991, https://www.washingtonpost.com/archive/opinions/1991/04/05/atwater-without-apologies/54f2513d-efaa-494c-a7b5-ce5c14434f3c/?utm_term=.8a6efc1364be.

64. S. Robert Lichter, "The Media," in *Understanding America: The Anatomy of an Exceptional Nation*, eds. Peter H. Shuck and James Q. Wilson (New York: Public Affairs, 2008), 210.

65. Ken Gormley, "William Jefferson Clinton," *The Presidents and the Constitution: A Living History*, ed. Ken Gormley (New York: New York University Press, 2016), 573–576, 584n32.

66. Gormley, "William Jefferson Clinton," 576–579.

67. Gormley, "William Jefferson Clinton," 580–581.

68. Elsa Walsh, "Blaming the Boss: A Former FBI Director Blasts the President Who Hired Him and Defends His Efforts Before 9/11," *Washington Post*, 16 October 2005, http://www.washingtonpost.com/wp-dyn/content/article/2005/10/13/AR2005101301588.html.

69. Don Van Natta Jr., "White House's All-out Attack on Starr Is Paying Off, with His Help," *New York Times*, 2 March 1998, https://www.nytimes.com/1998/03/02/us/white-house-s-all-out-attack-on-starr-is-paying-off-with-his-help.html.

70. Lauren Berlant and Lisa Duggan, eds., *Our Monica, Ourselves: The Clinton Affair and the National Interest* (New York: New York University Press, 2001), 86–87.

71. Shawn Boburg, "Enabler or Family Defender? How Hillary Clinton Responded to Her Husband's Accusers," *Washington Post*, 28 September 2016, https://www.washingtonpost.com/local/enabler-or-family-defender-how-hillary-clinton

-responded-to-husbands-accusers/2016/09/28/58dad5d4-6fb1-11e6-8533-6b0b0ded0253_story.html?utm_term=.972d5ea24599.

72. Amy Chozick, "'90s Scandals Threaten to Erode Hillary Clinton's Strength with Women," *New York Times*, 20 January 2016, https://www.nytimes.com/2016/01/21/us/politics/90s-scandals-threaten-to-erode-hillary-clintons-strength-with-women.html.

73. Julian Zelizer, "Bill Clinton Demonized Ken Starr—Can Trump Do the Same to Mueller?," *CNN Opinion*, 13 June 2017, https://www.cnn.com/2017/06/13/opinions/trump-mueller-clinton-starr-opinion-zelizer/index.html.

74. Joe Concha, "Bill Clinton Mocked on Twitter Following Explosive NBC Interview: 'He All but Set Himself on Fire,'" *Hill*, 4 June 2018, http://thehill.com/homenews/media/390548-bill-clinton-mocked-on-twitter-following-explosive-nbc-interview-he-all-but.

75. John F. Harris, "What Bill Clinton Was Really Thinking," *Politico Magazine*, 7 June 2018, https://www.politico.com/magazine/story/2018/06/07/bill-clinton-book-tour-218661.

76. Diane J. Heith, "The Polls: Polling for a Defense: The White House Public Opinion Apparatus and the Clinton Impeachment," *Presidential Studies Quarterly* vol. 30, no. 4 (December 2000): 783–790.

77. Jacob E. Cooke, ed., *Federalist*, no. 65 (Middletown, CT: Wesleyan University Press, 1961), 439–440.

78. John F. Harris, "'Washington Was about to Explode': The Clinton Scandal, 20 Years Later," *Politico Magazine*, 21 January 2018, https://www.politico.com/magazine/story/2018/01/21/clinton-lewinsky-scandal-20-years-later-me-too-216484.

79. William E. Leuchtenburg, *The American President: From Teddy Roosevelt to Bill Clinton* (New York: Oxford University Press, 2015), 795–796.

80. James Comey, *A Higher Loyalty: Truth, Lies, and Leadership* (New York: Flatiron Books, 2018), 159.

81. Jessica Taylor, "More Surprises: FBI Releases Files on Bill Clinton's Pardon of Marc Rich," *National Public Radio*, 1 November 2016, https://www.npr.org/2016/11/01/500297580/more-surprises-fbi-releases-files-on-bill-clintons-pardon-of-marc-rich; Comey, *A Higher Loyalty*, 160–161.

82. Josh Gerstein, "Clinton Camp Questions FBI Release of Marc Rich Pardon Files," *Politico*, 1 November 2016, https://www.politico.com/story/2016/11/marc-rich-pardon-files-230590.

83. George W. Bush, "Remarks to Police, Fireman, and Rescue Workers at the World Trade Center Site in New York City," 14 September 2001, http://www.presidency.ucsb.edu/ws/index.php?pid=65078; George W. Bush, "Remarks at the National Day of Prayer and Remembrance Service," 14 September 2001, http://www.presidency.ucsb.edu/ws/?pid=63645.

84. "Presidential Approval Ratings—Gallup Historical Statistics and Trends," *Gallup*, http://news.gallup.com/poll/116677/presidential-approval-ratings-gallup-historical-statistics-trends.aspx.

85. This is excluding natural disasters, such as the Galveston hurricane of 1900.

86. I deal with these issues in *Rush to Judgment: George W. Bush, the War on Terror, and His Critics.* It is my contention that Bush's extraordinary measures were in concert with the principles and practices of his presidential predecessors, and that Bush remained faithful to the framers' intentions in the realm of national security.

87. Julian E. Zelizer, "How Conservatives Learned to Stop Worrying and Love Presidential Power," in *The Presidency of George W. Bush: A First Historical Assessment* (Princeton, NJ: Princeton University Press, 2010), 36.

88. George W. Bush, "Inaugural Address," 20 January 2005, http://www.presidency.ucsb.edu/ws/index.php?pid=58745.

89. George W. Bush, "Remarks on Arrival at the White House and an Exchange with Reporters," 16 September 2001, http://www.presidency.ucsb.edu/ws/index.php?pid=63346.

90. Knott, *Rush to Judgment*, 17.

91. John J. Pitney Jr., "Asymmetric Warfare: Supporters and Opponents of President Obama," in *Transforming America: Barack Obama in the White House*, ed. Steven E. Schier (Lanham, MD: Rowman & Littlefield, 2011), 136.

92. "Fact Check: Did Obama Only Serve 300 Days in the Senate before He Became a Candidate?," *CNN Politics*, Political Ticker, 22 October 2008, http://politicalticker.blogs.cnn.com/2008/10/22/fact-check-did-obama-only-serve-300-days-in-the-senate-before-he-became-a-candidate/.

93. James W. Ceaser, "The Changing Face of Barack Obama's Leadership," in *The Obama Presidency in the Constitutional Order: A First Look*, eds. Carol McNamara and Melanie M. Marlowe (Lanham, MD: Rowman & Littlefield, 2011), 197.

94. Toby Harnden, "Barack Obama Vows to Change the World," *Telegraph*, 17 October 2007, https://www.telegraph.co.uk/news/worldnews/barackobama/3219308/Barack-Obama-vows-to-change-the-world.html; Adam Shatz, "Obama Hoped to Transform the World. It Transformed Him," *New York Times*, 12 January 2017, https://www.nytimes.com/2017/01/12/opinion/obama-hoped-to-transform-the-world-it-transformed-him.html.

95. Peter Wehner, "Eight Was Enough," *New York Times*, 14 January 2017, https://www.nytimes.com/2017/01/14/opinion/sunday/eight-was-enough.html.

96. Alan Kennedy-Shaffer, *The Obama Revolution* (Beverly Hills: Phoenix Books, 2009), 195.

97. Peter Hamby, "Obama: GOP Doesn't Own Faith Issue," *CNN Politics*, 8 October 2007, http://www.cnn.com/2007/POLITICS/10/08/obama.faith/.

98. "The Obama Cult," *Economist*, 23 July 2009, https://www.economist.com/node/14082968.

99. Stanley A. Renshon, *Barack Obama and the Politics of Redemption* (New York: Routledge, 2012), 278.

100. Paul Bedard, "First Newsweek, Now Foreign Policy, Calls Obama 'Second Coming,'" *Washington Examiner*, 8 February 2013, https://www.washingtonexaminer

.com/first-newsweek-now-foreign-policy-calls-obama-second-coming/article/2520973.

101. Mary Bruce, "YouTube Star Who Drinks Cereal from a Bathtub to Interview President Obama," *ABC News*, 22 January 2015, https://abcnews.go.com/Politics/youtube-star-drinks-cereal-bathtub-interview-obama-today/story?id=28398889.

102. Neetzan Zimmerman and Jesse Byrnes, "Silly Obama Uses Selfie Stick, and Asks 'Can I Live?' in New Video," *Hill*, 12 February 2015, http://thehill.com/homenews/administration/232629-silly-obama-uses-selfie-stick-asks-can-i-live-in-new-video.

103. Abe Greenwald, "I'm Ready for My Close-up, Mr. Obama," *Commentary*, 20 November 2018, https://www.commentarymagazine.com/american-society/im-ready-for-my-close-up-barack-obama/; Noah Rothman, "Our Famous Presidents," *Commentary*, 8 August 2018, https://www.commentarymagazine.com/politics-ideas/our-famous-presidents/; Jeremy Barr, "Ben Rhodes Says He and Others on the Obama Campaign Watched 'The West Wing' to Get Themselves 'Mentally Prepared' to Work There," https://twitter.com/jeremymbarr/status/1053787292479844352.

104. Jennifer Agiesta, "Most Say Race Relations Worsened under Obama, Poll Finds," *CNN Politics*, 5 October 2016, https://www.cnn.com/2016/10/05/politics/obama-race-relations-poll/index.html.

105. "Text: Obama's Remarks on Gates's Arrest," *New York Times*, 24 July 2009, https://www.nytimes.com/2009/07/24/us/politics/24obama.text.html.

106. "We the People: Your Voice in the White House," https://petitions.whitehouse.gov/responses; Brendon Bosworth and Emily Guerin, "Weird and Wacky White House Petitions," *High Country News*, 10 December 2012, https://www.hcn.org/issues/44.21/weird-and-wacky-white-house-petitions.

CHAPTER 9. THE APOTHEOSIS OF THE POPULAR PRESIDENCY: DONALD J. TRUMP

1. Nolan D. McCaskill, "Trump Accuses Cruz's Father of Helping JFK's Assassin," 3 May 2016, *Politico*, https://www.politico.com/blogs/2016-gop-primary-live-updates-and-results/2016/05/trump-ted-cruz-father-222730; Caitlin Yilek, "Trump Flirts with Suggestion That Scalia Was Murdered," *Hill*, 16 February 2016, http://thehill.com/blogs/ballot-box/presidential-races/donald-trump-justice-antonin-scalia-murdered-pillow-conspiracy-theory.

2. Danika Fears, "Trump Suggests Joe Scarborough Killed Intern," *New York Post*, 29 November 2017, https://nypost.com/2017/11/29/trump-suggests-joe-scarborough-killed-intern/.

3. Eliza Collins, "Trump Questions Rubio's Eligibility," *Politico*, 21 February 2016, https://www.politico.com/story/2016/02/trump-questions-rubios-eligibility-219586; Maxwell Tani and Michal Kranz, "18 Outlandish Conspiracy Theories Donald Trump Has Floated on the Campaign Trail and in the White House," *Business Insider*, 30 November 2017, http://www.businessinsider.com/donald-trump-conspiracy-theories-2016-5.

4. Brett Samuels, "Trump: 'Criminal Deep State' Caught Up in 'Major Spy Scandal,'" *Hill*, 23 May 2018, http://thehill.com/homenews/administration/388933-trump-criminal-deep-state-caught-up-in-major-spy-scandal.

5. Tim Hains, "Donald Trump on 9/11: 'You Will Find Out Who Really Knocked Down the World Trade Center,'" *Real Clear Politics*, 17 February 2016, https://www.realclearpolitics.com/video/2016/02/17/trump_you_will_find_out_who_really_knocked_down_the_world_trade_center_secret_papers_may_blame_saudis.html.

6. Andrew Buncombe, "Trump Claims Vaccine and Autism Are Linked but His Own Experts Vehemently Disagree," *Independent*, 5 May 2018, https://www.independent.co.uk/news/world/americas/trump-vaccines-autism-links-anti-vaxxer-us-president-false-vaccine-a8331836.html.

7. Alan Rappeport and Stacy M. Brown, "Trump Threatens Harley-Davidson, Saying It Surrendered," *New York Times*, 26 June 2018, https://www.nytimes.com/2018/06/26/business/trump-harley-davidson-tariffs.html.

8. Jacob T. Levy, "The Weight of the Words," *Niskanen Center*, 7 February 2018, https://niskanencenter.org/blog/the-weight-of-the-words/.

9. "Transcript: Donald Trump's Taped Comments about Women," *New York Times*, 7 October 2016, https://www.nytimes.com/2016/10/08/us/donald-trump-tape-transcript.html.

10. "30 of Donald Trump's Wildest Quotes," *CBS News*, https://www.cbsnews.com/pictures/wild-donald-trump-quotes/.

11. Ben Schreckinger, "Trump Attacks McCain: 'I Like People Who Weren't Captured,'" *Politico*, 18 July 2015, https://www.politico.com/story/2015/07/trump-attacks-mccain-i-like-people-who-werent-captured-120317.

12. Andrew Kaczynski, "Trump, Comparing Sex to Vietnam, Said in 1998 He Should Receive the Congressional Medal of Honor," *CNN Politics*, 14 October 2016, http://money.cnn.com/2016/10/14/media/trump-stern-vietnam-stds/index.html.

13. "30 of Donald Trump's Wildest Quotes."

14. Dan Merica, "Trump Boasts of a Higher IQ Than Tillerson," *CNN Politics*, 10 October 2017, https://www.cnn.com/2017/10/10/politics/donald-trump-forbes-interview-rex-tillerson/index.html.

15. Daniella Diaz, "Trump: 'I am a "Very Stable Genius,"'" *CNN Politics*, 6 January 2018, https://www.cnn.com/2018/01/06/politics/donald-trump-white-house-fitness-very-stable-genius/index.html.

16. "Trump: 'I Have the Best Words,'" *Washington Post*, 5 April 2017, https://www.washingtonpost.com/video/national/trump-i-have-the-best-words/2017/04/05/53a9ae4a-19fd-11e7-8598-9a99da559f9e_video.html; "30 of Donald Trump's Wildest Quotes."

17. Colin Dwyer, "Donald Trump: "'I Could . . . Shoot Somebody, and I Wouldn't Lose Any Voters,'" *National Public Radio*, 23 January 2016, https://www.npr.org/sections/thetwo-way/2016/01/23/464129029/donald-trump-i-could-shoot-somebody-and-i-wouldnt-lose-any-voters.

18. Aaron Blake, "19 Things Donald Trump Knows Better Than Anyone Else, According to Donald Trump," *Washington Post*, 4 October 2016, https://www.washingtonpost

.com/news/the-fix/wp/2016/10/04/17-issues-that-donald-trump-knows-better-than-anyone-else-according-to-donald-trump/?utm_term=.21c53a127f0d.

19. Michael Gerson, "Trump Is the Demagogue That Our Founding Fathers Feared," *Washington Post*, 10 March 2016.

20. "30 of Donald Trump's Wildest Quotes"; Brooke Seipel, "Trump: We Are Going to Say Merry Christmas Again," *Hill*, 12 December 2016, http://thehill.com/blogs/in-the-know/in-the-know/310311-trump-fulfills-merry-christmas-campaign-promise-at-wisconsin.

21. Nick Gass, "Trump's 'Haters and Losers' Sept. 11th Tweet Vanishes," *Politico*, 11 September 2015, https://www.politico.com/story/2015/09/donald-trump-9-11-sept-11-tweet-disappears-213546.

22. "Haters and Losers," Snopes.com, https://www.snopes.com/fact-check/donald-trump-haters-and-losers/.

23. Meghan Keneally, "A Look Back at Trump Comments Perceived as Encouraging Violence," *ABC News*, 3 July 2017, https://abcnews.go.com/Politics/back-trump-comments-perceived-encouraging-violence/story?id=48415766.

24. Madeline Conway, "Boy Scouts Chief Apologizes after Trump Speech," *Politico*, 27 July 2017, https://www.politico.com/story/2017/07/27/boy-scouts-apologizes-for-trump-speech-241036.

25. Katie Mettler and Derek Hawkins, "Trump's Boy Scouts Speech Broke with 80 Years of Presidential Tradition," *Washington Post*, 25 July 2017, https://www.washingtonpost.com/news/morning-mix/wp/2017/07/25/trumps-boy-scouts-speech-broke-with-80-years-of-presidential-tradition/?utm_term=.d2d7fdde8479.

26. Alexander Mallin, "Trump Says Critics of His Administration 'Better Just Take it Easy' with Language, 'Radical Ideas,'" *ABC News*, 1 July 2018, https://abcnews.go.com/Politics/trump-critics-administration-easy-language-radical-ideas/story?id=56297174.

27. Kevin Liptak, "Cabinet Members Give Trump Unusual Tribute," *CNN Politics*, 12 June 2017, https://www.cnn.com/2017/06/12/politics/trump-cabinet-tribute/index.html.

28. Helaine Olen, "Whether It Rises or Falls, Trump Owns the Stock Market. That's All His Own Fault," *Washington Post*, 6 February 2017, https://www.washingtonpost.com/blogs/plum-line/wp/2018/02/06/trump-owns-the-stock-market-thats-all-his-own-doing/?utm_term=.4adcfa6d2bd4; Jesse Byrnes, "Trump on Lack of Nominees: 'I'm the Only One That Matters,'" *Hill*, 2 November 2017, http://thehill.com/blogs/blog-briefing-room/news/358573-trump-on-lack-of-nominees-i-am-the-only-one-that-matters.

29. Brianna Gurciullo and Lauren Gardner, "Trump Takes Credit for Airline Safety Record," *Politico*, 2 January 2018, https://www.politico.com/story/2018/01/02/trump-airline-safety-262293.

30. Matt Ford, "Trump's Press Secretary Falsely Claims: 'Largest Audience Ever to Witness an Inauguration, Period,'" *Atlantic*, 21 January 2017, https://www.theatlantic.com/politics/archive/2017/01/inauguration-crowd-size/514058/.

31. David Nakamura and Lisa Rein, "'It's Very Gold': The Presidential Coin Undergoes a Trumpian Makeover," *Washington Post*, 22 December 2017, https://www.washingtonpost.com/politics/its-very-gold-the-presidential-coin-undergoes-a-trumpian-makeover/2017/12/22/23c8b11e-e5bb-11e7-ab50-621fe0588340_story.html?utm_term=.2fb280feba7c.

32. Travis M. Andrews, "From Elton John to Eminem to Peggy Lee: Trump's Bizarre History with Pop Music," *Washington Post*, 9 July 2018, https://www.washingtonpost.com/news/arts-and-entertainment/wp/2018/07/09/from-elton-john-to-eminem-to-peggy-lee-president-trumps-bizarre-history-with-pop-music/?utm_term=.23957d17bf3e.

33. "Opinion: The Republicans' Guide to Presidential Etiquette," *New York Times*, 20 January 2018, https://www.nytimes.com/interactive/2018/01/20/opinion/the-Republicans-Guide-to-Presidential-Etiquette.html?mtrref=www.google.com&gwh=CB5D5121B3479B84E0155BCBD8389F41&gwt=pay&assetType=opinion.

34. "Opinion: The Republicans' Guide to Presidential Etiquette."

35. Veronica Stracqualursi and Jessica Schneider, "Trump to DOJ: Don't Let Debbie Wasserman Schultz, Aide, 'Off the Hook,'" *CNN Politics*, 7 June 2018, https://www.cnn.com/2018/06/07/politics/trump-debbie-wasserman-schultz-it-aide-imran-awan/index.html.

36. Deanna Paul, "Trump's Latest Tweets Cross Clear Lines, Experts Say: Obstruction of Justice and Witness Tampering," *Washington Post*, 3 December 2018, https://www.washingtonpost.com/politics/2018/12/03/trumps-latest-tweets-cross-clear-lines-experts-say-obstruction-justice-witness-tampering/?utm_term=.6223474bfedd; Chris Cillizza, "The 35 Most Astounding Lines from Donald Trump's Jeanine Pirro Interview, *CNN Politics*, 15 January 2019, https://www.cnn.com/2019/01/14/politics/donald-trump-jeanine-pirro/index.html.

37. Bart Jansen, "Trump's Tweets: Judges in Government Secrecy Cases Say They Are 'Speculation' and Not 'Pure Fact,'" *USA Today*, 30 December 2018, https://www.usatoday.com/story/news/politics/2018/12/30/trump-tweets-judges-doj-lawyers-foia-lawsuits/2197524002/.

38. Ruth Marcus, "Trump's Dangerous Plot to Weaponize the Supreme Court," *Washington Post*, 30 March 2018, https://www.washingtonpost.com/opinions/trumps-dangerous-plot-to-weaponize-the-supreme-court/2018/03/30/60b53a04-343d-11e8-94fa-32d48460b955_story.html?utm_term=.f2fb5762e4d4; Adam Liptak, "Chief Justice Defends Judicial Independence after Trump Attacks 'Obama Judge,'" *New York Times*, 21 November 2018, https://www.nytimes.com/2018/11/21/us/politics/trump-chief-justice-roberts-rebuke.html.

39. Margot Hornblower, "Roy Cohn Is Disbarred by New York Court," *Washington Post*, 24 June 1986, https://www.washingtonpost.com/archive/politics/1986/06/24/roy-cohn-is-disbarred-by-new-york-court/c5ca9112-3245-48f0-ab01-c2c0f3c3fc2e/?utm_term=.c8a6f8222764;

40. James D. Zirin, "The Man Who First Fueled Donald Trump's Paranoid Politics," *Time*, 14 April 2017, http://time.com/4690261/donald-trump-paranoid/.

41. "30 of Donald Trump's Wildest Quotes."

42. David E. Sanger, "Trump Bets on 'Special Bond with Kim' to Deliver Nuclear Policy Shift," *New York Times*, 12 June 2018, https://www.nytimes.com/2018/06/12/world/asia/trump-kim-policy.html.

43. Quoted in Anna Palmer, Jake Sherman, and Daniel Lippman, "Trump Causes Chaos at NATO Summit," *Politico Playbook*, 12 July 2018, https://www.politico.com/newsletters/playbook/2018/07/12/trump-nato-withdraw-threat-285401.

44. Maggie Haberman, Glenn Thrush, and Peter Baker, "Inside Trump's Hour by Hour Battle for Self-Preservation," *New York Times*, 9 December 2017, https://www.nytimes.com/2017/12/09/us/politics/donald-trump-president.html.

45. Rick Klein, "Analysis: One Year in, Donald Trump Has Redefined the Presidency," *ABC News*, 14 January 2018, https://abcnews.go.com/Politics/analysis-year-donald-trump-redefined-presidency/story?id=52233867.

46. Justin Wise, "Trump Tweets Video of 2005 'Green Acres' Emmy Awards Performance to Hype Farm Bill Signing," *Hill*, 20 December 2018, https://thehill.com/blogs/in-the-know/in-the-know/422339-trump-tweets-video-of-green-acres-emmys-performance-to-hype.

47. Christina Zhao, "Donald Trump Says His Generals Are 'Better Looking Than Tom Cruise, and Stronger,'" *Newsweek*, 2 January 2019, https://www.newsweek.com/donald-trump-says-his-generals-are-better-looking-tom-cruise-and-stronger-1277581.

48. Kevin Liptak, Maegan Vazquez, and Betsy Klein, "Kim Kardashian Meets with Trump to Discuss Prison Reform," *CNN Politics*, 31 May 2018, https://www.cnn.com/2018/05/30/politics/kim-kardashian-jared-kushner-white-house/index.html.

49. Maria Puente, "Omarosa Gets Job in Trump White House as 'Public Liaison Leader,'" *USA Today*, 4 January 2017, https://www.usatoday.com/story/life/people/2017/01/04/omarosa-gets-job-trump-white-house-public-liaison-leader/96167028/.

50. Kathryn Cramer Brownell, "The Revolving Door between Reality TV and the Trump Administration," *Washington Post*, 15 January 2019, https://www.washingtonpost.com/outlook/2019/01/15/revolving-door-between-reality-tv-trump-administration/?utm_term=.b7f4f43e347f.

51. Kevin Williamson, "The Treasury Secretary's Wife," *National Review*, 19 November 2017, https://www.nationalreview.com/2017/11/steven-mnuchin-louise-linton-embarrassing/?utm_source=pantheon_stripped&utm_medium=pantheon_stripped?utm_source=pantheon_stripped.

52. Kevin Townsend, "A White House Troll 'Owning the Libs,'" *Radio Atlantic, Atlantic*, 1 June 2018, https://www.theatlantic.com/politics/archive/2018/06/radio-atlantic-a-white-house-troll-owning-the-libs/561827/.

53. Chris Cillizza, "Why Pro Wrestling Is the Perfect Metaphor for Donald Trump's Presidency," *CNN Politics*, 2 July 2017, https://www.cnn.com/2017/07/02/politics/trump-wrestling-tweet/index.html; "Donald Trump," WWE Hall of Fame, https://www.wwe.com/superstars/donald-trump.

54. Michael Anton, "The Flight 93 Election," *CRB Digital*, 5 September 2016, http://www.claremont.org/crb/basicpage/the-flight-93-election/.

55. Steve Inskeep, "Donald Trump and the Legacy of Andrew Jackson," *Atlantic*, 30 November 2016, https://www.theatlantic.com/politics/archive/2016/11/trump-and-andrew-jackson/508973/.

56. Linda J. Killian, "The New Old Hickory," *U.S. News and World Report*, 13 February 2017, https://www.usnews.com/opinion/op-ed/articles/2017-02-13/beware-the-similarities-between-donald-trump-and-andrew-jackson.

57. Jenna Johnson and Karen Tumulty, "Trump Cites Andrew Jackson as His Hero—and a Reflection of Himself," *Washington Post*, 15 March 2017, https://www.washingtonpost.com/politics/trump-cites-andrew-jackson-as-his-hero--and-a-reflection-of-himself/2017/03/15/4da8dc8c-0995-11e7-a15f-a58d4a988474_story.html?utm_term=.7940f519eb21.

CHAPTER 10. THE PROSPECTS FOR RENEWAL

1. David Greenberg, *Calvin Coolidge* (New York: Times Books, 2006), 63.

2. Jacob E. Cooke, ed., *Federalist*, no. 10 (Middletown, CT: Wesleyan University Press, 1961), 60.

3. For an insightful account of Van Buren's designs for the American party system and its important role in presidential selection, see James Ceaser, "Presidential Selection," in *The Presidency in the Constitutional Order*, eds. Joseph M. Bessette and Jeffrey Tulis (Baton Rouge: Louisiana State University Press, 1981), 251–262.

4. Quoted in Brian R. Dirck, *The Executive Branch of the Federal Government: People, Process, and Politics* (Santa Barbara: ABC-CLIO, 2007), 322.

5. Gene Healy, *The Cult of the Presidency: America's Dangerous Devotion to Executive Power* (Washington, DC: Cato Institute, 2008), 6.

6. Stephen F. Knott, "National Security and Foreign Policy," in *Debating Reform: Conflicting Perspectives on How to Fix the American Political System*, eds. Richard J. Ellis and Michael Nelson (Thousand Oaks, CA: Sage Publications, Inc., 2017), 394.

7. Knott, "National Security and Foreign Policy," 394–395; Stephen F. Knott, "When Everyone Agreed about Iraq," *Wall Street Journal*, 15 March 2013, http://www.wsj.com/articles/SB10001424127887324532004578360574070682516.

8. Knott, "National Security and Foreign Policy," 395; Final Report, National Geographic-Roper Public Affairs 2006 Geographic Literacy Study, http://www.nationalgeographic.com/roper2006/pdf/FINALReport2006GeogLitsurvey.pdf.

9. Knott, "National Security and Foreign Policy," 395; "Survey: Young People Lack Geography Skills," *USA Today*, 20 November 2002, http://usatoday30.usatoday.com/news/nation/2002-11-20-geography-quiz_x.htm.

10. Justin McCarthy, "Confidence in U.S. Branches of Government Remains Low," *Gallup*, 15 June 2015, http://www.gallup.com/poll/183605/confidence-branches-government-remains-low.aspx; Knott, "National Security and Foreign Policy," 395.

11. Philip Bump, "The Quintessential Trump Campaign Story: A Bag of Cash, Michael Cohen and a Rigged Online Poll," *Washington Post*, 17 January 2019, https://

www.washingtonpost.com/politics/2019/01/17/quintessential-trump-campaign-story-bag-cash-michael-cohen-rigged-online-poll/?utm_term=.f004bb96d92e.

12. Hugh Heclo, "Hyperdemocracy," *Wilson Quarterly* vol. 23, no. 1 (Winter 1999): 62–71; Stephen F. Knott, *Alexander Hamilton and the Persistence of Myth* (Lawrence: University Press of Kansas, 2002), 232; Knott, "National Security and Foreign Policy," 395.

13. Matthew Continetti, "The Book That Blew Up Washington," *Washington Free Beacon*, 5 January 2018, http://freebeacon.com/columns/book-blew-washington/.

14. James Kirchick, "Trump's Debt to Ron Paul's Paranoid Style," *New York Review of Books*, 17 January 2018, http://www.nybooks.com/daily/2018/01/17/trumps-debt-to-ron-pauls-paranoid-style/.

15. Knott, "National Security and Foreign Policy," 395–396; Stephen F. Knott, "The World of Justin Amash," *National Interest*, 30 October 2013, http://nationalinterest.org/commentary/the-world-justin-amash-9330.

16. Peter J. Stanlis, ed., *Edmund Burke, Selected Writings and Speeches* (New Brunswick, NJ: Transaction Publishers, 2009), 224.

17. Knott, "National Security and Foreign Policy," 396; Carol Morello and Karen DeYoung, "Secret U.S.-Cuba Diplomacy Ended in Landmark Deal on Prisoners, Future Ties," *Washington Post*, 17 December 2014, https://www.washingtonpost.com/world/national-security/secret-diplomacy-with-cuba-ended-in-breakthrough-deal/2014/12/17/c51b3ed8-8614-11e4-a702-fa31ff4ae98e_story.html.

18. See Tom Nichols, *The Death of Expertise: The Campaign against Established Knowledge and Why It Matters* (Oxford: Oxford University Press, 2017).

INDEX